Chasing Freedom

Chasing Freedom

Coming of Age at the End of Empire

SIMUKAI CHIGUDU

THE BODLEY HEAD
LONDON

1 3 5 7 9 10 8 6 4 2

The Bodley Head, an imprint of Vintage, is part of the Penguin Random House group of companies

Vintage, Penguin Random House UK, One Embassy Gardens, 8 Viaduct Gardens, London SW11 7BW

penguin.co.uk/vintage
global.penguinrandomhouse.com

First published by The Bodley Head in 2026

Copyright © Simukai Chigudu 2026

The moral right of the author has been asserted

Every effort has been made to contact all copyright holders. The publisher will be pleased to amend in future editions any errors or omissions brought to their attention.

Penguin Random House values and supports copyright. Copyright fuels creativity, encourages diverse voices, promotes freedom of expression and supports a vibrant culture. Thank you for purchasing an authorised edition of this book and for respecting intellectual property laws by not reproducing, scanning or distributing any part of it by any means without permission. You are supporting authors and enabling Penguin Random House to continue to publish books for everyone. No part of this book may be used or reproduced in any manner for the purpose of training artificial intelligence technologies or systems. In accordance with Article 4(3) of the DSM Directive 2019/790, Penguin Random House expressly reserves this work from the text and data mining exception.

Typeset in 11.9/14.2pt Fournier MT Pro by Six Red Marbles UK, Thetford, Norfolk
Printed and bound in Great Britain by Clays Ltd, Elcograf S.p.A.

The authorised representative in the EEA is Penguin Random House Ireland, Morrison Chambers, 32 Nassau Street, Dublin D02 YH68

A CIP catalogue record for this book is available from the British Library

ISBN 9781847927194

Penguin Random House is committed to a sustainable future
for our business, our readers and our planet. This book
is made from Forest Stewardship Council® certified paper.

To my parents: for everything, despite everything

Nations reel and stagger on their way; they make hideous mistakes; they commit frightful wrongs; they do great and beautiful things. And shall we not best guide humanity by telling the truth about all this, so far as the truth is ascertainable?

Black Reconstruction in America 1860–1880 by W. E. B. Du Bois

In bed, he tried to envision this freedom that was not quite freedom. That was and was not. That was 'here', but also 'not now' . . . His mind blanked at the paradox. As when that philosophic German stable boy had tried to describe a flying arrow that flew and yet somehow did not, was launched and yet never arrived at its target . . .

The Fraud by Zadie Smith

Contents

Author's Note   xi

Prologue   1

Book I: Origins and Echoes   13

Book II: Fire and Ashes   119

Book III: Exile and Arrival   213

Acknowledgements   329

Author's Note

This is a work of creative non-fiction – a blend of memoir, family story and political history. I draw on a diverse array of sources to tell this story, ranging from interviews to photo albums to books to conversations and much more. But, crucially, I rely on memories – mine and others'. What I present here is my version and understanding of events.

Where I didn't have access to written or recorded sources, the dialogue is necessarily an approximation of what was said or conveyed to me. Some of the characters that appear are composites of people I've known, and their names have been changed to guard their privacy.

I've moved between worlds throughout my life, and so this book does too. This complicates word choice and terminology. One issue that arose for me in the final stages of the book was whether or not to capitalise 'Black'. Given the centrality of race to this story, I have decided – against the prevailing convention – to use the lower case. This reflects the contexts in which I grew up, and where I first became conscious of race as a marker of social identity.

Prologue

In my home country, they call me a 'bornfree'. I belong to the first generation in the modern history of my native land that never lived under direct colonial rule. Unlike my father and his father before him, I have never been denied the vote based on my chocolate-coloured skin. I have never lived under a political system that dictated where I could lay my head at night. I have never fought in a war for my liberty. But even though I was born free, colonialism has marked the landscapes of my life with an eerie precision.

This is not an easy story to tell. It is messy and eventful and strange.

I could begin in 1871 when an eighteen-year-old Englishman, a boy really, arrived on the diamond fields of the southern African wilderness in search of fortune and glory. He was fair-haired and skinny; always clad in floppy hats and shabby tweed; inarticulate with a high-pitched, querulous voice; of weak physical constitution – they say he had been afflicted by a 'bad heart' all his life. No one who saw his gangly profile could have imagined that Cecil John Rhodes would one day become one of the world's richest men. Or that in decades to come he and his company would dispossess legions of Africans, including my family, of their homes and rename 150,000 square miles of land mass after himself. Or that the country he left in his wake, Rhodesia, would endure for ninety years as an apartheid state. That his legacy of expropriation and violence would be recast as munificence through a world-famous scholarship that bears his name at the University of Oxford, where I currently work as a professor.

I could also begin a century later, when my father joined a brutal war of liberation against the tin-pot, white supremacist Rhodesian government – a war that eventually paved the way for the independence in 1980 of a new country, Zimbabwe, the last nation in continental Africa to fly the British flag.

Or perhaps I could attempt to sum up the career of Zimbabwe's notorious and divisive first leader, His Excellency Comrade Robert Gabriel Mugabe, who came into office promising a new democratic era – and then refused to relinquish power. Mugabe's reign of thirty-seven years from 1980 to 2017 outlasted six US presidents, five British prime ministers, five secretaries-general of the United Nations, four actors who played James Bond in feature films, and two popes. His life encapsulated the exhilarating hopes and crushing disappointments of Africa's promises of freedom – promises he once championed, then shattered.

But I will begin with myself, on a frigid morning on 5 February 2019, a Tuesday, when I was running late for a hearing.

I planned to use my journey there to finesse my testimony and brace myself to deliver a subtle and judicious performance. It was, after all, a politically sensitive matter. But I had narrowly missed my train. I boarded the next one, scheduled to reach London King's Cross station at 9.45 a.m. That left me only fifteen minutes to make the twenty-minute trek to Westminster. I would be late for the ten o'clock start. I slumped into my seat. The train chugged out of the railway station. For at least the next hour, the only good use of my time would be to review my notes. But I was too flustered and annoyed with myself to concentrate. The words I had written melted into nonsense on the page. 'C'mon, c'mon,' I muttered under my breath, urging the train to move faster. When it arrived, I raced from platform to subway to footpath until I reached Portcullis House. I was sweating like a wrestler as I cleared security and trotted to the Thatcher Room.

The chair of the International Development Committee

PROLOGUE

in the House of Commons, who was leading the parliamentary hearing on the political crisis in Zimbabwe, sat in the centre of a horseshoe-shaped dais with three members of the select committee flanking him on either side. I stepped into the room gingerly and sidled into my designated seat next to the two other expert witnesses who had been called upon to testify before the British government. A solemn mood presided over the hearing as my colleagues delivered their opening statements.

* * *

I had missed my initial train that morning because I had woken up in an unfamiliar bed, feeling sluggish and disoriented. The night before, as I drifted into that grey zone between wakefulness and slumber, my consciousness had become a narrow, high-walled corridor crammed with everything troubling me recently. I was midway through my first year as an associate professor of African politics at Oxford and I was floundering. I didn't know how to do my job. My time management was hopeless, I had few boundaries, I was reeling from overwhelm and burnout. But I could not say no to invitations. There was more than a little ego and insecurity involved: I felt the pressing need to announce – no, to prove – myself as a new authority on African affairs. Two invitations to speak about Africa in two different cities, on consecutive days, to two very different audiences came my way. I, of course, said yes to both.

The first of these was from the University of Cambridge. Under growing pressure from students to 'decolonise' their teaching and research, the mostly white professors of African studies at Cambridge enlisted me to give a public lecture about white privilege and anti-blackness in our field, about what it might mean to decolonise. I had a reputation for speaking out against white supremacy in academia from my student days in an activist campaign group called Rhodes Must Fall in Oxford.

I left Oxford for Cambridge late on the morning of Monday, 4 February. While reviewing my PowerPoint slides on the train, I was interrupted by a phone call from an unknown number.

'Good afternoon, Professor Chigudu,' the voice on the line said. 'This is Bright Matonga. I understand that you are testifying tomorrow to the British parliament about our situation here in Zimbabwe. What are you going to say?' He was calling me about the second invitation I had received.

Bright Matonga had been deputy information minister in Robert Mugabe's cabinet. He still served in Zimbabwe's ruling party, the Zimbabwe African National Union – Patriotic Front, or ZANU(PF). I knew little about Matonga but had enough sense to deduce that propaganda was his remit. Strike an apolitical tone, I thought. I told him I would speak about problems like poor sanitation and diarrhoeal disease in Zimbabwe's cities and what donors could do to help. Uninterested in my attempts to steer the conversation to the neutral ground of public health, Matonga cut me off. He talked at me about the exaggerated claims in human rights reports that accused the Zimbabwean government of a recent 'campaign of terror' to quell civic dissent. He told me not to buy into such lies intended to undermine the legitimacy of the ruling party and enable a Western-backed regime-change agenda: a neo-colonial threat to the sovereignty of Zimbabwe. I had a duty, he reminded me, to be a patriot: 'You are the only Zimbabwean on that panel. It is important that you represent our people fairly,' he said. He stopped short of adding, 'We are watching you.'

The irony of being called upon as a representative of my people, albeit under subtle duress, did not escape me. For most of my life, I have been read by the world as quite the opposite. Black Zimbabweans have called me a 'salad' – someone who grew up in the country's formerly white neighbourhoods, was privately educated, and had adopted white cultural habits (like eating salad). White Zimbabweans have called me a *soutpiel* – an Afrikaans word meaning 'salt penis' – because I have one foot in Africa, one foot in Europe, and my genitals dangle in the Mediterranean Sea, pickling in the brine of cultural confusion. Americans have said I sound British. British people have asked me why I speak so well and concluded that I am the 'whitest black man' they know. And some of my colleagues at Oxford have suggested that I am not 'a *real* African'. This is partly why I have long felt a constant, gnawing need to prove myself. I used to think that the position of professor of African politics could compensate for my failed racial and national identity. Academic success was my way of covering up the bruises from cultural rejection and alienation.

I alighted from the train in Cambridge, tucked my phone into my jeans and hurried to my guest room. I had a few minutes to deposit my bags and catch my breath. In an hour, I would argue against derogatory and pessimistic ideas about Africa that abound in Western scholarship in front of a British university audience, having just been threatened by an African politician for testimony I would deliver the following day to British parliament about yet another crisis in Africa. My head was spinning.

I stared out of my guest-room window in an old Cambridge college. Before me was a finely manicured lawn resplendent with chrysanthemums, yarrow and roses. Cambridge looked surreal after that phone call. It felt so academic, abstract, removed from my concerns about Zimbabwe and the impending testimony. The old limestone buildings, the cobbled streets, the elegant courts, the pristine foliage all transported me to a world out of time.

***

'First let me apologise for my late arrival,' I said to the parliamentary committee. One of the MPs quickly posed a question – one I recognised was a trap: Had the UK government been too quick to endorse Emmerson Mnangagwa's presidency of Zimbabwe after a military coup that ousted his erstwhile friend and comrade, Robert Mugabe?

I shot a quick glance at Joss – my mentor, former PhD advisor and now colleague at Oxford – seated next to me. Our eyes met for long enough to agree that this was a loaded question. I looked over at the third expert witness, a professor of international politics at the University of London, on Joss' right. His eyes said it all too.

'Professor Chigudu, do you want to take that one?' the chair said to break our reticence.

No, I don't.

It was no secret that the British government hated Mugabe. There was a tendency in many portrayals of Zimbabwe to paint the early independence period of the 1980s in the aureate tones of halcyon days. The British certainly did so, as did the Americans, and pretty much every major Western power. It's easy to understand why. In 1980, a bloody war of liberation had just ended and Zimbabwe's new leader offered a magnanimous compact to hold the country together: 'If yesterday I fought you as an enemy, today you have become a friend and ally,' Mugabe said in a speech on 17 April that year, the eve of Zimbabwe's formal independence. 'It could never be a correct justification that because the whites oppressed us yesterday when they had the power, the blacks must oppress them today because they have the power. An evil remains an evil whether practised by white against blacks or by blacks against white.'

Forget the past. Focus on the future. And for a time, Zimbabwe flourished – or at least it appeared that way. Bubbling beneath the surface of Zimbabwe's apparent social progress and Mugabe's grandiloquent language of racial reconciliation were dark undercurrents. These became apparent by the turn of the millennium when Mugabe's tone radically shifted. No longer the great conciliator, Mugabe launched a scathing attack on European colonialism in Africa and the white settlers who had made their home on the continent. White settlers were guilty, Mugabe charged, of pillaging Africa's resources. In speeches full of vim and rhetorical flourish, Mugabe asserted that though Zimbabwe gained independence in 1980, the liberation struggle would never be over until all the white-owned land in the country had been returned to native black hands.

Criticisms from the West flew in like a storm of arrows in a medieval battle: according to his detractors Mugabe was a maestro of incitement, a splenetic prophet of self-sabotage stoking the rage of poor, black, ignorant hordes who, since 2000, had been occupying white-owned farms and calling themselves war veterans. When I was growing up, my father told me, repeatedly and often, just how much he hated this reading of Zimbabwe's politics. My father saw Mugabe as a proud black revolutionary leader and intellectual unafraid to stand up to the West. Whatever one's viewpoint, Mugabe lost all Western goodwill and was accused of punishing white people by stealing their lucrative farmland, thereby destroying Zimbabwe's economy. Investors withdrew from the country. Businesses shut down. International sanctions were applied. Zimbabwe spiralled into what economists call hyperinflation. I could not have guessed how bad this state of affairs would become. In just a few years, Zimbabwe sank into the entropy of systemic collapse: an economy so disintegrated and irrational that an individual egg cost trillions of dollars.

In 2015, at a private dinner party in London, the then British Ambassador to Zimbabwe said to me that it was time for Mugabe to go and that, despite a questionable human rights record, Emmerson Mnangagwa would make for a suitable successor. She insisted that Mnangagwa's plan for political and economic re-engagement with the West was what Zimbabwe needed. I wasn't convinced.

Mugabe was deposed in 2017. He died in 2019 in exile in Singapore. His death wasn't unexpected; he was withered, frail, and so very old. By that time, Mnangagwa's Zimbabwe was crumbling just as badly as his predecessor's. Arguably, it was worse. Idle young men, desperate and hungry mothers, frustrated civil servants and trade unionists were taking to the streets to protest a mismanaged economy and stolen elections. Time and again, Mnangagwa's government responded with a merciless crackdown. The parliamentary hearing I was attending on that cold February morning had been called in response to the latest of these crackdowns against protestors. Hundreds of people, including children as young as fourteen years old, had been detained without due process. They were locked up in cells dank with urine. Some protestors had been shot dead in the city streets by the military. Many others had fled the country.

'We were all relieved when Robert Mugabe was kicked out,' said another member of the select committee. 'But with President Mnangagwa, looking at what's happening in Zimbabwe, it just looks appalling. Is there any hope for the future of Zimbabwe?' The question bore the smug condescension and self-exoneration of an imperial power looking at its former colony as if to say, sotto voce, 'If only you'd left us in charge . . .' Gripped by the frustrating feeling the French call *l'esprit de l'escalier*, the predicament of thinking of the perfect reply too late, I have fantasised about returning to Parliament to quote John Milton: 'They who have put out people's eyes, reproach them for their blindness.' Wasn't it the British who championed Mnangagwa's presidency? Wasn't it the British who once championed his predecessor, Robert Mugabe? Wasn't it the British who colonised the country in the first place and set us on this dangerous path of one dictatorship after another? Zimbabwe's present circumstances stemmed from its colonial

PROLOGUE

history. But for all my righteous indignation, I had to admit that I too wondered whether there was any hope for the future of Zimbabwe.

* * *

I returned to Harare, Zimbabwe's capital, in December 2019, eleven months after the parliamentary hearing. It was the first time I'd been home in two years. My country had faded from the news cycle but not from my consciousness. I cradled a longing to see what had changed, and to divine some sense of where the country might be headed. I had also returned home to spend Christmas with my parents – a reunion that revealed itself to be an unravelling.

Like the nation at large, my childhood home was in decline. The front wall of our house, once beaming with a brilliant white finish, had succumbed to overgrown hedges and mud stains. A diesel generator rumbled grumpily in the background like an old locomotive, compensating for a routine power cut. These lasted eighteen hours at a stretch and occurred almost daily. Part of the patio ceiling had caved in and was too expensive to repair. My mother advised me to hold off on taking a shower, even though I was sweaty from my long-haul flight. With a citywide shortage of municipal water, a defunct borehole in our backyard and soaring rates of inflation, we had to ration the weekly provision of private water that we bought from some enterprising hustlers. While my mother kept the family home afloat, my father had his own money issues to worry about. He tried to keep his farm, where he spent most of his time, financially solvent. The government my father once loyally served had reduced him to humiliating penury in his old age. His pension and a lifetime of savings had been eroded to dust.

It was a weird Christmas. We had not gelled together as a

family unit for many years. The mood in our house was morgue-like, depleted of oxygen.

I left after three weeks, feeling unmoored from the comfort of my childhood home and confused about who I was and where I belonged. What was my relationship to Zimbabwe? What was my relationship to Britain? What was I to make of the slow but unspoken estrangement within my family, our plunge into a well of sadness and loss that we refused to acknowledge and that left me feeling empty and shaken? And how could I reconcile my outward persona of confidence and accomplishment with the inner turmoil brought on by loneliness and a deep sense of inadequacy?

* * *

In the years that followed, I began a quest to understand my story and that of my family in the wider sweep of the history that shaped us. I read books, I consulted archives, I visited historic sites in my family's lore, I cajoled my parents into telling me their life stories and I pored over the memories I carry within me.

As I said, this is not an easy story to tell. It stretches over time, through decades of conquests and uprisings, liberation struggles and Cold War rivalries. It's a story caught up in a vast and intricate web of romance, heartbreak, exile, aspiration and lost innocence. It's a story that hops all over the place. One moment we're in the hills and furrows between Uganda and Rwanda; the next we're in a small Catholic school of a quaint Irish village. We swerve just as quickly between the battlegrounds of eastern Mozambique during the civil wars of the 1970s and the Gothic churches of Transylvania. We make passing but important stops in San Francisco and Mexico City. But we will spend most of our time in Zimbabwe and the UK, between former colony and metropole. This is a story about memory, as much as anything else – what we remember, how we remember, whose memory lives on, whose is

PROLOGUE

forgotten. And it's a story about love. Not a love story in any saccharine sense. But the fragile, delicate love of a family burdened by a dark and terrible shame. A shame wrought by the violence of colonial history and its aftermath. It is this shame that I hope to heal in writing this story. Yes, I was born free, but I am still chasing freedom.

Book I: Origins and Echoes

CHAPTER 1

I was scarcely five years old and already collecting rejection letters. It was 1991 and my parents were trying to secure me a place at a primary school in Harare. They belonged to Harare's up-and-coming black middle class and were determined to make the most of the opportunities emerging from Zimbabwe's independence. Nothing focused their attention more than investing in my education. Education to them was everything. It meant social mobility. It meant respect.

In Zimbabwe in the nineties, for those who could afford it, education also meant a frantic, dog-eat-dog scramble to access the best private schools. Schools with names like St Michael's or St John's, like Bishopslea or Eaglesvale, not schools named Dzivarasekwa Primary No. 2. In other words, the 'best schools' were those that had, not so long ago, been run by white people for white children when Zimbabwe was still Rhodesia, when the white settler minority governed the country, when education was largely segregated. Since the fledgling nation was just over a decade old, the school system was riddled with the inequalities, enmities, allegiances and suspicions left by colonial rule and the war of liberation against it. And if all that wasn't difficult enough, my performance in school admissions interviews didn't help.

At one school interview, I asked my father if I could take home a trophy from the school's display cabinet. When he said no, I wept shamelessly and without restraint. The teachers looked on in choked disgust, concluding that I was too unruly for them. At another interview, I was asked to draw a picture of my mother.

My rendition in blue crayon was badly misshapen and compared poorly to the drawings of the other kids. The teachers there thought I was too dim-witted for outright admission but they were willing to offer me a spot on the waiting list. My mother turned it down. She was troubled by the teachers' proud embrace of the rod as an instrument to keep children in line. An interview at one of the most selective schools in the city seemed to go fine – it was incident-free, at any rate. But all the teachers there had been teaching since before independence and showed little sign of overcoming old prejudices. When we drove home from the school, a letter of rejection was already waiting for us in the mailbox. My parents complained for years to come about that letter. The school must have sent it earlier that week. Typical behaviour from Rhodies, they scoffed. Those conservative white Zimbabweans were trapped in the habits of mind of the Rhodesian era. They had no intention of assessing me fairly, given their arrogance, their ever-tumescent self-regard, their preference for their own.

* * *

Both my parents came from large families. My mother, Hope, was born in Uganda, the sixth in a brood of ten. My father, Tafi, was born in Rhodesia, the youngest of seven siblings. I was the first child born to my parents. They then tried and tried for another child. To their excitement and relief, my mother finally became pregnant again in 1990.

She was close to term when doctors in Harare went on strike against the government. The doctors demanded better working conditions and remuneration in the country's public hospitals. Meanwhile, my mother had started to worry that something was off in her pregnancy, though she struggled to articulate what exactly. It just didn't feel right. She tried to arrange a check-up with a doctor but there were no appointments available in the city's public clinics during the strike.

After many phone calls, favours and fistfuls of cash, a doctor in a private hospital agreed to see my mother on a Saturday.

In the doctor's room, my mother lay supine on the bed and exposed her large belly. The room's fluorescent light washed her in a brilliant white halo while the smell of carbolic acid soured the air. In slow, deliberate movements, the doctor lathered her abdomen with a cold gel before pressing an ultrasound probe onto her skin. Gently at first, then firmer and harder as he performed the scan.

She waited for him to say something. The intensity of his concentration chilled her to the marrow.

When, eventually, he looked at my mother, his eyes were full of sorrow.

'Mrs Chigudu, regretfully there are no signs of foetal life.'

A curtain of darkness descended.

'It would be unfortunate to cut you open under these circumstances,' the doctor said in reference to a Caesarean section. 'It would take many days for you to recover. I suggest that we book you in for an induction to deliver the stillborn.'

My mother called my father to tell him what had happened. As she tells it, my father's first – perhaps only – concern was how he would break the news to his mother, who was eagerly expecting another grandchild. I'm sure my father remembers it differently, but that phone call is etched in bitter recall for my mother.

An anxious wait followed because of the ongoing doctors' strike. At the time, my mother was employed by a Danish organisation giving development aid in Zimbabwe. Her well-meaning European expat colleagues offered to buy her a ticket to Botswana and to pay for the procedure there, away from the uncertainty in Zimbabwe's health system. But the mere thought of packing her bags, boarding a flight, travelling to an unknown country, finding a new doctor, conveying her medical history, and most likely doing all this alone, enervated my mother. Instead she went back to the private hospital in Harare four days later with a friend who stayed with her through the induction. When the baby was delivered, my mother shut her eyes, refusing to look at her lifeless daughter, at the dead sister I would never meet. Her friend held the body tenderly for a few moments before handing the swaddled child over to the midwife.

My mother came home from the hospital, anguished and alone. I sat with her, took her hand and said, 'I'm still here.' I was four years old and don't remember this, of course, but it's what she tells me. The two of us were bound in a melancholy whose depth I could not comprehend, aware only that my mother needed to be soothed. My father cried too. But not with us. He cried with his own mother. Despite their shared affliction, my parents could not find comfort in each other.

Grief, as rendered by the poet Denise Riley, is time lived, without its flow. To escape the smothering feeling of suspended vitality, my mother decided to return to Uganda. She was hired for a two-week consultancy there and took me with her. It would also be a chance for us to be with her family. My father stayed behind. We were not in the habit of travelling together as a family.

From as far back as I can remember, I wanted nothing more than to please my mother. Her sadness was crushing to me; I would do anything to make her happy. Throughout my childhood, then my adolescence and well into my adult years, I would see myself as her ambassador and steady companion, someone she could always count on and who would make her proud.

My mother and I ended up staying in Uganda for several months after the stillbirth. When we returned to Zimbabwe, my mother used the money from the consultancy to buy my father his first car: a sky-blue Toyota Corolla.

After the months in Uganda, I had changed in one fundamental way: I had forgotten every word of Shona I knew. Before my mother and I left, I used to speak to her in English and to my father in Shona – the most widely spoken vernacular language in the country, the language my father grew up speaking, my native tongue. Now, my attempts to speak Shona left me feeling like a short-sighted driver trying to find my way at night through a maze of side streets and narrow passageways in a foreign city, in an unfamiliar car. From then on, we only spoke their shared language in the house: English.

* * *

There is nothing unusual about an unhappy couple trying to rescue their relationship by focusing on their child. In my family, this added another subterranean layer of meaning to my education: investing in my education was not only about my future, it was also about saving my parents' union. I suspect that this is why my parents had enrolled me in an exclusive, racially mixed nursery school called Head Start even before the hunt for a primary school began.

One day, my father picked me up at around lunchtime. I must still have been about four years old at the time. I was sullen during the car journey. He tried to coax me into opening up but I refused to speak. As he parked the Toyota and turned off the engine, I started to cry. I pointed at my skin: 'Is this black?' I asked.

'I can't quite remember how I answered you,' my father says now, 'but I knew what had happened.' He picked up his keys and drove back to the nursery to confront my teacher, a white woman in her mid-twenties called Debbie. She wasn't surprised to see my father charging into her classroom that afternoon; she was expecting him. She looked at him with a mournful expression, not unlike a concerned physician delivering a cancer diagnosis.

'Mr Chigudu,' she said, 'we recently admitted eight new children to the school. They grew up on farms, you see.'

As she continued, my father tuned her out. He noticed for

the first time the flamboyant colours painted on the walls: lilac, pistachio and hibiscus pink, crowded with clusters of children's drawings. He didn't need to parse Debbie's words, he'd already got the gist of it. The new children were Rhodies. He knew the type. They had been raised to take black people for granted, to see us as farm workers, domestic helpers, not as neighbours with whom they now shared the country on an equal footing. Their mothers no doubt kept them from playing with black children. Rhodie farmers were notorious for letting their dogs chase black men up a tree or down the road. Their kids grew up laughing at black people's indignity. My father clucked in disgust. Rhodie parents passed on their racism to their Rhodie children with near-genetic efficiency, like a dominant allele on an X chromosome.

My own memories of the nursery-school episode are misty. What's vivid to me is the feeling of inadequacy that accompanied it and that has dogged me since: the sense of being forever out of place, prone to humiliation, my dignity a fragile and easily broken thing.

Towards the end of 1991, my father heard about a new school that was about to open. To help launch the project, he joined the school's board of trustees, most of whom belonged to Harare's small diasporic community of people from the Indian subcontinent. It was a secular school, but they named it Twin Rivers in honour of the twin rivers of Hinduism and Islam. Incongruously, the school was located behind a hexagon-shaped church, on grounds owned by the Holy Trinity Church Community. I joined Twin Rivers as part of its first cohort of pupils. 'You're a pioneer,' my father said to me chock-full of enthusiasm. I didn't know what it meant but I liked the sound of the word. When anyone asked me what school I went to, I told them I was a *pioneer*. In the early days, our school uniform was entirely grey, apart from our brown leather shoes. But in time and in keeping with the riverine motif, the school adopted turquoise as its official colour. Soon we were wearing turquoise hats, ties and jumpers. I liked the sound of the word 'turquoise' too.

The drive to school with my father was a sacred time in which he told me stories. He told me about Muhammad Ali and how he'd watched the great boxer dance around George Foreman during their rumble-in-the-jungle fight in Zaire in 1974. 'Float like a butterfly, sting like a bee!' my father said, his face a picture of glee. He told me about Pelé, who also danced but did so impishly around defenders on soccer pitches across the globe when he led Brazil to World Cup triumph in 1958, 1962 and 1970. My father would play music in the car too. Among his darlings was Tracy Chapman. I was mesmerised by her sultry, contralto crooning. I liked the looping rise and fall in tempo of 'Fast Car', the haunting a cappella of 'Behind the Wall', the elegiac lament of 'I Used to be a Sailor'. My favourite song was 'Bang, Bang, Bang'. I liked the clean simplicity and repetitiveness of its chorus. When I heard Tracy sing, I pictured a white woman with permed blonde curly hair; the image of Dolly Parton was my mental template for all American women. My father corrected the picture in my head. He told me that Tracy was black like us. She was a revolutionary spirit uninterested in fame for fame's sake. She had dreadlocks and wore jeans and a T-shirt when she performed. She sang about important things like making the world a better place for other black people.

'Your name, Simukai, it means to *stand up*,' my father said. It does literally mean that but my father had a more figurative, more nationalist connotation in mind when he named me. I was born in 1986, and while I was 'born free' in independent Zimbabwe, the struggle against white settler rule in southern Africa was still ongoing in the eighties. Across the world, in churches and trade unions, on American college campuses, in the Congressional Black Caucus, at music festivals, there were calls for the end of Apartheid in South Africa and the release of Nelson Mandela from prison. On the ground, the anti-Apartheid struggle appeared to be reaching some kind of apogee: an all-out civil war or a negotiated political settlement or escalating street violence; these were all on the table. Elsewhere in the region, the South West Africa People's Organisation was campaigning for independence against the South African Defence Force that occupied Namibia. I was too young to understand that my father's selfhood had been forged in the gyre of anti-colonial conflict, that the cause of African liberation was my father's lifeblood. It was essential to his identity, to the persona he presented to the world. More than anything, it was what he wanted me to know about him, so much so that he commemorated his politics through my name: Simukai, to *stand up* against colonialism in all its forms. I felt even back then that through my name a solemn and heavy mantle had been draped on my shoulders.

It was no small paradox, then, that my father took me to a school that aspired to educational elitism modelled on the recent colonial past. Despite Twin Rivers' patronage from Harare's South Asian community, the headmistress, the teachers, the secretary-cum-bursar were all middle-aged white women. Only the groundskeepers and cleaning staff were black. Nothing about the school was recognisably African when it started. For my first two years at the school, we didn't have a Shona teacher. When I entered grade three, the school moved to a new building in a different suburb. The number of staff and pupils increased and we finally had two or three black teachers join the school. We now started learning Shona but only as an afterthought, a token acknowledgement that we were in fact in Zimbabwe. Shona lessons lasted a mere thirty minutes each day and revolved around singing songs and naming animals. Most of us would go on to fail the government's mandatory Shona exam in grade seven.

My cultural education consisted of playing white people's sports like field hockey and cricket. We sang English folk songs about Henry VIII, the First World War and the streets of London. We held bake sales. We read about meadows and castles and kings. We learned to speak proper English. Assiduous attention to syntax was key, as was affecting a delicate, papery accent that linguists call Received Pronunciation. Before ever having left the African continent, I was learning to speak like the landed gentry of southern England, with the prestigious accent of the BBC. Etiquette at Twin Rivers mattered a great deal too: always walk in single file when moving from one room to the next, don't run; walk with your back straight, don't slouch; cover your mouth when you yawn, otherwise flies will come in; stand up when a teacher enters the class and salute her in unison, 'Good morning, ma'am'; don't shout; and most importantly, wherever you are and at all times, strive to be a credit to the school.

When my father dropped me off each morning, I would grow apprehensive about the day ahead. He had to cajole me to get out of the car. I feared my grade-one teacher. She was a severe woman who wore frilly, fuchsia-coloured dresses. She had curly hair and a wart on her nose that reminded me of the witch from Disney's *Snow White and the Seven Dwarfs*. My fear of her was so great that even when I was desperate, I didn't dare ask her permission to go to the toilet during classes. The consequences were . . . well, there is no dignified way of saying this: I shat myself.

'Ma'am,' one of the kids said to the teacher, 'something stinks.' The other kids hovered around my desk, pinching their noses and making pee-ew gestures. 'What?' I said, shrugging my shoulders and playing innocent, ignoring the mess in my pants. The teacher came over to me. 'Let's go outside, Simukai,' she said.

We walked out of the room, and I pretended that I didn't know what was going on, but I could only feign ignorance for so long. With each step, we walked closer to acknowledging the mortifying truth.

'Let's see if you trod on something.'

Dutifully, I raised my right foot to show her the sole of my shoe. Clean.

'And now the other one.'

I raised my left foot. That too was clean.

'Ma'am. I didn't step on anything. I did a mistake.'

She tried to be kind and didn't even correct my grammar on this occasion. She found a spare pair of clean briefs for me to wear, but the school was out of spare shorts. And so, I spent the rest of the day wearing brown leather shoes, grey knee socks, a grey shirt but no shorts, only turquoise underpants.

I had a meltdown before every new school term. Sometimes I doubled over with crippling stomach-aches of no medically demonstrable cause, but these would nevertheless cause me to miss school. Other times, I couldn't sleep for days before school restarted because I had nightmares about witches and snakes hunting me down. My mother dreaded these periods. She often felt powerless and frustrated, shuffling me between doctors' appointments and going to meetings with my teachers to tell them I tended to get 'nervous' in new situations. Maybe, she asked, they could go easy on me. This attenuated my nervousness. But, at the same time, my mother signed me up to a slew of extra lessons – in French, maths, pottery and horse-riding – which only heightened my nervousness all over again. I dropped out of every extra-curricular activity she enrolled me in, with nothing to show for it. At the time, my mother complained that I was 'very sensitive', just like my father.

What springs to my mind as I reflect on my meltdowns is a game I used to play with my father that he found repetitive and annoying. We sat in the living room on a quiet evening, and I said to him, 'Daddy, what will we do when the giant comes?' He rose and gestured for me to follow him. I trailed him to the kitchen where he kept a series of garden tools behind the fridge. There was a garden hoe and a pitchfork, both were taller than me. 'We will use these to defeat the giant,' my father said. I grew giddy with excitement and felt safe and reassured. Within moments of returning to the living room, I asked him, 'Daddy, can you show me again? What will we do when the giant comes?' He sighed and took me back to the kitchen.

All the fear I carried with me was a symptom of how I had learned to read the world as impossibly overwhelming. I was not much bigger than a chair, but I had an impression, however vague, of the enormous weightiness of every expectation and task set before me, of the contradiction of having to honour my proud black name while flourishing in a white-run school, of my family's fragility and my desperate need to keep us together. It was as if the world was saying to me: *I am powerful and you are not; I am big and you are small; now find a way to deal with that.*

What if the giant came when I was all alone, left to face him with nothing but my puny hands? Everything I loved would fall apart.

CHAPTER 2

When my mother first moved to Zimbabwe in 1984, she had a short-lived and unhappy career as a high-school teacher. She left that job for a position as civil servant in a government ministry, where she spent the last four years of the eighties. It was exciting at first – and far better than teaching – but she gradually lost interest in that work too. 'I would go to the office, close the door, put two chairs together and lie down,' she said to me. 'One day, I decided that I was not going back.' Indeed, she walked out of the ministry without a word of goodbye and never returned.

Soon after, she landed a job with the Danish Association for International Cooperation. She loved the work and culture of the organisation; she had never encountered such a flat hierarchy before. She may have been a programme staff member working on an important portfolio but she helped around the office too, as everyone did. She wrote high-level funding reports one minute, and in the next she delivered the post and helped with washing the company cars.

Within a year of starting this role, though, she was offered another new job, this time with the UN Industrial Development Organization. They were looking for African women with experience in small-scale commodity production who were willing to work weekends. My mother fit the bill because she had once worked in a leather tannery before she emigrated from Uganda.

My father, who had set himself on the path of a career bureaucrat in government, did not understand how my mother could flit so haphazardly from one job to another. This was an important source of tension between them, but one that belied deeper and more difficult frustrations. My mother disregarded my father's constraining voice as her confidence grew in lock-step with her professional success.

Once, when I was about nine years old, she took me out to lunch at the Meikles Hotel as a treat on a sleepy Sunday afternoon. I was eager to visit Zimbabwe's most glamorous hotel: a colonial relic for sure, dating back to 1915, that in the mid-nineties was still a rarefied playground for the wealthy and a meeting spot for foreign dignitaries. Mercedes-Benzes and Jaguars were always parked outside. The hotel's main entrance was flanked by two intricately sculpted lions, sitting there like sentries, propping up the fiction of enduring colonial grandeur. The hotel's cafe heaved with tourists. I studied the menu forensically and made the considered decision to order the steak sandwich with fries and a double-thick vanilla milkshake. We were ready to order but the waiter brushed past us several times, making fleeting eye contact before attending to other guests. 'Excuse me,' my mother called to him. He ignored her and raced to welcome a white couple walking into the cafe. The waiter addressed them as sir and ma'am, he implored them to take a seat, asked how their Sunday was going, offered them still or sparkling water.

I watched irritation ripple across my mother's face. 'Okay, that's it,' she said to me, and she shouted for the waiter's attention. '*Ndiri kuuya*. I am coming,' he muttered, not even looking at us. My mother pushed her seat back with a screech. She leaped to her feet and stood in the waiter's path, blocking his way. She sneered and raised her voice in an ugly snarl. 'Ndiri kuuya! Ndiri kuuya!' she said, mocking him, her hands on her hips. 'You say you're coming, but we've been waiting for you for twenty minutes. Twenty minutes!' She pointed a finger at the white couple and said, 'You fall over to serve these white people but you ignore us. Is our money not good enough for you? Huh? You should be ashamed of yourself. Colonial mentality!'

She picked up her handbag. 'Come, Simu, we're leaving. We

don't need to wait for these self-hating blacks to serve us.' She spoke with such theatre and force. The waiter was dumbfounded. The cafe's guests averted their eyes from us in a spasm of social discomfort. On the drive home, I told her I was proud of her – what else could I say? But boy did I want that sandwich.

My mother took joy in such displays of defiance and in the humbling of men; they endowed her with an oomph and gravitas that I admired and feared. I studied how she moved through the world, ever her faithful apprentice. Her force of personality clung, membrane-like, to my entire being. We were so close that I often had trouble distinguishing her thoughts from my own. I took everything she said seriously and literally. According to my mother, women were all, without exception, noble: they were loving despite being exploited; they suffered humiliation with compassion; they bore the brunt of patriarchy and male insanities. When I was young, my mother was fond of saying, 'Women never lie.' I believed her – how could I not, since women never lie? – and I ignored all evidence to the contrary.

My mother's favourite word was 'exposed'. She knew that, compared to those she grew up with, she was 'exposed', in the sense of worldly. Her career took off in the nineties; she eventually left the UN and helped start a women's rights non-governmental organisation based in Harare. From there, she worked in various capacities as a gender and international development consultant. It was work that opened up the world to her. She jetted around Africa, then Europe, the United States and Asia. She always came back more fashionable than before she left. She changed her hairstyles frequently: plaits, braids, Bantu locks, double-stranded twists, even a bald shave. She wore designer skirts with high-waist belts, harlequin maxi dresses and jeans from The Gap. She brought me back toys and stationery, which I loved.

The waiter at the Meikles Hotel, my mother told me, had internalised an inferiority complex from Rhodesian rule and he still saw white people as our masters. This is why he ignored us and attended to the whites, she explained. He was not 'exposed' to other ways of thinking. If someone spoke too loudly or chewed food with an open mouth or came to visit empty-handed or didn't use deodorant when they could afford to, my mother would shake her head and pronounce that this person was not 'exposed'. If a woman believed she was inferior to her husband, she needed to be 'exposed' to feminism. Poor manners, ignorance, antiquated views, belief in old wives' tales: all signs of a lack of exposure. It was her way of teaching me the value of expanding my horizons and appreciating that not everyone would have the same opportunities as me.

* * *

During my primary-school holidays, I visited Uganda once or twice a year, usually with my mother. These trips overwhelmed me. As soon as the flight from Harare landed at Entebbe international airport, my senses were assailed from all directions. Stepping out of the plane, I was hit with a hydraulic blast of hot air, no matter the time of day. At immigration and baggage reclaim, throbbing crowds moved like a stampede under fluorescent light. I felt swallowed up by the tide of humanity. It was all too close. When we left the airport, the traffic from Entebbe to my auntie's house in Kampala was thick, cacophonous, bad-tempered and far worse than anything I had encountered in Zimbabwe. My heart rate galloped at the spectacle of *boda bodas* on the road – motorcycle taxis laden with passengers and suitcases and large jerrycans of water or gasoline performing death-defying manoeuvres to weave their way between lorries and minivans. I was a fussy eater back then and I hated the texture and taste of *matoke*, Uganda's staple of steamed bananas typically served with an oily groundnut sauce. And then there was the wet equatorial heat, the wail of mosquitoes, the eye-watering smells of smoke and sweat that pervaded the atmosphere.

My parents first met in Uganda, when they were undergraduate students at Makerere University in Kampala, 'the Harvard of East Africa', as it used to be nicknamed. My father was a student refugee at the time, exiled from Rhodesia for his political activism. At Makerere, he distinguished himself as a long-distance runner. He regaled me with tales of his running prowess when I was a child. I loved one story more than any other, and I would ask him to retell it again and again. I imagined his words as if I were watching a film. An opening wide-angle shot of an expansive stadium gradually homes in on two athletes. My father, the newcomer in Makerere, is gearing up to challenge the university's reigning champion. My father stands tall, his lean body is primed for the race. His rival, Opiyo Orono from northern Uganda, is sinewy with dark and polished skin as smooth as sea-washed stone. Lap after lap around the track, my father keeps pace with Orono. Their bodies are tightly locked against each other, refusing to relinquish even an inch of space, each heel strike synchronised between the two men. In my childhood imagination, there are no other runners. The crowd roars for the plucky underdog: 'Tafi! Tafi! Tafi!' My mother watches with stars in her eyes. My father, spurred on by the cheering crowd, starts to pull ahead. At the bend of the track, as he approaches the final straight, he breaks into a sprint. He is unleashed. Orono tries to catch him but can't. He watches helplessly as my father's lithe figure glides across the finish line. My victorious father extends a handshake to his opponent and nods to the crowd. My mental projection ends with the spectators in jubilation. I would ask my father, 'Daddy, can you tell me again? How did you beat Opiyo Orono?' When he'd sigh and start over, I would squeal with delight.

For all that my father would talk fondly about his time in Uganda, he never seemed to want to go back. If anything, he seemed to look down on Uganda, often taking casual jabs at the country for being less developed than Zimbabwe or making fun of the Ugandan accent, much to my mother's chagrin. I only remember one childhood trip to Uganda where I travelled with both my parents. I was five years old and obsessed with swords. He-Man was in vogue at the time. To mollify me ahead of the long journey, my parents bought me a plastic sword that could light up in yellow, green or red. When I held the sword, I felt powerful. I made the sounds of clashing metal and imagined myself slashing an army of barbarians in just a few skilful blows. The fantasy of invincibility carried me all the way from Harare, through transit in Nairobi, and then finally to Kampala.

It would be at least another decade before my father and I were in Uganda together again. As in so many other aspects of my family life, I took for granted that I spent time with one parent (usually my mother) or the other, so seldom with both at the same time.

The trips to Uganda with my mother were loaded with meaning beyond my grasp. She was always trying to teach me something about the importance of family or culture or about my identity. She wanted me to think of myself as both Zimbabwean *and* Ugandan, as a child of Africa. Sometimes when we were with family in Kampala, my mother would abruptly announce that she and I were leaving the city for Kabale, a small town some 260 miles away from the capital, in the south-west of the country, bordering Rwanda, the same small town where my mother had spent much of her childhood. Not only would we meet more family (and more people who were family-adjacent) in Kabale, it would also be a chance, my mother said, for me to get to *know* Africa. The Africa my mother had in mind belonged to her own idiosyncratic psychogeography. It was as much a physical place rich with food and humidity as it was an idea rich with memories. She wanted to dislodge me from the middle-class comfort of our quiet life in Zimbabwe and offer me passage into the world in which she grew up.

On a couple of occasions, my mother insisted that we make the trip from Kampala to Kabale by bus rather than by car. She thought this more authentic somehow. For over eight hours, I sat face-to-armpit among fellow passengers. The roof of the bus sank overhead under the weight of its cargo. Babies and chickens were shuffled around the carriage to make room for people to alight from the bus or squeeze themselves into it. My mother wanted me to take notice of the changing landscape as we moved out of the city. The sprawl of wood-and-brick shacks at Kampala's edge gave way to a deeply folded countryside: expansive valleys of cultivated fields and steep hillsides, some covered with grass, others quilted with groves of eucalyptus and banana trees and dotted with tiny houses roofed with corrugated iron or thatch. 'The green of the trees,' my mother observed, 'is so luminous, it hurts the eyes.' And she was right, the green refracted every felicitation of light. In sporadic patches, the forests dwindled to reveal a lovely rustic landscape of clumpy red earth. The colour palette was made all the more vivid by the acres of azure sky above us.

We would arrive in Kabale at dusk and stay with one of my mother's sisters. That Auntie Faith was a most gracious host did not stop me from worrying about the prospect of pit latrines and parasites at her house – I was squeamish and hated travelling outside cities for fear of poor plumbing and disease in the more rural parts of Africa. At Christmas, Auntie Faith hosted a mess of cousins and relatives, only a fraction of whom I could name. My attempts to proffer greetings in Rukiga, my mother's language, were indulged and gently mocked by my extended family who predicted that I would grow up to marry a *mzungu* – a Swahili word for white person. Auntie Faith also took care of my grandmother, whom we called Kaka. I remember Kaka as hunched over and frail. And she spoke no English. It was important to my mother that Kaka and I spend time together, even if it was just sitting in the same room nodding and smiling at each other.

At family gatherings my mother's charisma was on full display. She stood up to be seen. She charmed and corralled with energy and exuberance as she initiated then stage-managed rounds of speeches. My mother was a kind of lynchpin in the family: a confidante to my aunts and uncles, a patron to my cousins. She was both a feminist extolling empowerment and a matriarch preserving generational hierarchy. Her balancing of these multiple roles was something to behold. I began to understand that in my mother's family, achievement had been distributed with stark inequality. My mother had defied the wizards of poverty and provincialism to become something large.

* * *

Because my mother wanted me to be 'exposed', she would try to bring me with her on some of her work trips. In addition to Uganda, we went together to Kenya, Ethiopia, Swaziland and South Africa. Tireless in my quest for praise from grown-ups, I set out to impress my mother's colleagues and friends. I was a little show-off, a non-stop performer who had to steal all the attention in every conversation. As a respectable conformist without brothers or sisters to keep me in check, I concurred when my mother's friends called me intelligent or thoughtful or quick-witted.

My mother wanted me to learn how to fly on my own as young as possible. 'Really, my child must get everything I didn't get. It must be the very, very best,' she would say to me. 'You must travel, you must see the world.' I took my first domestic flight from Harare to Bulawayo, Zimbabwe's second city, at age five; my first international flight from Zimbabwe to Swaziland at age six; and my first overseas flight from Zimbabwe to Ireland at age nine.

An Irishman called Gerard had come to our home in Harare for dinner one night in 1995. He was an academic from a university in Cork who was researching the role of agriculture in

Zimbabwe's development and my mother collaborated with him on the gender aspects of his work. As with all my mother's guests, I tried to fascinate and entertain him. With greying hair, a full beard, rosy cheeks, a generous paunch, an abundance of guffaws and a strange accent, Gerard reminded me of the Santa Clauses I had seen on TV. It was fitting, then, that he invited me to spend Christmas that year with his family. I leaped at the opportunity and my mother thought it would be good 'exposure' for me to see somewhere beyond Africa, though she herself had never been to Ireland. I can't remember how my father felt about this trip. His relationship with Gerard was stilted but that was true of all my father's interactions with my mother's friends. It had not occurred to me that, in other families, the parents might have mutual friends who were not in-laws.

I flew to Ireland that December of 1995 as an unaccompanied minor under the care of KLM's flight attendants. In transit through Schiphol airport in Amsterdam, I was dumped in a room full of toys and sweets. I devoured Toblerone chocolate until I was almost sick. Carol, Gerard's wife, met me at the airport when I finally landed, bleary-eyed and confused, in Cork City. She looked stiff and uncomfortable. Her shoulders were tense and her manner curt. What would she do with this little African kid for a whole month? The day was sluggish and grey but the thrill of being in the First World, as we called it back then, lent a radiance to every building, statue, road, car or bridge I saw. And there were white people *everywhere*. We stopped at a mall where Carol bought me a cheeseburger for lunch. To my astonishment, I didn't have to wait half an hour for my order as I would in Zimbabwe, it was ready instantly. And it was served by a white person. After lunch, we drove ten miles out of the city into the deep, verdant valleys of County Cork. The further we went, the lanes became narrower and the hedgerows on either side of the road came closer and larger as if the earth was caving in on itself. The clouds didn't alter. They hung low above us, darkly shaded and thickly interlaced. The ambient wetness of freshly fallen rain made the air damp and sharp.

Gerard and Carol's house smelled of burning peat and hot food. Gerard liked to cook bowls of thick, steaming stew and potato casseroles dripping with melted cheese and béchamel. He introduced me to black pudding: congealed masses of fat, oatmeal, sausage and blood. I shared a room with Séamus, Gerard and Carol's son with long, golden hair. Everyone mistook him for a girl but he didn't care. He was the same age as me, nine years old, but so much more intent on being himself. He had tastes in music and confidence in his opinions, which I didn't. I was all too happy to follow his lead. His room was plastered with images of Eric Cantona and Ryan Giggs of Manchester United. Thus I became a Manchester United fan.

My immersion into Gerard's family felt like a betrayal of my own. I noticed how Gerard and Carol would sometimes kiss to say hello or goodbye. These tiny, fleeting moments made me think about how scrupulously my parents avoided any physical contact, any touch of skin.

* * *

After Ireland, during my next school holiday in 1996, I went back to Uganda on my own. Like a medical student rotating through different clinical placements, I stayed with my mother's siblings and friends in quick succession, spending time with their families in Kampala. I regularly spoke to my mother on the phone but my father was peripheral to this whole operation. Every now and then, he would call my Auntie Lilian and Uncle Jo, always my first stop when visiting Uganda, and the conversation went something like this:

'Hello.'

'Hello. Is that Lilian?'

'Speaking.'
'It's Tafi here, in Harare.'
'Yes, Tafi, good morning, it's Lilian. How are you?'
'Everything is fine. The rains have come.'
'God is good.'
'How's the going?'
'Everyone is fine. We thank God.'
'So . . . Jo has gone to work?'
'Hold on for Simu.'

Afterwards, my auntie laughed at the awkwardness of the call. I didn't understand how hard it was for them – my father, my mother, my extended family – to express feelings to each other. I had heard them talk – loudly, restlessly, argumentatively – about colonialism, 'the agrarian question', 'the national question', the land, the struggle, the International Monetary Fund, the government. But the moment the conversation turned to something more intimate, what came out was moistureless, even frightened, the result of generation upon generation of repression.

After staying with Auntie Lilian and Uncle Jo for a few days, I went to stay with family friends called the Lubegas. They were a Ugandan family who had lived in Zimbabwe for several years before returning home to Kampala. I was especially close to their youngest of seven children. Andrew was seventeen years old and still attending a boarding school in Harare called St George's College, one of the oldest and most prestigious all-boys schools in the country. Like me, he was in Uganda for the vacation. He was also the coolest person I had ever met. Andrew introduced me to code-switching. As a product of a Zimbabwean education, he spoke with due deference and in Received Pronunciation to the grown-ups. He was my model for how a fine young man should carry himself. But when it was just the two of us, he became slack and easy-going, speaking to me in a dialect I didn't quite understand.

'Simu, bra, what's cutting?' he said.

I hesitated. 'Cutting what?'

Andrew threw his head back in laughter. 'Yoh! My guy, you need serious help.'

'Why? What did I do?'

He shook his head: 'You're still speaking like the olds are around. Loosen up, ekse. Chune me your rosties.'

'My what?'

'Your *rosties*, my guy. Your stories! What's been going on?'

'Oh,' I said. 'Uh . . . not much. What are your rosties?'

'Eish, I've been here for span. I'm ready to og cab to the Miz.'

'The Miz?'

'The Miz, dude! Zimbabwe! Ah, Simu, you're killing me.'

I laughed. I needed a decoder to understand Andrew.

'I can't understand the way you speak,' I said, 'but can you teach me?'

'Now you're talking,' Andrew said, rubbing his hands together. 'First, you don't say, *What's going on?* You say, *What's cutting?*'

Andrew continued like this. He used a mix of slang words drawn from Zimbabwean and South African street lingo, Jamaican patois and African American Vernacular English, all remixed together in a style that black teenagers in Harare called 'vererse'. In 'vererse', you typically flip the main consonants of a word – *stories* became *rosties*, *funny* became *nuffy*, *back* became *cab*, *Zim(babwe)* turned into *(the) Miz* and *reverse* became *vererse*. But there was no rigid formula. Andrew and his friends played with this language constantly, bending and breaking and inventing new words on the fly. 'Once you learn it, bra,' Andrew assured me, 'you can speak proper to your teachers, then rap in vererse with the oans at school.' I wanted that. I wanted to be like Andrew, fluent in both worlds and slipping between them with ease.

In Uganda, Christianity was the air we breathed and even among the least religious, atheism was unthinkable – could there be anything more abhorrent than believing there was no God? At every gathering and dinner I went to, I was asked if I was 'saved'? I didn't know how to answer. I liked the story of Samson and Delilah, told to me by my father more as a bedtime fable than a parable, but I knew little else of scripture. The Lubegas took their creed to frightening extremes. Before bed each night, they held prayer vigils in the TV room. These sessions started tamely with a reading from the Bible but the prayers soon accelerated from conversational pace to near-unintelligible speed, with volume and pitch rising to a crescendo that shook the walls of the house. Each line of supplication was followed by a chorus of 'mmmhhh-mmm yes Lord!', the words themselves drenched in the sweat of vigorous, gasping worship. 'We rebuke the devil and all his work,' Mrs Lubega said one night in prayer. I trembled with fear, worried about how the devil might be working through me. Every fibre of my body tightened at the thought. That night, having heard enough about the eternity of torture awaiting those who had not accepted Jesus Christ as their Lord and Saviour, I said, 'I want to be saved.'

Mrs Lubega glowed with the pride of winning over a new convert. Her eyes were hot when she said to me, 'Little Simukai, all the angels are singing songs of joyous celebration because of you!' And then Andrew added, 'The powerful thing about the Bible, the best thing about the Bible, is that it's all true. Every single word. *You* now have the power of this gift of truth.'

The distinction between feeling alive in Christ and feeling absolute terror at the prospect of going to hell was hard for me to draw. I read the Book of Revelation. I discovered that on Judgement Day at the end of time, anyone whose name was not found written in the book of life would be thrown into a lake of fire. I felt ashamed of all the things I had done wrong and thought wrong, as if my entire being were contaminated by failure and sin.

When I returned to Zimbabwe, I knocked on the door of my mother's office one morning.

'Come in,' she said. I walked in and found her typing furiously.

The office was long and narrow. To my mother's left were stacks of books and papers that flavoured the room with a sweet, almond-like smell.

'What is it, Simu? I'm very busy.'

'I got saved. When I was in Uganda. By Mrs Lubega. I mean by Jesus.'

It was more a confession than a declaration. I didn't think my parents would object but I suspected that they wouldn't be enthusiastic either. In truth, I didn't know what my parents believed.

My mother said nothing, provoking my worst fears: that she was not saved, that her name was nowhere to be found in the book of life.

'Are you saved?' I asked.

'Not any more.'

She turned her back to me and continued typing. My lip started to quiver and my mother could hear me whimpering behind her but she ignored me. I ran out of her office, down the corridor, and threw myself face down onto my bed. My mother followed after me. She turned me over to face her and said, 'I was saved a long time ago but nowadays, I don't think it's for me.'

'But you will go to hell!' I wailed.

She shrugged and said that these things are not straightforward. She didn't want to talk about it any further. She left my room. I lay crumpled on the bed.

***

Underneath all my mother's preacherly confidence about gender and exposure and the various other lessons she was trying to impart to me, underneath her career ambition and her desire that I see the world, lay a complicated and often conflicted inner state. My mother was the most important person in my life but my need for her affection and reassurance was not always requited.

Consciously or not, my mother played an emotional sleight of hand. She loved me in an engulfing way one moment, only to pawn me off to other families the next. There were times she treated me as a helpless, impressionable child in need of her guiding hand. At other times, she acted as if I were an autonomous mini-adult capable of figuring out the world on my own. These shifts in my mother's moods and attention were governed by forces I could neither name nor understand as a child; I could only bid for her adoration by being whatever I thought she needed me to be in the moment. Even now, it would be extravagant for me to speculate too much about the workings of her psyche. Still, I can't help but see, through the clear-sighted lens of hindsight, a busy and distracted woman yearning for escape, desperate to build an identity – a life, actually – outside the confines of a faltering marriage. She was confused about how to raise her sensitive and precocious only child with a husband she did not fully trust. Deep down, in some impossible-to-articulate way, my childhood self already knew that I was her blessing and her burden.

CHAPTER 3

For many years, a childhood memory draped over me like a blanket of shame. I was almost ten, and had arrived at school one day feeling tense and brittle. This must have been a few months after the Ireland trip, around May 1996. I can't be certain. It was about 7.30 in the morning, and classes started at 8.00, leaving enough time for a quick game of tag in the playground. I joined the game with the other kids but was eliminated almost immediately. I started to sob – hopelessly and helplessly. My friends tried to comfort me but I was inconsolable. A girl called Susan ran over and tried to tag me again. She didn't know I was already out. I lashed out at her. Two slaps, one on either cheek. Her neck twisted to one side then the other. The rush of blood to her face turned her white cheeks florid. Behind a curtain of tears, I saw her eyes raked with fear and shock. I kicked her leg, then wailed at the top of my lungs, 'I hate you!' She fled. My body went limp and I collapsed, like an empty garbage bag, into a trembling mess. *What have I done? What have I done?*

The scene sent one of the boys into an uproar: 'Yoh!! Did you see what Simukai did? *Pap-pap, I hate you!*' He sniggered. Horror split my mind from my body. I took stock of the damage: I had let the school down, hurt Susan, and sinned against God. My parents would be mortified, and I feared I'd ruined my life in just a few minutes.

My teachers were dumbfounded. To my knowledge, the school did not inform my parents of my outburst. By now, my habitual nervousness notwithstanding, I was a star pupil at Twin Rivers: a teacher's pet and serial winner of awards for academic merit. I can only guess that my teachers thought this was a one-off incident and it was best not to probe too deeply into whatever happened on the playground.

A few days later, my class was going on a camping trip for a week. As we waited to board the bus, my grade-five teacher walked over to me, her arms folded, her gait tentative, a hesitant and inquiring smile on her face. She was a tiny woman with bronze skin and jet-black hair. Her family came from Pakistan but had lived in Zimbabwe for many years. She normally wore gold bangles on her wrists and an elegant shalwar kameez in different colours for each day of the week. On this occasion, she wore white sneakers and an aquamarine tracksuit, all set for the camping trip. 'Simukai,' she said, almost meekly, 'did you hit Susan?' I confessed that I had. I don't remember what she said. But I know I wasn't punished. Next, the headmistress – short, frumpy, grey-haired – pulled me aside and said, 'Don't do that again.' We boarded the bus and took the three-hour journey to a large conservation area full of woodland, streams and rocky outcrops, and home to our campsite for the week. Dense, white cumulus clouds massed and dispersed in the blue arc above, small black swallows swooped and dived through the trees lining the road.

***

My memory, usually so reliable, turns mercurial when I reflect on this time; dark gaps fill the blanks between fragments of remembrance.

I remember, for instance, my father's first car, the sky-blue Toyota Corolla, in which he took me to nursery and primary school. It was in this car when he first played Tracy Chapman for me. But I remember too that one day it disappeared and we had a new car. That too disappeared, then came another. We cycled through Toyotas, Nissans, Peugeots, through sedans, station wagons, hatchbacks and trucks. Every now and then I heard my mother shout at my father about another accident. He took it, as always, in silence.

Sometimes we forget because our mind is trying to shield us from what is too painful to remember. And sometimes memories spring forth vividly and unexpectedly, years later, soliciting the attention of our adult consciousness, inviting us to revisit the past with mature awareness.

I remember lying in bed unable to sleep because the late-night screaming from my parents' room was keeping me up. I folded my pillow over my ears and prayed for it to stop. But the squabbles and harsh words – *I hate you!* – dribbled under my door like a rising flood of water, creating a pool of distress around me. My sleep became fitful. I was anxious about what might happen each night. I remember hearing my mother in a fit of rage, how she shouted at my father, 'This is not good for the child!' I knew I was involved in their unhappiness. I eavesdropped, understanding only a fraction of what they were saying and, as children do, I invented the rest. I took responsibility for their predicament. I took my parents' anger and grief and shame and made them my own.

One evening, my mother and I talked in the living room. I don't remember if she told me that we had lost another car or whether I imagined that she did because I now know this is what happened. I was in my brown, paisley-patterned pyjamas. She wore a pastel-pink nightdress. As she did every night before bed, my mother covered her skin with shea butter that had a nutty, earthy aroma. I went to my room and fell asleep promptly that night, only to be woken a few hours later. The screaming had started again. My mother did most of the shouting. Louder than usual. This was one of those nights when it got out of hand. I prayed for it to end. Loud noises followed by muffled thuds. A soft thump. Then a chilling silence.

I rushed out of bed. I burst into my parents' room. It was dim with only trickles of light peeping into the room. I saw a figure on the floor draped in pastel pink. I was too late. My knees buckled. My hands shook.

Before I could bend down to touch the pink cotton, my father picked up the rolled-up pile of bed sheets and blankets on the floor that I had mistaken for my mother's body. He threw them back on the bed. I couldn't see my mother anywhere. Then I noticed a yellow light under the bathroom door. She had locked herself in the en suite bathroom. My father told me to go back to bed.

The next morning, like so many mornings during this time, I woke up distraught and confused. This pattern went on for years yet I only remember it in pieces. I tried to be brave, but I often burst into tears soon after being dropped off at school. If my father picked me up later, I gave him the silent treatment for as long as possible, and when I did speak to him, I uttered no more than what needed to be said.

For a year or two, maybe longer, I cannot recall, I did not sleep through the night. I had recurrent nightmares that I would burn in hell or that my mother would get shot and killed, the imagery for this latter dream coming from the film *Set It Off* – a crime caper in which four desperate black women start robbing banks to provide for their families, three of them ending up dead, gunned down by the police in the closing act of the film. I suffered from vague stomach-aches and had to miss many days of school.

***

My parents and I didn't talk about their fighting at night. They hoped I might forget it but when it was clear that I had been affected, my father tried to make it up to me. Not knowing what else to do, he took me to England in 1996 as a Christmas present.

It was the first time I can recall the pair of us travelling together alone. My mother stayed home.

London's city streets were lit up in a splendid display of festive colour. My father took me to Hamley's toy store on Regent Street and the Disney Store. He spared no expense. The highlight of the trip was going to Manchester. Man United had just won the 1995/96 FA Carling Premiership title, having made an improbable comeback against rivals Newcastle United. Now I got to see my team's legendary home stadium, Old Trafford, the theatre of dreams. We went on the official tour and saw the dressing room and the pitch. We had two photos framed from that tour. In one, we are standing pitch-side, bundled up in our coats and looking in awe at the grass. In the other, an official portrait, we are holding the Premier League trophy, both of us looking at the camera with wide grins.

I wanted to absorb every morsel of information I could about the club and its history and to take in all the gossip about the players. By the end of the trip, I was only dressing in United's colours: red, black and white. I had the full Man United kit, Man United underwear, a Man United team poster, an Eric Cantona baseball cap and mug, a Man United toilet bag, a Man United alarm clock, and my most treasured keepsake: a pair of Man United sneakers. When paying for this haul at the Man United megastore, a whopping £200 (or nearly £400 in today's money), my father smiled at the two young women at the till and said, 'I love my son.'

My father understood parenting to mean providing for his child, not communicating with him. On our first trip to England, he pulled out all the stops he could to provide an entertaining and lavish holiday. But no amount of material indulgence could clear the mess nor assuage the anxiety in our family.

I never did tell my parents about what happened with Susan. Not until recently, well into my adulthood, could I make the connection between the distress I was experiencing at home and how it burst out of me in my behaviour on the playground. As a child I reached instead for the language of sin, that was what I knew. I knew I was short-tempered and emotionally fragile, apt to lose control, which made me vulnerable to the devil and all his works. I committed the sin of anger when I hit a girl. And I committed the sin of cowardice when I didn't tell my parents about it. The shame was unbearable. I felt a self-loathing deep in the pit of my stomach.

***

When my mother was away on one of her trips, my father would try, with only modest success, to come home early from work during the week. We had a housekeeper, a kindly man whom we called Mr J. He babysat me until I went to bed if my father had not returned from town. I would wake up in the middle of the night to check whether my father had come home. Often, I found him asleep on the couch, his face lit up by the bright glow of the television. I would nudge him awake and he would look at me with swimming rheumy eyes, his eyelids drooping, his speech less than eloquent, his breath tart and fruity.

In my mother's absence, my father would try to find things for me to do during the weekend. He took me swimming at the club or deposited me at the cinema. Once, when I was about six years old, my father ushered me into a film theatre midway through the screening of a gun-slinging Western deemed unsuitable by the local film board for anyone under the age of eighteen. He left me in a seat and said he would pay for my ticket. I sat alone for a few minutes in the dark, unable to follow the narrative on screen and feeling restless and panicked. An attendant came into the theatre looking for me. I was swiftly ejected but my father was nowhere to be seen. I sat outside on the kerb. I studied the three promotional posters on the wall. I looked at the wall's peeling blue paint, its cracks and crevices with insects and the occasional lizard zipping through. And I waited. I was too young to know where my father had gone. I didn't know what a bar was. But I knew that sooner or later he would collect me when he thought the film was finished. I played fantasy games in my head and escaped into my imagination.

Like many men of his generation, my father survived the violent cataclysm of the liberation struggle but did not emerge unscathed. He had seen too much, and been through too much. He had marched with hundreds and thousands of other soldiers, all of them dry as bones on a field of slaughter, surrounded by fire and sulphur and blood. Who knows what my father saw when he closed his eyes? What memories came back to him unbidden? Who knows what he was trying to anaesthetise himself from feeling, or what his soul was longing for when he guzzled down bottles of beer or tumblers of whisky?

No form of counselling or rehabilitation existed for veterans like him. My father's wounds were his own to nurse.

All I knew as a boy was that sometimes I had to wait when he didn't show up on time to pick me up. And sometimes late at night, I had to wake up, check if my father was passed out on the couch, put him to bed, and then double-check that all the doors were closed and locked and the television and the lights were turned off before going back to sleep myself.

It took nearly three decades before I realised that one of the reasons we kept cycling through cars was that my father kept crashing them when he was drunk-driving.

CHAPTER 4

We lived in a bungalow on a four-acre compound on the southern fringes of the city. We had moved there when I was eight years old. The area was still under development. Ours was the last in a row of compounds. Turning left out of our front gate led to a tarmac road and the other homes in the neighbourhood, while on the right was a dusty track lined with scattered building materials, heaps of sand, mounds of scaffolding, sacks of cement and coils of wire for fencing. Beyond that was brushwood in a stunted forest.

I would spend hours on end walking around our yard with a stick in my hand and creating imaginary worlds where I was the hero of the story: a Jedi Knight, a star striker for Manchester United, an African Wolverine leading the X-Men against the forces of evil and hatred. We grew guava and mulberry trees that whispered to each other whenever there was a breeze. When the sun set, it didn't take long for the sky to be covered in stars like a canvas of crushed glass. As was typical for a middle-class family like ours, we provided housing on our compound for our domestic help, Mr J and his family. Every morning at six o'clock, Mr J arrived for work. The creak of the door and his unmistakable shuffle announced the start of the day. For the next several hours, Mr J did all the housework himself, ably and with a slow deliberateness despite his right leg being shorter than his left, a residual effect from a childhood polio infection that left him with a lopsided limp. I liked to follow Mr J around the house as he spent each morning sweeping, cleaning, cooking, washing, drying, ironing and folding until the whole place was gleaming. He gathered and saved loose items and scraps, whether old milk cartons, bottle tops, dated newspapers or torn wrapping paper. His inability to let things go, no matter how worn or tattered or useless, came from never having had much. He was dutiful to the point of compulsive in his determination not to be wasteful. When he was done with the chores, a smile of satisfaction spread across his face, a parting of the lips revealing poor dentition. He would look over his handiwork with his gentle eyes and draw on his limited English to say, 'It's good like that.'

On the days I spent walking around the garden, holding my stick and inhabiting my elaborate fantasies before spending time with Mr J, life could be placid.

But in the background was a country moving ineluctably to disaster.

As a child, I only caught hints of what was brewing. From our new bungalow, everything was now further away. There was a great deal more driving to do to get to work or school or to see friends. I began to notice sometime in 1997 the lengthening queues for fuel, like a trail of giant millipedes, along the banks of major highways. My father occasionally dragged me with him to hunt for diesel. These were shaggy-dog expeditions: hustling around the city, bouncing from one gas station to the next, encountering rumours of magic men who could divine diesel from stones, all leading to the anticlimax of being told at one station after another to come back the next day when we might be lucky.

I was frustrated too by how often power cuts happened. They interrupted my cartoon-viewing schedule for the afternoon. I would call my father when he was at work and ask him to fix it. This was a child's reasoning since I didn't understand my father's job. I knew he wore a tie, an Oxford shirt and a charcoal-grey suit when he went to work at a place called the National Economic Planning Commission in the Old Mutual building in downtown Harare. The lobby at his workplace always smelled like a new car, and it had a scale replica of the building in a glass case, which mesmerised me every time I saw it.

I heard my father use polysyllabic words that were meaningless to me. Words and phrases such as 'civil servant', 'economy', 'finance', 'state enterprises', 'para-statal organisations' and the like. I had no inkling of how my father saw himself – as part of a cadre of liberation-fighters-turned-bureaucrats whose mission was to deliver on the promise of Zimbabwean independence. But the country's vision of unity and broad prosperity had been supplanted by the rise of unrelenting, vulgar corruption by a coterie of political elites. Personal enrichment in the upper echelons of government had superseded public spiritedness and redress for colonial injustices.

My father stayed loyal to the government. Loyalty for him was to the ruling party and it was anchored in history, in sacrifice, in his need to believe that the struggle for liberation hadn't been in vain. He held this belief firmly, even as scandal after scandal made it harder to justify. It wasn't just one scandal. It wasn't even two. It was a litany, touching every part of government. You could barely keep track.

For instance, the National Housing Fund, established to build dwellings for lower-paid civil servants, was reportedly looted to build extravagant homes for senior government officials – pot-bellied, heavy-jowled men who drove air-conditioned SUVs from their offices to the city's affluent northern neighbourhoods. Their homes came replete with swimming pools and tennis courts, protected by high masonry walls topped with broken glass to shred the hands of intruders. If that wasn't enough, electric fences sat on top of the glass. Ominous signs were affixed to the gates of such properties: *Chenjera Imbwa*. Beware of the Dog.

And then, one of my mother's friends, a politician called Margaret Dongo, revealed in parliament that a fund set up to compensate war veterans injured during the liberation struggle had been looted by high-level functionaries of Zimbabwe's ruling party, ZANU(PF). 'We should be celebrating our independence and the end of white minority rule, but our people are asking themselves why our leaders are enriching themselves shamelessly while most of the real war veterans are living in abject poverty,' she said. War veterans camped outside the president's official residence and stormed the headquarters of the ruling party. Members of the war veterans' association delivered blistering public speeches about the 'fat stomachs' and 'luxury yachts' of Zimbabwe's oligarchy while those who brought them to power languished in squalor: 'Is this the ZANU(PF) I trusted with my life?' At the Heroes' Day celebrations in 1997 – a national holiday commemorating the revolutionaries and guerilla soldiers of the liberation war, people like my father – Mugabe was booed off stage during his speech. To regain political favour, Mugabe paid out a hefty and unbudgeted compensation package to the war veterans: a one-time disbursement followed by monthly cheques, free medical care, free access to education, and land. This payout made a huge difference to the lives of war vets, though there were fierce disagreements about who counted as a war vet and who didn't. I have no idea if my father was a beneficiary. The package cost 4 billion Zim dollars. The local currency crashed the day after the initial payout – a day now known as 'Black Friday'.

And then, again: money allocated to government agencies, such as the District Development Fund, intended for farming and digging boreholes, was instead used to buy cars and high-tech farming equipment for senior officials' personal use.

The list goes on: bribery, nepotism, embezzlement.

Tension in the country was rising. The Zimbabwe Congress of Trade Unions called for national stay-aways – a form of non-violent strike action where workers across multiple sectors temporarily boycotted their jobs as a strategy to bring the country to a halt. Food riots and street protests erupted with increasing frequency throughout the city. The country was in open revolt. The people were losing faith. My father? He never did. Or, if he did, he never admitted it.

***

The changes afoot in Zimbabwe presaged a much more devastating period that would come to be known as 'the crisis'. But politics was a world apart from my immediate concerns.

I was in my penultimate year of primary school. My mother, being the astute judge of character that she was, did *not* like my grade-six teacher. Mrs Ramasamy had moved to Zimbabwe from Mauritius and carried herself like a dictator in a silk blouse. 'Mrs Ramasamy is not a serious person,' my mother complained, her tone sharp as a German paring knife. And my mother had a point. Among other offences, Mrs Ramasamy thought it was appropriate to teach us about racial traits based on an old anthropology textbook. She sprinkled in some extra nonsense for good measure. According to her grand classification system, I was part of the 'Negroid' group because of my dark skin, coiled hair, wide nose, large teeth and what she called my 'tendency to prognathism'. I obviously didn't know what prognathism was but it didn't sound like something you wanted to have. I later learned that the word describes the facial bone structure of Neanderthals. That revelation upset me. It's hard to enjoy your school days when your teacher turns you into a racist caricature from nineteenth-century ideas about phrenology. But this was also the same woman who instead of lessons made us have potluck parties, where we danced the Macarena. At the end of each party, she shamelessly hoarded all the leftover snacks including Mr J's exquisite samosas that I had brought to class. It was, to say the least, uncouth for a teacher to take a child's food after calling him a 'Negroid'.

One morning on the way to school, my mother and I stopped

by my mother's office so she could collect some documents. As I was playing solitaire on the computer at reception, my mother said, 'Simu, I've been speaking to Gerard. How would you feel about going back to Ireland to finish the school year?' Without a hint of hesitation, I said yes. The prospect of four months in Ireland, to spend so long out of Africa, thrilled me. My mother talked of the benefits that would come from this exposure and I wanted to prove that I had the maturity and independence to spend so much time away from my parents.

I don't know if my mother consulted my father before speaking with Gerard about this plan. I do know that he was not enthusiastic and that he objected, but to no avail; my mother's mind was made up. He eventually accepted my mother's decision with brooding resignation.

In late August, the night before I left for Ireland, two of my cousins came over to our house for a sleepover. We laid out mattresses in the living room and gorged on a large stash of sweet things. We planned on watching TV late into the night and telling stories.

A scream from down the hallway broke the magic of the evening.

'SIMU!' My mother called my name.

I sprang up from the mattress and raced down the corridor. *It's happening again. I must stop it.*

My parents were in the spare bedroom. I barged in. Their arms were raised and tangled like they were struggling. My father held something. An extension cord, maybe?

I forced myself between them and wrapped my arms around my mother's waist as tight as I could. I placed my body in front of hers as a protective shield.

I couldn't breathe. I uttered quivering, threadlike sounds as if my voice would break in two if I tried to speak.

'What's wrong?' my father asked in a voice dressed in innocence.

I looked at him with disbelief, fear, confusion. I held my mother tighter.

'He's terrified,' my father now said. His change of tone registered my alarm. He raised his eyebrows in a show of concern.

I squeezed my mother's waist tighter still.

'We were just playing,' my mother said.

'No . . . you . . . weren't . . .' I managed.

'We were just playing a game and I said, I'm going to call Simu. And so I called you. There's nothing to worry about. Go back to the living room with your cousins.'

That moment hung heavily in the air. Why did this keep happening? Something was wrong. Or had I misunderstood? I didn't know. No, no, no, I wanted to say. But I just didn't know.

I loosened my grip on my mother's waist and recoiled as a kicked dog. I walked back down the corridor to the living room. One hesitant step in front of the other.

Years later, I spoke to both cousins who had been there about that night. One of them had no recollection of the sleepover. The other, when prodded, mustered a vague but uncomfortable felt memory, a terrible dreamlike sequence of a scream, me running after it, the feeling of not knowing what to do, the awkwardness that followed. 'This is not a memory I would ever go back to,' she said to me, 'but I remember thinking, *I am not supposed to be here. I am not supposed to see this.*'

The next day, I boarded a plane and flew to Ireland.

CHAPTER 5

Ireland greeted me, at the end of August, with the last days of a northern summer. The afternoons were calm and balmy. It would stay light as late as nine in the evening. I had never seen the sun at that hour. I had never seen dusk unfold with great ease, taking its time to welcome the night. On the brightest of afternoons, we visited the nearby stony beaches for a few hours. The water was too cold for a swim but I loved watching the serene tide lapping on the pebbled shore. I loved dipping my bare feet into the cool, grey sand.

I was absorbed into Gerard's family again. I went to a small, Catholic school in the village with his son Séamus and daughter Ciara. I was the first black person most people had ever laid eyes on. Normally, my nerves were at their rawest and most intense when I entered a new class but they would usually subside after a few weeks. But in Ireland, this time round, tension settled into my body, made a home there and refused to leave. My teacher, a man of dour comportment, wore the same outfit every day: black trousers, white shirt, green blazer and tie. His nose was cavernous, his eyes pious and impassive, his voice baritone and mirthless. I was once again too frightened to ask for permission to use the toilet. I would sit at my desk, my whole body shaking as the pressure in my bladder became unbearable, and I wet myself in class. During the breaks, the kids would ask me if Conor had had a go at me with his water pistol as they pointed to the wet patch over my crotch. Séamus, concerned but not knowing what to do, said, 'You know, Simu, you can tell Mr O'Hanlon when you need to use the toilet.'

At home, I didn't know how to handle Gerard. My father was sometimes loving and present, but more often he was absent and detached. Gerard, on the other hand, was always present, always overbearing. He was full of song and food and gross humour. He would tell me to pull his pinkie then he would fart on cue. He was also terribly irascible. I could not predict what would set him off but he could erupt into bellows of resounding thunder. Like some kind of traffic light warning system, his face changed from white to pink to red. Each change of hue was my only clue that a thunderstorm was about to break.

When Princess Diana died, a few days after I arrived in Ireland, I was stricken and upset but Gerard would have none of it. 'Sure enough, it's because you go to a posh school in Harare,' he said, his face starting to glow pink. 'The only thing they teach you in a place like that is how to be more English than the English.' I could feel shame rising in me. For hours at home and then at the pub over Sunday dinner, which confusingly was at mid-afternoon, he talked about the superciliousness of the English, the inglorious history of the Crown, the gaudy pageantry of regal affairs, and how thoroughly undeserving the royal family was of my sympathies. His face now an unforgiving red. Celtic nationalism was important in his household. As kids, we were rarely allowed to watch TV but Gerard relaxed the rules so I could watch videotapes of *Michael Collins* and *Braveheart*, as a corrective to a tedious tradition of English self-congratulation. I didn't understand the political or historical contexts depicted in these films but I understood that in Gerard's world, the English were the baddies of history despite what the Queen and Twin Rivers would have me believe.

Gerard thought too that I was spoiled. He would turn red when I didn't know how things worked. 'There's no Mr J in this house,' he would say. At school and at home, my mind would sometimes go blank for long spells. In my mental truancy, I inhabited a fantasy world where I was a troubled hero like Batman, an orphan who turned his fear into a source of physical strength and intellectual acuity. Gerard would snap me out of my dissociation and accuse me of lacking initiative. He told me to write out in my diary a hundred times, 'I must learn to think for myself. I must learn to think for myself. I must learn to think for myself . . .'

* * *

In the autumn Gerard volunteered me to appear on a children's edutainment variety show called *Echo Island*, on Irish national TV, to talk about agriculture and land in Zimbabwe – a subject about which I knew nothing. The producers of the show had been running a series on Zimbabwe and they thought it would be cool to film a real, flesh-and-blood Zimbabwean meeting some Irish children to talk about cultural and geographic differences when it came to food. I happily agreed. Gerard patiently prepared me for the segment. He instructed me each step of the way about what to say during the recording. Filming the five-minute segment took about four hours at a school in Dublin. Between shots, I spoke to the other kids.

'Is it true you're from Africa?' a blonde-haired girl in pigtails asked.

'Yes,' I said. She let out a tiny gasp and cast a gesturing look at her classmates that said: *See, I told you.* The other kids whispered among themselves and inched a little closer to me.

'But sure, how do you know English?' asked a freckled boy. But before I could answer, more questions were fired my way.

'How come the palms of your hands are white but the rest of you is black?'

'I don't know,' I said.

'Did you wear normal clothes in Africa, or like . . . I don't know, different ones?'

'Do you eat normal food in Africa?'

'What did you do with your spear?'

They were all excited and drawing even closer to me. Then the director said we had to start filming again.

I won't forget how Gerard looked at me before the last take, his eyes moist with pride, his voice full of sweetness when he said, 'You've done an amazing job, lad. Nine out of ten. Now go and make it ten out of ten.' It was a moment of unbridled joy. I felt high on parental approval.

When the episode aired a few weeks later, I became the most popular kid in school. Even Mr O'Hanlon watched it.

This happened around the same time that land had become a renewed topic of national debate at home in Zimbabwe. The original sin lay in the country's founding as the colony of Rhodesia in the 1890s through conquest by Cecil John Rhodes and his men, who displaced hundreds of thousands of Africans and massacred tens of thousands while annexing their land. Rhodesia was ruled by a white settler minority that established a civil order based on European economic dominance and racial segregation – as they did in Australia, Canada and the United States, countries that were more successful iterations of settler colonialism and that achieved a much greater decimation of native cultures. It took years of agitation to end colonial rule, including militant insurgencies and a deadly liberation struggle for Zimbabwe to gain independence. But despite this, land hunger persisted in the country and had long been a source of political grievance among the rural black majority. The dream of a full complement of civil rights and the equitable distribution of resources for all Zimbabweans had been deferred. But why? Neither Mugabe nor his party were ever consistent champions of rectifying land dispossession from the colonial era. In the eighties, nationalism in Zimbabwe was not really about universal human rights, political pluralism and the restitution of lost land. Nationalism was, to a great extent, about eliminating dissent from ZANU(PF) rule and consolidating power in what effectively became a one-party state. It's trite and oversimplified to say this, but authoritarian rule begets authoritarian rule. Nationalism was also about creating a modern and productive economy through bureaucracy and centralised planning – the work my father did.

Much like the Rhodies before them, Mugabe's government swiftly and harshly evicted then punished poor black people who 'squatted' on land they didn't own – no matter how poor, hungry or desperate the so-called squatters were – and embarked on ambitious social programmes to transform the country according to the ruling party's vision of orderliness and progress. But this agenda was slowed by a mountain of debt, part of which was inherited from the former colonial masters. Needing to service this debt, Mugabe's government adopted an economic austerity package called the Economic Structural Adjustment Programme in 1990. Implemented under the direction of the World Bank, the package allowed the government to sell off various national industries to private companies and invite more foreign investment. The country's elite saw a huge payday as they rigged the contracts and selling of tenders. But these neoliberal reforms also gutted public resources, cut social services, and curtailed mass redistribution of wealth including land ownership. The government dealt with the land question by claiming it had shelved plans for radical land reform in the early nineties for fear of scaring off the remaining white people in the country. The potential emigration of white people from Zimbabwe would send a dangerous signal to neighbouring South Africa about the changes that could come if white people relinquished too much to black leaders in the negotiated settlement to end Apartheid. In other words, not pursuing land reform before the end of Apartheid was, they said, a shrewd diplomatic move to maintain stability in the region.

Given the growing pressure on the land question and the fall in ZANU(PF)'s reputation and popularity, Mugabe's government had to do something. The president and his ministers appealed to the freshly elected New Labour government in Britain in 1997, with a youthful Tony Blair as prime minister, for financial support to aid the redistribution of farmland in Zimbabwe. The British demurred. In a now infamous letter, Clare Short, the UK's international development secretary, wrote to Zimbabwe's minister of agriculture on 5 November to say, 'I should make it clear that we do not accept that Britain has a special responsibility to meet the costs of land purchase in Zimbabwe. We are a new government from diverse backgrounds without links to former colonial interests. My own origins are Irish, and as you know, we were colonised, not colonisers.' Allow me to paraphrase: we have bigger things to worry about than the inane mess and petty grievances of a tiny African country. Lord Peter Carrington, who brokered the 1979 Lancaster House agreement that brought the liberation war for Zimbabwean independence to a close, was aghast at Short's letter. 'Surely,' he said in an interview with an Oxford academic in 2012, 'the Labour government would have known you could not write that. It is absolutely true that we promised Mugabe at Lancaster help to fix the land problem between whites and Africans.'

Had I asked Gerard about the Clare Short letter, I imagine he would have discoursed at length about the habitual flow of Britain's self-deception when it came to its colonial history, about the country's convenient amnesia whenever accountability for past wrongs was raised. But I didn't ask because I hadn't the faintest clue who Clare Short was.

***

My friendship with Séamus sustained me during my four months in Ireland. He taught me how to play Gaelic football and how to change gears on a bike so I could ride uphill. Once every week or two, Séamus and I walked, sometimes raced, up the road to a small, isolated house on the corner of a country lane. While we walked, we whispered about the girls we fancied at school. When we reached the house down at the end of the lane, we dropped off milk and other sundries for Old Man Munro, a quiet but friendly loner with gaunt and ashen cheeks, thinning white hair and large, thick glasses. I never saw him without tobacco on his lips. Old Man Munro thanked us profusely and then retreated into his front room. He had two daughters who lived in Cork City. They babysat Séamus, Ciara and me on Gerard and Carol's date nights.

One winter evening, there was a blackout at home. A common occurrence in Zimbabwe but this was the first one I had experienced in Ireland. Carol was home with us and decided to put us to bed early when, from an upstairs window, Ciara saw a thick gauze of smoke and a dull orange glow beneath it lighting up the deep blue of the night sky. We looked at this strange and marvellous sight for what felt like hours but must have only been a few moments. Carol realised what we didn't: it was a fire at Old Man Munro's house.

She ran downstairs to the landline.

'Help! I need the police,' she said into the phone, her voice breathless, her heartbeat audible; beads of sweat rolled down her forehead. She then called Old Man Munro's daughters to join us in the house while we waited for the emergency services to put out the fire. They appeared in no time. I remember seeing these two young women crying in low, shallow whimpers all night, a constant stream of tears pouring down their faces. Carol tried repeatedly to phone the old man but his line was dead.

The police and fire brigade did their best but the house was destroyed. Old Man Munro had died, the coroner said, from smoke inhalation. His body burned in the vestibule at the front of the house where he had tried and failed to escape.

His was my first funeral. It drizzled that day. Ciara and I stood next to each other and she held my hand. The wet air swirled and blew around us, mingling with our tears. I squeezed Ciara's hand. She looked up at me with sorry blue eyes.

I didn't know what to make of Old Man Munro's death at the time. To some extent I still don't, other than to say I experienced it as part of a pattern. Emotionally weighty things happened in my life that were never talked about; whatever was difficult or painful lay dormant in the dark shadows of my soul.

*　*　*

In the run-up to Christmas, Séamus, Ciara and I made wish lists for Santa Claus. I was sceptical of this ritual. So far as I knew, Mr Claus had never deigned to come to Africa. But I became a believer when I heard Santa's heavy breathing and percussive footfalls echoing through the house in the middle of the night on Christmas Eve. We woke up the next morning to find that Santa had eaten the mince pies we'd left out for him. He had drunk the glass of milk by the fireplace. He had filled our large stockings with trinkets. And he'd delivered every item on our wish lists – amazingly this included a Batman figurine that I had admired at a toy store in Cork just a few days earlier.

My parents came to Ireland for Christmas in what felt like an uncanny merger of my two families. At the end of December, I flew home with my mother and my father made his own way back. We still didn't travel together as a family.

Back in Harare, the atmosphere in the house was suspended between calm and chaos. Soon, the four months that I had spent in Ireland were put behind us, quickly shed and forgotten like a graduation gown.

The late-night noises returned.

There is a kind of magical thinking that children possess, in which they believe in the talismanic power of certain acts to prevent disaster. I came to believe in the talismanic power of my own good behaviour. I must not complain and I must keep my hands where they can be seen and I must protect my mother. And, knowing how much my parents valued education, I must be really good at school.

* * *

I returned to Twin Rivers for grade seven, the final year of primary school. For the first time ever, I was not debilitated by dread at the start of a new school year. I had returned from Ireland full of stories and confidence, ready to receive a hero's welcome from my classmates. We had a new teacher. When we first laid eyes on her, a middle-aged white woman with a pixie cut wearing a crimson-and-black frock, walking purposefully down the path that led to the grade-seven block, we stared at her as children do. She made an abrupt stop, sensing the pairs of eyes on her. Her body rotated slowly until she was facing us directly. She leaned forward with her shoulders hunched, let her mouth hang open, then stuck her tongue out and grunted like a bull. We scuttled off in fear. She chuckled sardonically and carried on walking to the classroom.

Mrs Palmer, it turned out, was a dedicated teacher. She was attentive to me and told my parents of my unrealised potential. She said I was smart – the smartest kid in the class, which pleased me no end – but I had not yet learned how to apply myself in a disciplined and sustained way. Her voice, her manner, her arresting use of the English language were more polished than fine leather. I so wanted to please her. She tested our spelling every day and little made me happier than when I scored highest on these quizzes. She reinforced the school's emphasis on Received Pronunciation, warding us off common Zimbabwean pitfalls of the tongue. 'It's *thir*teen,' she said, 'not *thay*teen. You should say, *excuse me*. Not *scuse*. And never ever call for someone's attention by hissing. *Sssss! Sssss!* What is that? Disgusting.' 'Yes, ma'am,' we all agreed. Gerard was not wrong, my school was teaching us to be more English than the English.

What comes to mind now as I look back is something the Zimbabwean writer Dambudzo Marechera said of his youth in a township in Rhodesia: 'The English language was automatically connected with the plush and seeming splendour of the white side of town.' As apt in the nineties as it was in the sixties. Mrs Palmer embodied for me this plushness and splendour via the medium of language. And much like Marechera, 'I took to the English language as a duck takes to water. I was therefore a keen accomplice and student in my own mental colonisation.'

Twin Rivers, still only seven years old, was intent on building a reputation as a leading private school for primary education in Harare. To do so, it needed to send as many of us as possible to the top high schools in the country. In Zimbabwe, you can't start a conversation with an accomplished, well-connected person without first asking, 'And where did you go to high school?' Mrs Palmer and the other teachers made clear to us that we were in a crucial and formative year in our schooling and in our lives, a make-or-break year that would ultimately determine our future trajectories. To succeed, our teachers said, we would have to pass gruelling exams to earn admission into a good high school with pedigree and history (code for traditionally white schools).

'Getting into these schools is hard. Do you think any girl can get into Arundel or Chisipite or the Convent? Do you think any boy can get into St John's or St George's or Peterhouse?' Mrs Palmer said. 'They only take the cream of the crop. Because you are here at Twin Rivers and not at one of their junior schools, you will have to work twice as hard and do that much better on the admissions test. You just have to be the cream of the crop, that's the only way to get in. If not, you can go to a government school. They will be happy to have you, I'm sure.'

I wanted to be the cream of the crop. Government schools, forever stained by blackness, were less an option than a punchline.

Following the example of Andrew Lubega, I applied to St George's College, or Saints as I would learn to call it. Saints appealed to my parents, as it did to many middle-class black families like ours, because it provided a cultural and social foothold in Zimbabwe's fast-evolving class structure. Boys from Saints regularly went on to study at Oxford or play on Zimbabwe's celebrated national cricket team. My father had started telling me that girls around Harare said, 'St George's boys are gorgeous boys.'

In mid-June, I sat the school's admissions test: four papers in maths and English, notoriously difficult to complete in the allotted time. Of the fifteen of us from Twin Rivers who applied, I was one of only two pupils accepted into Saints. I proved myself a credit to the school. I made Mrs Palmer proud. I made my parents proud. I felt that I had earned my place in the world.

I had no way of grasping this at the time, but my education was priming me for life *outside* Zimbabwe. One obvious clue was that Shona wasn't taught in any serious way at Twin Rivers. What mattered were more 'universal' subjects like English and maths. But it cut deeper than that. Earlier in the decade, private education guaranteed a comfortable life in Zimbabwe but by 1998 a series of events was foreshortening the prospects of my generation. There was 'Black Friday', when Mugabe made the massive payout to war veterans' pensions, which shocked the economy. There were the fuel shortages and food riots. There was the worrying rate of inflation, the corruption and outstanding debts. There was the economic austerity and the consequent fall in the quality and coverage of social services. And then the government sent troops to the Democratic Republic of the Congo to support Congolese President Laurent Kabila, who was under fire from rebels in his military allied with Rwanda and Uganda. That my mother's home country backed a rebellion against the regime of a former liberation fighter supported by my father's home country was like watching our family drama play out on a geopolitical canvas. Even at age twelve, I could see the symmetry. Mugabe asserted his authority as leader of the Southern African Development Community, which obliges member states to assist each other in the event of foreign invasion. He also feared that if the rebel forces took over the country, they would not honour the debts that DRC owed Zimbabwe. Plus Mugabe saw a chance to secure access to minerals that he would dole out to his cronies as patronage. Involvement in this war cost the Zimbabwean treasury US$3 million per month. Adding to our financial woes, the World Bank and other donors cancelled vast sums of aid to Zimbabwe as punishment for meddling in the DRC. The Zim dollar continued to plummet in value. Kids at school showed off their $1 bills with George Washington on the note and bragged that this was worth $14 in local currency. The next week it was worth $21, then $28, and so on. My teachers could be overheard saying that the country was going to the dogs.

Education – especially one oriented to the West – was both a ticket to a better life and a safety net in case of disaster. There was a dark side to this thought: what happened to those who were not educated? This prospect haunted my parents. They were terrified that I might fail and become resigned to subservience to other human beings. They put everything they could into my schooling.

The state newspaper, *The Herald*, a mouthpiece for the government's increasingly jingoistic messaging, criticised Harare's private schools for producing 'export quality' students. The paper accused such schools of inculcating a form of racism more subtle than the old-fashioned kind but no less damaging to the nation; this was racism turned inwards, marked by self-disregard and a disdain for all things African. Despite its partisan sympathies, *The Herald* had a point. I wasn't just excelling at Twin Rivers, I was being primed to abandon the country of my birth.

CHAPTER 6

We arrived just before seven, an early start but the sun was already luminous and fierce. The journey there had taken half an hour from our home on the outskirts of Harare, enough time for my father to dispense platitudes about my upcoming rite of passage. It was January 1999. I was twelve years old and, my father insisted, edging closer and closer to manhood. But to get there, I would have to weather the tumult of adolescence. Starting Form One, the first year of high school, was an important step in my development. My mother concurred. As we drove through the school's imposing black gates, she also insisted that she just wanted me to have a good first day, both an encouragement and a challenge.

Trepidation and excitement stirred in me. When our car climbed the steep driveway towards the main part of St George's College, I peered in awe at the granite castle tower, crowned with a full set of crenellations, that dominates the grounds and offers a presiding view of Harare. I felt like I had stepped out of Twin Rivers' pantomime version of an elite private school and into the real thing.

Saints was established by Jesuit missionaries in 1896, in the middle of the colonial wars that preceded the formal founding of Rhodesia. Moulded after Oxford University and English boarding schools, Saints prepared young white Rhodesians to carry on the country's political and economic regime. For nearly a century, the school educated scions of the country's wealthy white settlers. Beginning in 1963, the college also accepted a select few boys from the country's small black upper class. After independence in 1980, the school opened its doors to sons of the country's emerging and aspirant black middle classes, sons of doctors and lawyers, sons of accountants and small-business owners, sons of NGO workers and mid-rank civil servants.

I was dressed in the school's iconic red blazer as well as a red-and-grey-striped tie, khaki shirt and shorts, grey knee-high socks (supported by white garters) and a cartoonishly floppy hat. I looked like an English schoolboy on safari. The bell rang promptly at 7.25 a.m. and I joined the throng of other boys in their red blazers filing into the Beit Hall – a spacious, neo-classical structure named after Alfred Beit, an Anglo-German mining magnate and colonialist who arrived in southern Africa during the diamond rush of the 1880s. As I glanced upward to an interior balcony, I noticed a display of polished mahogany panels with gilt lettering bearing the names of Old Georgians who had won the Rhodes Scholarship, which sends about a hundred international graduates to study at Oxford every year. I could see that most of the names belonged to white students.

During the assembly, we met the headmaster, a stern white man whose hair was silver and charcoal in hue. He had a protruding stomach and a pockmarked and rubbery face. He was a true son of St George. He had studied at Saints in the late fifties and early sixties when he captained the school's First XV rugby team. Rugby and cricket, two quintessential colonial sports, commanded a level of devotion second only to the Catholic faith at Saints. The school's best rugby team, its First XV, held the same status as the Praetorian Guard in the Roman Republic. Our headmaster had been working in this role since 1980; his tenure was as old as the country itself. Rumour had it that he spoke to one of the other teachers in Latin during his smoking breaks. He introduced us to the strange world of this single-sex institution with its rules, peculiar traditions and hierarchies. The school was governed by an elaborate and inviolable system of privileges that were denied to junior students and that accrued as you progressed through the school or distinguished yourself on the field or in the classroom: particular lawns you could walk on or stairwells you could use or articles of clothing you could wear. Even the toilets were arranged hierarchically, with juniors restricted to a small section of stalls and urinals in the toilet block.

As new pupils, we were granted a two-week grace period to master the school's rules. We would then be tested on school history and expected to follow the local custom to a T. Over the grace period, I anxiously crammed the college mottoes, the names of all the captains of sport, the history of the founding fathers, the names of the first six pupils to attend the college, the number of Old Georgians who had died fighting for Britain during the First and Second World Wars. At Saints, this was the past that mattered most and the school jealously guarded its version of history, its apparent status as one of the last redoubts of Britain's global imperium.

Discipline was important too. A careless misstep could result in manual labour – a routine punishment where you had to dig fields and carry bricks for hours while the sun pummelled you like a fist. More significant misdemeanours were drubbed out by the catechism and the cane. The thought of being sent to the headmaster for 'cuts' terrified me; I imagined his cane slicing across my tender buttocks, raising a fine welt of swollen tissue.

I quickly learned to cower before the prefects, senior boys entrusted with meting out punishments for even the most minor transgressions. They could call offenders (or even just pick boys at random) to 'Preez Room' (the prefects' room) for an exercise called 'military', where, for instance, they might ask you to run around to avoid being hit by tennis balls that they hurled at you, or to do push-ups while running arithmetic sums on a calculator using your nose. One afternoon, I was hanging around with a few boys on the first-year parapet when an older boy – he looked like a man to me – walked past. He was tall with rippling muscles, accentuated by tight-fitting white shorts and a yellow tank top. He had just been playing sport and a sheen of sweat coated his body like a fresh lick of paint. He stopped abruptly and then turned back to us.

'Do you know who I am?'

'First of all,' said one of my friends, 'are you a prefect?'

The face of this towering man grew dark with menace.

'You have the cheek to ask me if I'm a prefect!' he thundered. 'Go to the notice board. GO! Look at the list of prefects. Tell me if you see the name: Zimunya.'

'Yes, sir,' we said in chorus. And after looking at the notice board, 'You are Mr Zimunya, sir.'

'And?'

'We're sorry, sir. We will not forget your name, sir.'

'Because it is the grace period, I will let you off with a warning. Now get out of my sight.'

We had committed the cardinal sin of failing to salute a prefect but had narrowly escaped humiliating punishment. We dashed off the parapet and ran down to the car park where we finally stopped. I could hear nothing over my desperate gasps for air, until someone said in a high-pitched screech, 'You have THE CHEEK to ask me if I'm a PREFECT!!' Laughter tore through us.

In subsequent months, the prefects were not so clement. To evade them, I moved through the school with the supreme awareness of someone walking in a strange forest for the first time. Whenever a senior boy passed by me, I clipped my conversations mid-sentence until the danger had subsided. At the merest provocation, prefects could stop and survey us as if they were studying fruit at a market stand – appraising our uniforms, testing our knowledge of school history – trying to find a ripe one to devour.

Men for Others on our tongues. *Ex Fide Fiducia*, from faith comes confidence, on our breast pockets. *Ad Maiorem Dei Gloriam*, to the greater glory of God, written out as AMDG on the top left-hand corner of every page of every exercise book of every Saints boy.

We were in a hotbed of Catholicism, one that suited my predilections for tremendous guilt and sanctimony. I abided by the school rules with a marvellous talent for conformity. I became more Catholic than the Catholics, just as I had become more English than the English. I began each school day with individual prayer in the chapel. I joined the Christian Life Community, a Bible study group. I could recite the St Ignatius prayer for generosity and often volunteered to help conduct the weekly Mass. I internalised the school's logic of elitism and hierarchy, of discipline and punishment. Wasn't it only natural that older students ought to wield power over younger ones, or that those who excelled at sports and schoolwork be granted privileges denied to lesser children? Wasn't it right that those who stepped out of line be forced to labour or even be whipped? The essence of this colonial model of education was to normalise a self-perpetuating and rigid social order in which we, as students, moved through rites of passage from terrified to terrifier, to repeat as if by compulsion what we had experienced, to do unto others as had been done to us. (All without any girls to distract us, of course.)

'St George's is trying to turn you into Little Mugabes,' my mother said to me before launching into a disquisition about patriarchy and other abstract nouns. Mugabe might have been a militant anti-colonial nationalist but he was paradoxically an ardent Anglophile with an unimaginative penchant for Savile Row suits, the Queen's English, a Victorian sense of orderliness. Implicit in my mother's charge – and far beyond me at the time – was how Mugabe embodied and how Saints institutionalised all the contradictions of colonial rule: the genteel cultural affectedness and the capacity for ruthless violence; the ability to speak of equality while lording over those deemed lesser; the pompous projection of power undercut by a constant fear of subversion.

Like other spaces of confinement, such as prisons or military camps, Saints was governed by more than its formal rules and religious diktats. In addition to being a good albeit faux Catholic boy, I had to learn a vast array of competing, overlapping codes – many of them unspoken – about making the transition from boy to man.

We were at a 'war-cry' practice one day. Eight hundred boys huddled in a quad during the mid-morning break. For twenty-five minutes, we practised chants ('war-cries') to spur on the First XV rugby team that weekend, in a show of fearsome unity, when they played against our arch-rivals, Prince Edward School, the country's leading government all-boys school. We sang a combative, drill-like version of 'When the Saints Go Marching In'. We practised various call-and-response anthems to announce our team. We appropriated songs from Zimbabwe's liberation war of the sixties and seventies when guerilla soldiers set up choirs to sing embattled versions of folk hymns. Revolutionaries sang these songs in all-night vigils called *pungwes* – mesmeric and frightful rituals intended to inspire, politicise and educate the masses about the war for independence. Much like reggae, this was music of social commentary and cultural preservation. But from our lips, what had once been songs of bloodshed and sacrifice against the despotism of colonial rule became just another way to insult other school kids. And for me, it was the closest I came to learning about the liberation war as a student at Saints.

A short prefect with a bald head and a cherubic face led the war-cry practice. He looked like a large baby. He shouted at us, 'You oans need to sing as loud as you can.' Murmurs spread through the crowd. 'You oans think I'm jamming?' he said. 'I'm chuning you now: I might be short but I got the biggest fucking dick in the whole school!'

He pointed at someone near me, another Form One boy who was shy of puberty by some way, and told him to come to the front of the crowd.

'Fast Masikati, now!'

The boy wanted to cry, fear was written all over his face. In a whiny falsetto he sang as fast and as loud as he could:

> Masikati Makadii
> This is what we've come to see
> Dragon fire, dragon flame
> Watch St George's play the game
> Waaaaaaaaahhhh!

The whole school roared in laughter at his tiny voice. I was relieved when the humiliating display was over, not so much for his sake but mine. There, but for the grace of God, go I.

My goal was to get by at Saints by being unobtrusive without being pathetic, a delicate balancing act. I kept a low profile and maintained a steady, unremarkable performance in all aspects of school life.

Like everything else at Saints, academic life followed a hierarchy. Our year group was divided into five different classes called sets, which were determined by exam performance and which we inevitably took to be a stratification of our intelligence. The geniuses were in set one, the Darwinian failures in set five, the rest of us fell somewhere in between. There was something of a self-fulfilling prophecy in these rankings. As the recognised brightest, the set-one students worked hard to keep up this impression. I was ranked forty-third out of 150 students, which placed me in set two – we saw ourselves as naturally smart but didn't feel the need to apply ourselves, much like Mrs Palmer had said about me at Twin Rivers, and it was uncool to try too hard. The students in set three, cast as neither particularly smart nor lazy, merely average, acted accordingly. The students in sets four and five internalised the message that they were stupid, lazy and lacking in discipline; they too acted accordingly and, to no one's surprise, these students had the worst behavioural problems and attracted the most punishments.

At sports practice, I couldn't keep up with the other boys. A few laps on the track during warm-up left me knock-kneed and gagging for air as if someone had poured acid on my lungs. But I had to do just enough to not be the worst. I grew resentful of Twin Rivers for not preparing me for this.

Then there was the small matter of race. Saints signalled its prestige through its racial makeup. We had a white headmaster and a white rector. The teachers with the strongest reputations for excellence were white. We also had a high percentage of white students, about half the student body in a country where white people made up less than one per cent of the population. A significant portion of the white boys were sons of farmers who owned large-scale commercial farmland in different parts of the country. They were the Rhodies. But there were also white boys from more liberal corners of the populace like the expatriate community of Eastern European Jews, or those whose parents had opposed the worst vagaries of the Rhodesian government's segregationist rule. Nearly two decades into independence, Saints remained a traditionally white school. In his memoir about growing up white in Africa, the Zimbabwean writer Peter Godwin recalls meeting a few black students at Saints in the sixties: 'They didn't want to discuss African things. They wanted to be like whites. They spoke English without much of an African accent.' I was much the same. I barely spoke Shona, my father's first language, nor did I sound at all like either of my parents – my accent having been exquisitely crafted by my training in Received Pronunciation. The school placed me in the first-language Shona speakers' class with the other black kids. The Shona lessons were less a pedagogical experience than a ritual witnessing of my classmates speaking in tongues. I sat in silence, eyes trained on my lap, praying that the teacher would not ask me anything.

The shame of not speaking my own language was compounded by my simultaneous resentment of white racism and my aspiration to the cultural capital of whiteness. The white people who didn't flee Zimbabwe immediately in 1980 – to be sure, a lot of them did, about 100,000 in the first six years of black majority government – still owned over half the country's land and the lion's share of industry and commerce. They sent their kids to schools like Saints, and enjoyed sundowner cocktails when the sky was rosy and orange. They played cricket and swam at private clubs that once excluded black people for fear we might contaminate the water. They passed dreamy days behind high walls. Most Rhodies had accepted Zimbabwe's independence without changing their way of thinking. At school, it was obvious how the Rhodies saw me, whether I wore Saints' red blazer or not. 'Chigudu,' one white classmate said to me, 'what's the difference between a nigger and a bucket of shit?' I looked at him blankly. 'The bucket,' he chortled.

We were studying *Romeo and Juliet* in my English class. Our teacher, a stocky white man with an impressively square jaw and expansive chest, asked one of my classmates to read Mercutio's famous monologue, the Queen Mab speech, out loud to the class.

'And please don't ruin the poetry of the speech as you read it.'

'You're saying that just cos I'm black,' my classmate said, kissing his teeth.

My teacher slammed his copy of the play on his desk in exaggerated indignation. 'That's it! That's all you black oans ever say,' he charged.

The class descended into a raucous argument about which race was 'better': white or black. It was as asinine as that. I laughed gleefully at the bravado as we compared the races according to various criteria. Our teacher threw himself into the fray, giving his insight as coach of the First XV rugby team: 'The black oans like Mugeyi and Chisora are the brawn of the team. They are fast and strong, hey. But they are not the brains of the team. That's where you need white oans like Dobson, Shaw, Croker, Hanssen who can follow tactics and kick the ball skilfully. The white oans can do much more than run fast and bash other oans. They can think strategically about the game.'

Soon, the tenor of the conversation shifted from boisterous to belligerent. The evangelists of white supremacy have a tradition of mourning nations that no longer exist, like the Confederate States of America or the Boer Republics of South Africa or indeed Rhodesia. This peculiar genre of nostalgia surfaced among the Rhodies in my class, who argued that it was white people who built up the country and black people who were now ruining it. Before colonialism, they said, this land was little more than bush with tiny villages of mud-walled, grass-roofed huts sporadically interrupting the emptiness. Then the Rhodesians built fine and functioning railways and roads. The colonial towns were clean and the farms could grow anything: sunflowers, cotton, mangoes, passion fruit, apples, plums, bananas, and the country's staple food, maize. The Rhodesian mines extracted gold and platinum, asbestos and chromium. Rhodesia, they said, was a paradise but Zimbabwe was going to the dogs, just like the rest of Africa before it. 'It is sometimes said that the worst thing to happen to Africa was the arrival of the white man,' writes Peter Godwin. 'And the second worst was his departure.'

I didn't know what to say. I sat and waited for the bell to ring.

CHAPTER 7

The turn of the millennium seemed like the right time to make a change, to reinvent myself. Yes, I knew how on-the-nose it sounded but that didn't matter to me. I was determined to make a success of myself in my second year at Saints.

My mother and I spent the long school holiday over Christmas in Uganda. To my considerable dismay, my mother announced that we would usher in the new year in Kabale, hundreds of miles away from all the Y2K parties that my friends in Harare would be going to. 'But, Mummy,' I whined, 'I don't want to go to Kabale.' How could we spend this once-in-a-lifetime calendrical turning point in the least exciting place in the world? I pleaded. My protests fell on deaf ears. My mother was intent on making me spend time with her side of the family and imparting wisdom for how I should approach the new year. 'Saints is the kind of place that can make or break you. Schools like that are ruthless and they only reward achievement.' And in case there was any doubt in my mind, she added, 'You're not going to make it in sports, that's not your talent. But you can distinguish yourself in academics. Remember what Mrs Palmer said? Simu, please work hard this year.'

While we were in Uganda, I caught up with Andrew Lubega, still my role model and my initial inspiration for attending Saints.

'It's really hard, Andrew,' I said. 'I just can't keep up with all the other oans at Saints. Bra, those oans are all faster than me and stronger than me and cleverer than me. There's this one oan called Williams whose average was like ninety-three per cent then another oan called Mhuka with an average at like eighty-nine per cent and this guy Kok who was also at like eighty-seven to eighty-eight per cent. Those are like the baddest oans. To even get into set one, you need an average in the seventies. And then there's me with an average of sixty-seven per cent. That's wack. I'm chuning you, bra, I'm seeing flames. It was not like this at Twin Rivers.' To say that I was 'seeing flames' was my way of describing how hard my first year at the school had been, how I felt out of my depth. We were ranked in class according to our average percentage across all subjects and these averages were both a point of comparison and a stark reminder of my own mediocrity. Andrew laughed and shook his head. He was still rake-thin.

'When you go back, you must punish the books,' Andrew said, refusing to entertain my self-doubt. He combed his fingers through his hair that he had grown into matted, chunky dreadlocks. I wondered how his ultra-Christian mother felt about his rasta hairstyle. 'Don't worry about any other oans. You must chune the books – *No, my name is Simukai*. You hear me, bra? You must punish the books.'

Punish the books. Andrew had said this while pounding the open palm of his right hand against his left fist. I repeated the phrase to myself like an incantation. I felt buoyed by Andrew's resolute faith in me, his belief that I could excel if I put my mind to it.

In my dairy, I wrote down my goal for the year: earn promotion from set two into set one. Beneath that, I wrote several motivational quotes – gathered haphazardly from rap songs, Bible verses, self-help books and Hallmark greeting cards. One quote in particular became my motto, from Isaac D'Israeli: 'It is a wretched taste to be gratified with mediocrity when the excellent lies before us.'

***

The start of Form Two was less daunting than Form One. I was thirteen going on fourteen and I walked with a little more strut now. We were no longer the youngest boys in school, there were 'lighties' – those poor Form Ones – beneath us, who had no idea what was waiting for them.

On the first day of the new school year, my class filed into registration. Our form tutor was a tall and lanky man who wore skinny ties that looked like strips of ribbon dangling from his neck. He spoke English with a thick, guttural accent; his first language was Shona. He mangled his pronunciation of English words, extending vowel sounds that ought to have been short and clipped – at least in the mannered way that I had learned to speak. When he told us off, we laughed condescendingly. I would put on an accent and mock him, 'I foh-goat to main-shun the bade behaviour cohnsayning the cohnduct een the chaypel.' We called him 'gwash' and an 'SRB', someone with a strong rural background. We were snobs. It's not lost on me that I felt shame for not being able to speak Shona, yet here I was mocking a Shona speaker for not speaking English with the same polish as those of us who grew up in the city and went to private schools.

Our class prefect, nicknamed 'Piggy', was 'coloured': a term for mixed-race people in southern Africa that was coined and codified in colonial law and had now been trawled into common vernacular. Piggy was effeminate and he was an award-winning choral singer. Surely, my class speculated, he must be gay, or at the very least a sissy. We held incorrigible views about what makes a man.

I began to execute my masterplan to get into set one. In Form One, during my first Shona exam, I made guesswork of the multiple-choice portion of the paper, then ignored the tests of comprehension and essay writing. Instead, I laid both my pen and head down on the desk and slept for an hour. I scored five per cent. In the next set of exams I did a little better, scoring a whopping twelve per cent. In between the formal assessments, I asked Mr J's nephew to complete my homework for me. Neither my Shona teacher nor my class tutor asked why I was performing so poorly in Shona. I went in to the last exam of my first year determined to do better. I thought that if I could write an essay then I might double or even triple my previous score. In the exam, we had to choose an essay to write from a selection of five prompts. I didn't understand the first four but the last one asked us to write a story that ended with a phrase I couldn't translate. This was the prompt I attempted. I wrote a story that was simple but coherent and grammatically correct. And I was proud of myself for trying. My Shona teacher gave me zero per cent for the essay because I had clearly not understood the meaning of the phrase I used at the end of the essay, and he offered no reward for effort. My overall mark for that exam was thirteen per cent. These marks crippled my grade average in Form One, and I could not afford to continue failing my exams if I wanted to be promoted to set one. The first step in my plan was to ask my father to write to my teachers requesting that I be transferred to the second-language Shona speakers' class with the white, coloured and Indian kids. This would have been embarrassing, unbearably so, were it not for the comforting fact that my best friend, who was also black, did the same thing.

Step two was to enrol in extra French lessons every Saturday at the Alliance Française. My mother delighted in my new-found fervour for academic study and she thought that learning to speak French would be good exposure for me. For reasons I couldn't explain, French came more naturally to me than Shona. Or, at least, I didn't feel ashamed for being a novice.

The most important was the third step: waking up early every day, initially at 5 a.m., then at 4.30 a.m. and sometimes at 4 a.m., to study for an hour or two before school started. In my monkish discipline, I abstained from watching TV for the six weeks before exams. If I had to walk into the living room to speak to my father, I closed my eyes until he turned off the screen before I talked to him. My mother was impressed. 'Simu, you've always been disciplined when you decide to do something. I wish I had your discipline.'

I took to the arts: French, Latin, history, English and religious studies. My pale-skinned, wispy-haired Latin teacher had us sit before him in alphabetical order by surname. He started each lesson by shaking an old tin of travel sweets filled with scraps of paper bearing our names. He pulled out a scrap at random and tested that student on Latin grammar and vocabulary.

'Today . . . we shall have . . . Chiguduuuuuu,' he said, stretching the last syllable of my name in a long exhale that keened into a fine whistle.

'Chiguduuuuuu, do you know your Latin?'

'Yes, sir.'

'Conjugate *amare*, *regere* and *videre*.'

'*Amo, amas, amat . . .*'

I performed on command like a well-drilled corporal. Soon enough, when my teacher pulled my name from the tin, he said, much to my satisfaction, 'We don't need to test Chiguduuuuuu because he already knows his Latin.' My classmates rolled their eyes at me; I was violating the set-two code of not working too hard.

I approached classes like fierce competition, a contest to make the best impression on the teacher or show that I had the largest vocabulary or could come up with the most insightful reading of a book. I refused to be defeated by Thomas Hardy's dense prose, I agonised over the difference between ionic and covalent bonds, I memorised Woodrow Wilson's Fourteen Points, I drew elaborate sketches of the formation of igneous rocks. I was punishing the books.

I began to excel academically and found the success intoxicating. After the first major set of exams, midway through the year, I ranked second in class – bested only by my closest friend – and among the top ten students in the entire year group. We were invited to dine with the headmaster at Imperator's Breakfast, a celebratory meal honouring the top two students in every class throughout the school. And, more important to me, we were both promoted to set one. I still remember the morning that the set-one form tutor, Mrs Baxter, a frumpy woman of large proportions, came to find us to tell us the news. When we walked into our new class, the set-one boys applauded. My heart raced, gooseflesh swept across my skin. It was the first time that I had worked towards a goal and achieved it, and it was the most exhilarating feeling I had ever had.

But in my growing enthusiasm for Saints, I had failed to notice an important way that colonialism was still operating at the college: we were learning almost nothing about the troubled country that lay beyond the school's black gates.

* * *

In February 2000, the country went to the polls for a referendum on a new constitution proposed by President Mugabe – a constitution that would concentrate more power in the executive; extend presidential term limits; and mandate the transfer of white-owned farms to the state. At the last minute, a clause was added obliging Britain, as the former coloniser, to foot the bill for the land transfer from white farmers to the Zimbabwean government. Support for the president and his ruling ZANU(PF) party had been declining, and the new constitution helped Mugabe to revivify his claims of being Zimbabwe's true liberator and to galvanise his base. ZANU(PF) portrayed the new constitution as an essential part of the country's incomplete decolonisation agenda; they would finally rid Zimbabwe of the colonial vestiges of the Lancaster House constitution of 1979. Free at last.

But a hodgepodge of trade unions, human rights organisations, women and youth groups, churches, farmers and businesses coalesced under the umbrella of the National Constitutional Assembly to oppose the government. They spearheaded a successful 'No' campaign against the new constitution and advocated for democracy, civil rights and an end to corruption. This coalition then took the form of a new political party, the Movement for Democratic Change (MDC), led by a charismatic trade unionist and former nickel miner, Morgan Tsvangirai.

The electoral defeat of the president's proposed constitutional reforms was a humiliating rejection for Mugabe and signalled the loudest call in the country's twenty years of independence for a change in leadership.

This was a watershed moment. Mugabe took to political rallies, clad in military fatigues, to denounce his enemies. He evoked, then skilfully manipulated, a pungent wash of bitter remembrance about the evils of white supremacy. Histories of black people's brutal experience of the liberation struggle and of slavery and colonial exploitation were recited again and again until they were stripped of context and complexity and repackaged in service of ZANU(PF). He turned trauma into propaganda. On television and radio broadcasts, in newspaper broadsheets and political pamphlets, at national museums and galas, on Heroes' Day and Independence Day celebrations, on every occasion of public commemoration, the party told a simple story about the nation's struggle for freedom. There was the first uprising of the late nineteenth century against Cecil John Rhodes and his rapacious British South Africa Company. Known as the First Chimurenga, meaning revolutionary struggle, it ended in tragedy. The liberation war of the sixties and seventies against the hardline Rhodesian Front led by Ian Smith that won us independence was known as the Second Chimurenga. And now, we had entered the Third Chimurenga – the finale in an epic lineage of revolutionary wars, this time against white farmers in Zimbabwe and their supporters, who represented the last traces of colonialism in the nation. In April 2000, Mugabe warned white farmers, 'You are now our enemies because you really have behaved as enemies of Zimbabwe, and we are full of anger.' The white farmers, he said, were to blame for the country's economic inequalities; and the new opposition party, the MDC, were un-African stooges enthralled by their colonial masters. It didn't matter that ninety-seven per cent of MDC voters and candidates were black, since Mugabe argued that the values of his political rivals were a cover for neoliberal policies that, like colonialism before them, would serve to exploit Zimbabwe on behalf of the West. This story accommodated only one set of heroes: Mugabe's ZANU(PF) government, who ordained themselves guardians over Zimbabwe's past, present and future.

As parliamentary elections approached in June, a few months after the constitutional referendum, the country's politics heated up. Bolstered by Mugabe's rhetoric – and the Central Intelligence Organisation, the country's national intelligence agency – black 'war vets' quickly began to occupy white-owned commercial farmland despite the results of the referendum. The term 'war vets' is something of a misnomer when applied to all the people who occupied white farmland. Many of these so-called 'war vets' were in fact young people, some just a few years older than me, but they were out of school, unemployed and staring at grim futures robbed of opportunity.

Election day had the feel of a carnival, at least in the city. I remember seeing the long lines form at polling stations. Some people had been waiting for days but most had arrived in the depth of night, hours before the stations opened. Amid the throngs there was singing and chanting, the roasting of maize, the selling of salted corn snacks and frozen flavoured drinks in little plastic sheaths. Some people sat on folding chairs waiting for the queue to inch forward.

Mugabe's political equation was straightforward: to vote for ZANU(PF) was to be patriotic, and loyal to the cause of black freedom. But to vote for the opposition, the MDC, was to be a puppet of the white man.

This message did not land in urban areas, where his party was trounced, nor did it land in the two Matabeleland provinces in the west of the country – a region intimately familiar with the ruling party's capacity for violence – where ZANU(PF) failed to win a single seat. This legacy of violence in Matabeleland was a history of which I was wholly ignorant and would not learn about until many years later. It was only in rural areas with a Shona majority where ZANU(PF) won enough seats to narrowly hold on to a parliamentary majority.

After the election, Mugabe told his ZANU(PF) central committee that the MDC represented 'the resurgence of white power' and 'the revulsive ideology of return to white settler rule'. The MDC, he asserted, was the old Rhodesian enemy reappearing in blackface to act as 'a counterrevolutionary Trojan horse contrived and nurtured by the very inimical forces that enslaved and oppressed our people yesterday'.

I didn't have any understanding of what the MDC actually was. I knew that the party had emerged from the coalition that had killed Mugabe's constitutional reform earlier in the year but I didn't know if this was a good or a bad thing; nor did I have room to think about it for myself because I lived in a ZANU(PF) household. At home, my father's idea of connecting with me was to talk at me in long, winding monologues about soccer and politics. He praised Alex Ferguson with a reverence usually reserved for prophets, and he praised Robert Mugabe as if our president had been anointed to save Zimbabwe, Africa and all black people everywhere. Then his voice would rise to a pitch that was cold and sharp as he condemned the hypocrisy of the West. 'Their so-called democracy', he said, 'is only for themselves. They want to keep us weak and indebted.' He would vociferate about the callousness, greed, cynicism, insouciance of European colonialism in Africa. He would then rattle until breathless about how colonialism had never really ended; it had merely changed shape. The new masters sat in European parliaments and Washington boardrooms, orchestrating the decline of Africa through aid traps that bred dependency on foreign charity and unfair trade agreements that stifled Africa's growth. 'Neo-colonialism', he called it. He railed against the IMF and the World Bank, against the capitalist thieves who stole Africa's wealth and stashed it in Swiss bank accounts, against CIA and MI6 spies who engineered coups to topple left-wing governments in Africa and Latin America. Sometimes, when he was especially worked up, dogs came into his diatribes: those imperialist dogs; that dog Tony Blair; that pro-Western son-of-a-bitch leader of the MDC; the Rhodie dogs who taught me at Saints. My father spoke in a way that brooked no disagreement. There was no room for me to figure out for myself how to make sense of the world around me and my place within it.

CHAPTER 8

I wasn't really following the news. If anything, all the media's election coverage was a nuisance; it interrupted my favourite programming. I used to love listening to Radio 3, with its signature jingle: 'Radio 3, it's the only place to be, when I listen to the songs you play, it helps me through the day.' At 6 p.m. every weekday, I tuned in to the countdown charts show *Hitsville* hosted by DJ Peter Johns. This was where I found out what hip-hop, RnB, Kwaito or dancehall was popular in Zimbabwe. My cousin and I built up a stacked collection of audio cassettes recorded from the radio, our *Hitsville* mixtapes. We wore the tapes out listening to Ginuwine's 'Same Ol' G' with Timbaland's ab libs between the verses, to the divine harps on Brandy and Monica's 'The Boy is Mine', to the dulcet sensuality of K-Ci and Jojo's 'All My Life' – songs that indexed being true to yourself, heartbreak, the ecstasy of romantic love. The radio was a portal into glossy tales about coming of age. But all that was lost when the government banned foreign music in favour of seventy-five per cent national and twenty-five per cent regional content. Most of that content was about the greatness of the president and his version of history.

At Saints, the country's politics widened the chasm between black and white. When the MDC called for nationwide stay-aways in protest against the government, the white kids and teachers took heed while most black kids, me included, came to school as if nothing had changed.

Saints made no effort to hide its allegiance to the MDC. The school decreed that at 1 p.m. each day, before the lunch bell at 1.05 p.m., every class had to say a prayer for Zimbabwe: 'Our country is in great peril. And we and all its people are concerned about the future.' That November, I won my first academic awards at Saints for overall merit and religious studies. The keynote speech at our annual prize-giving ceremony was delivered by Trudy Stevenson, a new parliamentarian elected earlier in the year on the MDC ticket. She looked so brittle when she stood at the podium. She had the delicate frame of a swallow, accentuated by her short hair and bony features. Yet what came out of her mouth was bullish. She spoke of her decision to enter politics and her resolve to learn Shona. I now cannot recall much else about the substance of her speech. When Stevenson died in 2018, she was widely quoted in obituaries as saying, 'Mugabe does not frighten me, I feel it is my duty to stand up for the rights of all.' I suspect she said something similar at Saints on that temperate November night. What I do remember was the vague unease I felt about the partisan messaging of her speech. My parents tut-tutted afterwards about how shameless but predictable it was that Saints had turned a school ceremony into a political rally for the MDC. 'That's Rhodies for you,' they said. A battle over history, a battle over the symbols and institutions of the country, a battle over who gets to tell the nation's story was underway in Zimbabwe.

***

Race infected every aspect of school life. Sports were racially codified. White kids swam and played water polo, cricket and field hockey. I still have a copy of the school's annual magazine, *The Chronicle*, from 2001, the cover of which features the school's rowing team: a group of nine linen-white boys on a pewter-coloured lake. They look virile in their Lycra suits, stern with intense scowls of concentration etched on their faces. This was the image the 'fifth best school in Africa' projected to the world.

There were no black students on the rowing team; we dismissed it as a Rhodie sport. Rugby was a mixed sport, and even that gave rise to heated arguments about which race contributed more to the school's teams. Black people, we played basketball and soccer. We dominated track events, especially the sprints. The only black kids who played white sports were either exceptional athletes, in which case they could get away with it, or they were coconuts (brown on the outside, white on the inside), in which case they lost their racial credibility.

My mother was right, I was not an athlete. I played soccer with a farcical lack of control and had no power in my skinny-maningi legs to strike the ball. I was selected into the 'B' team for my age group. When I was in Form One, my team conceded eight goals in two twenty-minute halves against Prince Edward but we managed to score a consolation goal and celebrated as if we had won the UEFA Champions League final. In Form Two, Churchill School thrashed us 15-0, provoking the games master at Saints to call us 'the worst team in the whole school in any sporting discipline' – of which Saints had at least twelve. Through all my years at Saints, we were thumped by St John's, by Allan Wilson, by Eaglesvale and by Oriel Boys' among a host of other Zimbabwean schools with European names.

Not being an athlete, I had to find other ways of performing my blackness for my peers. My goody-two-shoes classroom self wouldn't cut it. Blackness, as I was learning to inhabit it, was not only what I looked like – that was a starting point but what mattered was a way of speaking, of style and self-presentation. Blackness was swagger. It was quick-witted put-downs of peers and teachers. It was code-switching into slang, a stud in the earlobe (which my father forbade me from getting), a comically subversive nonchalance, a love of the music on BET. It was taking Black American culture and modifying it with your own words and references and context. When my classmate Ooozi started barking at school and summoning his dogs like a madman, I learned that he was quoting the most popular rapper on the planet. The first DMX song I ever heard was the lead single, 'Slippin'', from his sophomore album. It changed me. The conceit is simple. DMX opens the song with an epigraph, a quote from Friedrich Nietzsche: 'To live is to suffer, to survive is to find meaning in the suffering.' What then follows is a biography in miniature as DMX recounts his abusive upbringing before he spurned his family for a life on the streets as a stick-up kid with only a dog for company. And then after a cycle of addiction and imprisonment, he eventually makes it as a rapper. I was entranced by DMX's gruff delivery, his muscular throatiness spitting cathartic bars over an unsparing and harsh beat. The oppressive darkness, the anger, the tales of crime were like nothing I had heard before. DMX's unrelenting will to survive became my solace when I felt fear or loneliness. When my mother next travelled, I asked her to buy me his first two albums. I studied his lyrics with hermeneutic rigour and within days I could recite his words track by track, line by line. Anytime DMX's music videos came on MTV or BET or Channel O via our satellite dish, I yelled, 'My nigga, turn that shit up!' even when I was alone. I wanted to hear that voice and that bass so loud that it soaked into the skin and slowed the heart.

I bought DMX's third album myself, on my first trip to the United States. My mother was attending a meeting of the Global Fund for Women in San Francisco and she brought me along with her. It was my dream to visit America. I wanted to be somewhere that mattered, somewhere central and vital in a way that Zimbabwe simply wasn't. America was like the full moon: distant, unattainable but glowing with mystery and delight. To live there one day, like landing on the moon, would be arduous and improbable. But I dreamed of it all the same.

My mother arranged for me to stay in Palo Alto for a few days with the Hewlett family, of the Hewlett-Packard information technology company, who were donors to the Global Fund. At breakfast one day, Esther Hewlett made pancakes and toast and asked, 'What's going on in Zimbabwe? It's been on the news a lot. Is it true that they are just taking white people's farms? Do you know why?'

'Well, yes, they are taking the farms. But what the news won't tell you is that land reform in Zimbabwe has been long overdue. You must keep in mind that many of those white people got their farms in the first place when they colonised Zimbabwe. Now, they must give back what they stole.'

'How fascinating.'

I was pleased with myself for having this very grown-up conversation. And the pancakes were fluffy and delicious, coated with maple syrup and melted white butter. To top it off, Esther laid out a small bowl of fresh strawberries with a dusting of powdered sugar.

'What about the other guy? You know, the one who is campaigning against Mugabe. He's black but it looks like he supports the white farmers.'

'You mean Morgan Tsvangirai? I don't know much about him, to be honest. But I can tell you that the opposition has no clear vision of its own. They are defined by what they are not. It's all in the name: Movement for Democratic Change, but change for what?'

'How fascinating,' Esther said again. 'But what about the violence?'

'The Western media exaggerates these things. There have been some isolated incidents here and there, but nothing more than that. The media has an agenda. They're afraid of Mugabe because he is a strong black leader.'

When I finished my breakfast, Esther took me on a tour of Stanford University before we went into San Francisco for the day. Later, Esther told my mother that I was such a smart young man and that I even knew about politics. My mother smiled, taking the compliment but thinking to herself, hmm, but what does Simu know about politics?

Nothing. I knew nothing about politics.

***

Being a city boy, I had no interest in farming. But I was happy for my father when, like other war veterans, he was allocated a farm from the government as a reward for his contributions to the country's liberation. This was part of the land reform programme. It did not occur to me to ask my father if the farm he was given had been confiscated from a white farmer.

The version of nationalism I was absorbing at home jibed, however awkwardly, with my ideas of race and my emerging sense of who I was. There was an unlikely consistency between Robert Mugabe's fierce anti-colonial persona, the occupations of white-owned farms, the racial polarisation at school, my father's nationalist speeches in our living room, and my immersion in rap music with its assertion of a pugnacious and charismatic black masculinity that I fantasised about making my own – of course I never would, since I was much too driven to do well at school and please my teachers. I also hated the Rhodie kids at school. They were racists and bullies, as far as I was concerned. Their fathers turned up at major sports days or for weekend events at Saints wearing the uniform of the white farmer: blue short-sleeved shirts and khaki shorts with red and knobbly knees above long fawn socks, faces tanned and mottled from a lifetime in the sun. It was not uncommon to overhear them ranting about how the 'Afs' couldn't run a bicycle store, let alone a country.

Did I feel a blush of pride when such people were 'war vetted' – that is to say when their land was taken through forceful occupation? Mugabe was, in his way, inspiring. A figure of defiance against the West and their 'kith and kin' in Zimbabwe. (In later years, after I had left Zimbabwe, I made many black friends from other parts of Africa, the UK and the US who lavished praise on Mugabe as an icon against white hegemony.) I smiled to myself when I saw one of the farmers' boys crying at school because his family's land had been taken and they would have to leave the country. How to explain the *Schadenfreude* at work in me?

There is a story Frantz Fanon tells in his book *Black Skin, White Masks*. Born in Martinique, a Caribbean island and an overseas department of France, and raised there in the 1920s and 30s, Fanon would go on to spend his adult life in France and Algeria, working as a psychiatrist before becoming one of the world's most compelling writers on the human, social and cultural consequences of decolonisation. Before reaching intellectual fame and political influence, Fanon was a young medical student in the French city of Lyon shortly after the end of the Second World War. He had not been in the country long when, one day, he was travelling by train. He brushed past a white woman and her small child, momentarily locking eyes with the boy. There was fear in the child's face. 'Look, Mum, a negro!' the boy shouted. 'I am afraid!'

It was a life-defining moment for Fanon, a horrifying epiphany, when he understood in his marrow what it was to be black in a white world – it was to be hypervisible because of one's skin colour yet simultaneously to have one's individual humanity rendered invisible, even in the eyes of an innocent child. Fanon writes that violent resistance against oppression is medicinal; it's a purging of the passivity and diffidence born of seeing oneself through the eyes of the coloniser. When one casts off the mask of obedience, a psychological rebirth occurs. Is it a stretch to say that as a politically naive and historically illiterate fourteen-year-old watching Rhodies lose their land, I felt this restoration-through-violence that Fanon describes? We had a copy of *Black Skin, White Masks* lying around the house. My father asked me to read it and I ignored him. Many years passed before I read any of Fanon's arguments about the role of violence in anti-colonial struggle, let alone his prescient warnings about the nativism that might come after the winning of independence. I didn't know that the most important part of Fanon's philosophy was his impassioned and humanist plea for the defeat of race as a construct.

For good reason, the public deliberation about the Third Chimurenga revolved around the occupation and reclamation of white farmland. In less than five years, the number of white farmers farming the land dwindled from about 4,500 to under 500. But race was not the whole story in Zimbabwe – far from it.

Many more black people were affected by the farm occupations than white farm owners – as many as 200,000 black farm workers, who had been working on white-owned farms, lost their jobs and often their homes. Some white farmers had been killed, about ten of them in what I had described to Esther Hewlett as isolated incidents. But I had no idea that the number of black farm workers killed by the same ZANU(PF) militias was close to 200, with many thousands more suffering violent assaults. While the plight of white farmers seized global attention, especially when they fled the country, it was black farm workers who stayed behind to be dispossessed and cast as 'sellouts' – in language harking back to the liberation war – for being too close to their white employers. So many of them were left destitute and drifting. Their predicament was nothing short of a major humanitarian catastrophe.

The suffering of black farm workers found parallels in the struggles of other key MDC supporters, including black youth in high-density urban townships and among trade unionists. It was mass disenfranchisement that cut so much deeper than Mugabe's populist framing of a revolutionary struggle against white farmers. Indeed, by focusing people's attention on white land ownership, Mugabe and ZANU(PF) hid how they were changing the core structures of government. In addition to the violence on the farms, the ruling party disregarded the rule of law, sacked technical experts in government bureaucracies, replacing them with party loyalists, and plundered public resources to further entrench their autocracy. I thought the Third Chimurenga was part of an ongoing anti-colonial uprising and I could not see what it was ultimately all about: an authoritarian clinging to power.

CHAPTER 9

Ignorance of history serves many ends. Sometimes it papers over the crimes of the present, by attributing too much power to the past, like when Mugabe said all of the country's problems stemmed from colonialism and not the corruption of his regime. Sometimes it covers up past crimes, like when the Rhodies downplayed the harm done by their segregationist rule and talked instead about how they developed the country as a way of justifying and preserving the economic and cultural privileges of white Zimbabweans.

Throughout my second year of high school, fights in my class between the black and white kids broke out all the time. We were raucous teenage boys caught up in a maelstrom of political and economic change that we did not understand and that was upending our world as we knew it. It was much easier to resort to name-calling. When I was still in set two before my promotion, our prefect, Piggy, exasperated with the bad blood in the class, forced us to write an essay on the detriment of racial barriers. As a coloured student, he tried to act as a bridge between the races. When that exercise failed to cool temperatures, Piggy sent us to 'Preez Room' for punishment by humiliation.

Piggy singled me out, as he knew I was a goody-two-shoes: 'Chigudu, you and I are going for a little walk. As we do so, you will pick out all the troublemakers in this wretched Form Two, set-two class. The hour of reckoning, dear friends, is upon us. Who shall be left standing and who will fall?'

'Yes, sir,' I said, looking at the boys lined up before me. They stood straight as pencils with the top button of their blazers buttoned, their hats off and held behind their backs, their knees touching, their feet pointing ahead of them. Some of the faces staring back at me were defiant, others petrified. Piggy and I began our walk. It was overly slow and dramatic. He asked me to look into each boy's eyes and then give a thumbs-up to those who would be spared and a thumbs-down to those condemned for hazing, as if I were Commodus deciding a gladiator's fate.

In hindsight, I should have refused to grass on my classmates and insisted that we all go down together but, being a compulsive rule-follower, I did as Piggy instructed. The boys I picked out stayed behind for their punishment. '*Mfana!*' the prefects shouted at a classmate, using the Shona word for small boy but here drenched in contempt, 'drop down and give me ten. I will count for you. One! One! One! . . .'; or 'Dance with this tree like you're dancing with your babe. You must grind with it, you horny bastard!'; or 'I just tore this piece of paper. It is dead now and you must cry for it. Do you hear me, you little wanker? I want to see tears.'

An important reason why my classmates didn't beat my ass afterwards was that I picked on the least popular boy in our group. A kid called Reed, who cried for the paltriest of reasons. In hindsight, he must have been a sensitive boy like me but, unlike me, he had no survival instincts. I only cried at home, lying in bed at night when I dreaded going back to school the next day. But Reed cried openly and drew attention to himself, becoming an easy target. To pick on him was a cruel move on my part and also a self-preserving stroke of genius. Another one of my classmates, a tall, imposing coloured boy, cornered me later that day and said, 'Chigudu, you're a fucking dick for picking me.' He let the moment hang, allowing me to panic, before adding, 'But at least you picked Reed too.' He laughed and walked away. I was vindicated.

* * *

ZANU(PF) had begun training youth militias to unleash a reign of terror against their enemies. The party reinstated pungwes, those frightful and mesmeric political vigils that had emerged during the war of liberation, to induct young people into this next phase of the struggle. This political education was made up of ZANU(PF) campaign materials and Mugabe's speeches. It was crude in the extreme. The ruling party recounted some of the most monstrous acts committed by the Rhodies during the war — for instance, the killing of black people by pouring boiling beer on them — and then asserted that this would happen again if the MDC were elected.

New legislation was passed to legalise the farm occupations after the fact. When the courts challenged the government, the president said to his base, 'This land is your land. Don't let them use the courts and constitution against the masses.' Judges who refused to toe the ruling party's line were disciplined for alleged misconduct. My English teacher's husband, Justice Fergus Blackie, had sentenced Patrick Chinamasa, the justice minister, to three months in prison for contempt of court after the minister had repeatedly failed to appear for previous charges. Chinamasa's son also attended Saints. Blackie was arrested at his home, detained in a squalid prison cell and denied access to food, his diabetes medication and legal representation. The ordeal was a form of political theatre, a retributive performance to send a clear message to all established and newly appointed judges about the consequences of defying the government.

ZANU(PF)'s violations of human rights and its flagrant manipulation of the law, in addition to the farm seizures, attracted sanctions from the United States, the United Kingdom, Australia, Canada and the European Union. Western governments, the international media and NGOs all condemned Mugabe. The pro-ZANU(PF) intellectuals described this targeted attention on Zimbabwe as a threat to our hard-won sovereignty as a nation. Sovereignty: the word was nothing less than sacred. My father took this position. Besides, Mugabe and my father argued that all the West's shrill protests about human rights abuses were a fig leaf to cover up a more nefarious agenda: continued access to Zimbabwe's resources, and regime change. After 11 September 2001, prominent journalists and academics in Zimbabwe criticised the 'US–UK terror war' as the real axis of evil, a pretext for a resurgent Western imperialism bent on toppling governments they found unfavourable, like ours. Every political pronouncement from the West ought to be regarded with suspicion, my father told me – it was all lies and hypocrisy.

'And this is where I get sick with people not understanding the politics of the world,' my father said. We were the victims of a great historical injustice and they were the evil wolves thirsty for our blood. Like Mugabe, my father invoked anti-colonialism to take aim at all Western-aligned organisations in the country, including non-governmental and international development agencies. The kinds of organisations my mother worked for. 'He sees NGOs as agents of imperialism, he sees them as sellouts, as non-patriotic,' my mother said of my father. Despite her own deep belief that colonialism in Zimbabwe had never really ended, my mother was disgusted by the machismo of the ruling party, how they scrubbed women out of the country's liberation history, how they abused women with impunity, how they used violence to dispatch challengers.

My mother's friend the politician Margaret Dongo attempted to lead a small opposition party to compete with ZANU(PF). For her troubles, she was rewarded with a visit from the ruling party's youth militia who left her with a battered face and fractured bones. To make sure that Margaret understood the message, the youth militia locked her in her house and set it on fire. Terrified about whom to trust, Margaret called my mother. She croaked on the phone, her voice raspy from the smoke. Hungry flames devoured the carpets, the photos of Margaret's children on the walls, the thick and pleated curtains with floral patterns that hung in the windows. A great dark column arose from the house and blackened the sky above it. My mother had no choice but to summon the police. What happened next is unclear to me. Perhaps the details are less important than the fact that Margaret survived, even if the arson left her destitute. My father was unmoved when my mother told him what had happened, what his beloved party had done to Margaret. His face, hard as a knuckle, betrayed no sympathy.

What is politics if not war by other means? My father had long been haunted by his time as a guerrilla soldier. He often brought up this period of his life when I was a child, yet he spoke of it laconically. He didn't relay coherent memories so much as emanations of wartime experiences, abrupt and fragmented phrases about suffering, duty, and how much he missed my grandfather. But he was not one to openly share his fears or his needs. I've never been sure where the line between stoicism and trauma is drawn within him. Or indeed if such a line exists at all. Maybe it's just how men – black men, African men – are. Then again, the fault might have been mine for not taking enough interest, for not being curious enough about my father. Growing up, I only gleaned sparse details of his political imprisonment and time fighting in the bush. I knew he had been held captive by Rhodesian security forces. They flogged him – a punishment that they called 'cuts', the same word used at Saints for caning, testament to the ugly bond between corporal punishment and colonial violence – until his ragged beige uniform had turned burgundy and he cried in hushed agony, the taste of blood and dust on his tongue. He mentioned to me his time in the rear bases in Chimoio and Mudzingadzi where the Rhodies dropped bombs on guerrillas and civilians indiscriminately. The deafening explosions left an eerie tinnitus in his ear. The bodies of his comrades were ravaged all around him. In that moment, he believed that he was dying, perhaps that he was already dead.

* * *

Around this time, during the first couple of years of high school, I started to see much less of my father. It happened covertly. He drifted in and out of the family house like a ghost or a tourist. He was around late at night during the week but went to his farm every weekend. When we were together, his mind was elsewhere. I could understand why he wanted to work on his farm but not why he and I no longer laughed together. I reminisced about our trips to Manchester and London and then felt the strange and slow sadness of missing someone who was still in my life, an uncertain but ineluctable loss. It was an unhappiness that I did not know how to voice. My father was opaque to me, and I was opaque to him.

I did not allow myself to dwell on this, or if I did then I have repressed the felt memory of our emotional cleavage. I remember instead believing that my mother needed me more than I needed my dad. I saw her working harder and harder, trying to keep our household steady even as inflation hit the country at a shocking rate of 115 per cent — a figure that now looks quaint, knowing what was to come in just a few years. I had to be the perfect son and her best friend: she more or less told me as much.

School took over my life. The thrill of earning promotion to set one was gradually superseded by an anxious desire to keep performing well in my studies. If I did brilliantly enough in my public examinations at the end of Form Four, called O-levels ('ordinary-level') — subject-based public exams taken by high-school students at about the age of sixteen — then I would earn the award of 'full colours' and the school would honour me with a white blazer instead of the red one. I wanted the prestige and recognition of that blazer; the mere thought of it was a motivator and a security blanket. I began waking up earlier and earlier, sometimes as early as 3.30 a.m. during the week. On Saturdays, I woke up at 5 a.m. and tried to study for upwards of eight hours. I stopped taking breaks, apart from watching a single twenty-two-minute episode of *Frasier* every Saturday at 9 p.m. I had no days off. My natural inclinations were towards the arts, but I now began to focus on the sciences. I was determined to prove myself as clever and to do that meant conquering mathematics, physics and chemistry even though I had no real passion for atomic numbers of the elements or the properties of light and sound.

I was trying to model myself after an older boy at school. I doubt he ever knew who I was but I still remember his name, Tawanda Sibanda. He was the most academically gifted student at Saints and in his final year at the annual prize-giving ceremony he won a medal for excellence that was only awarded under exceptional circumstances. I had never heard an ovation like that, it was thunderous. He was tall, erect and proud as he walked with grace and confidence to collect his medal. Everyone was so impressed by him and I wanted to know what that felt like. Rumours flew around the school that Sibanda's mind worked like a computer, that he scored 104 per cent on a chemistry exam because he answered all the questions correctly and then threw in some extra details for fun. When we found out that he had been accepted to the Massachusetts Institute of Technology, that seemed to me to be the high water-mark of human achievement and I decided that I wanted to achieve the same thing.

My mother was pleased. 'Africa needs more scientists,' she said. My mother knew I had an affinity for words and, when I was younger, she suggested that I might grow up to be a journalist. But she quietly withdrew this encouragement in favour of the solidity of science and its promise of a future in a fast-paced and technology-obsessed world. An education in the humanities or a career in writing seemed unreliable, incapable of giving me the safety she wanted me to have.

We had moved from the southern fringes of the city to a house in a northern suburb. When my mother arrived home from work, she and I would often walk around the neighbourhood. On a late-afternoon walk, when the jacarandas were in full purple blossom, I said, 'Mummy, I want to tell you something.'

She fixed her gaze on the road ahead. 'Yes, Simu, what is it?'

'I don't know how to say this. But I don't think we are a family—'

'What do you mean? Of course we are!'

'Mummy, please let me finish . . .'

'Okay. Sorry. Go ahead.'

'I don't think we are a family. You know, we never eat together—'

'But that's because we have different schedules. You need to eat when you come home from school. I like to eat vegetables before going to bed early. Tafi comes home late—'

'Mummy! I said please let me finish!'

'Okay. Okay. Relax, Simu.'

'I'm saying that we are not really a family. We don't eat together. Even at Christmas, which is really the only time we eat together, it feels awkward. And we don't do anything else together. We never bond. And Daddy is never really around. I mean, is he good to you? Is he there for you? I sometimes wonder . . .'

Our pace had slowed down but not come to a stop. We were on a quiet backstreet in a part of the neighbourhood with the large residential houses of various foreign ambassadors behind high walls.

'I sometimes wonder if you should get a divorce . . .'

'No, Simu.'

'Why not? Why are you still married to him?'

'There are things about Tafi that I love.'

This, like everything my mother said about the marriage, was elliptical. She didn't specify what she loved about my father. I was perplexed. My parents held each other at a distance, like partners in a minuet, only speaking to each other with cold detachment. What was I to do with my parents' marriage? What was I to do with myself?

* * *

I aspired to a kind of saintliness, not only of a religious type, though I did serve multiple terms as president of the Christian Life Community at school. But I wanted to be saintly in my ability to do no harm, to say nothing wrong, to cloak myself in an armour of irreproachability. I took no interest in alcohol or smoking. I became vegetarian, which was highly unusual and terribly mocked by my schoolmates at the time: 'Chigudu is an embarrassment to negroes. How can you have a black vegetarian?' But that didn't matter to me. I needed to be in control, to have total mastery over my discipline. I didn't want to sneak into nightclubs or stay out late with friends. I was in no rush to learn how to drive. As for sex, I couldn't control the urges roiling in me but I didn't dare act on them. Besides, I was too timid and naive even if I'd wanted to. I received no meaningful sex education. At school, we were instructed to avoid the twin calamities of getting a girl pregnant and getting ourselves infected with HIV. My father's approach to talking to me about the birds and the bees was to hand me a seventies-era encyclopaedia, *The A to Z of Sex*, and flee. I used it as masturbatory fodder then felt terrible guilt. Because I listened to so much rap music, my favourite insult at school was to call students I didn't like 'no-pussy-getting niggas', even though my most erotic experience was fleeting eye contact with a cute girl at church that had my pulse galloping for days.

Everyone kept telling me how good I was, how disciplined and serious beyond my years. My father bragged about my work ethic to his friends. My mother told me she was envious of my ability to keep pushing myself.

In the run-up to my O-level mock exams midway through Form Four, a bothersome feeling started to creep up on me. I began to feel a weariness in my body. I struggled to retain what I was reading in my textbooks. The exams, which were only practice for the real thing, looked impossibly difficult and an overwhelming sense of apprehension set in my bones, akin to deep rot in old wood.

When temperatures cooled during the Zimbabwean winter, over the months of June and July, I developed itchy, swollen, painful lumps on my fingers and toes. The urge to scratch them was irrepressible, but this only made it worse. My fingers became even more swollen. At school, I felt a compulsion to puncture my fingers with the compasses from my geometry set. I could not account for this, it was just something I did. I punctured my skin over and over until my fingers bled. I then wrapped them in bandages, which I told people I was using for my chilblains. A friend saw me doing this once and he let out an awful groan of panic and disgust. 'What the fuck are you doing?' Something hot and bitter rose inside me when he said this but I ignored it. And I ignored him. I didn't know how to say, 'Please help me.' Maybe because I knew he couldn't. No one could.

One evening, after a long day of lessons and soccer practice, I came home exhausted and fragile. I had a shower and tried to motivate myself for a few hours of study but I couldn't do it. A shower normally soothed and revived me but I felt breathless and tight under the stream of hot water. I turned off the tap and dried myself and returned to my room. I sat on the edge of the bed, still wrapped in a towel, and tried to steady the shaking of my limbs and the fluttering sensation in my chest. I felt a crushing, fearful despair plunging me into terror. My father came into my room without knocking. He never knocked.

'GET OUT!' I screamed. I hurled a candle at the door. Tears poured out of me. I couldn't breathe or think. I collapsed onto the bed and wept.

A few days later, my mother took me to see a counsellor after school. We pulled into a driveway made of gravel and shaded by acacia trees. Not knowing what to expect, I walked tentatively into the counsellor's meeting room. It was inundated with natural light. Stone sculptures and potted plants lined the windowsills; the coffee table was draped with a wax print cloth. The counsellor, much younger than I expected, was pretty with saddle-brown hair.

She told me that I needed more than six hours sleep a night because I was burned out, a phrase I didn't understand. I told her that it would be impossible – impossible! – for me to stay on top of my studies if I slept for any longer. She gave me breathing exercises to help me with the panic attacks. It didn't occur to me to tell the counsellor about my sadness at home. Only now that I am looking back am I able to take stock of how much fear and loss and confusion I had stowed away in me. Something shocking and tragic had happened at school the year before. One of my classmates didn't come to school one day; in fact, he was absent for several days before we learned that he had died by suicide. I remember going to his funeral but apart from the eulogies in the church and one discussion with a teacher, this was something that was never discussed or processed. I didn't think to mention this to the counsellor. Likewise, both my parents had lost siblings to the HIV epidemic. I had seen but could not express how these losses had affected them – or me.

I passed my mock exams, finishing third in the whole year group (I was still obsessed with class rankings). My counsellor looked at my exam results. She saw that I was good at maths but asked why I was so intent on physics and chemistry too when I clearly had an aptitude for languages, history and other arts subjects. I told her that I wanted to go to the Massachusetts

Institute of Technology one day and become a chemical engineer. She asked me to keep an open mind about the future.

Now that I had passed my mock exams, I had no reason to keep going to counselling. I didn't go back, nor did I ever talk about my counselling sessions with my parents.

CHAPTER 10

I am sure my father doesn't remember anything about the first time I went to counselling. He was preoccupied with Zimbabwean politics to the exclusion of all else. The country's high inflation and devastating food and fuel shortages dominated international headlines. The explanation in the foreign media for what was going wrong in Zimbabwe was always the same. Samantha Power, the Pulitzer Prize-winning academic and diplomat, encapsulated it: 'The country's economy in 1997 was the fastest growing in all of Africa; now it is the fastest shrinking . . . How could the breadbasket of Africa have deteriorated so quickly into the continent's basket case? The answer is Robert Mugabe.'

Samantha Power was being clever. But still, to reduce an entire country's problems to one man was much too simple – and much too dangerous – an explanation. Certainly, Mugabe and ZANU(PF)'s desperation to hold on to power at all costs had precipitated the country's economic crisis. But this was not the whole story. The Lancaster House agreement that negotiated the end of the liberation war and paved the way for Zimbabwe's first democratic election in 1980 had also preserved the economic privileges of the country's white minority. The changing of the political guard without more comprehensive economic redistribution was like giving black Zimbabweans the keys to the house but not the combination to the safe. To boot, the new government inherited the colonial regime's debt. Not only did this political reality smack of unresolved colonial legacy, but it was also fertile ground for demagogues trying to rouse nationalist sentiment.

My father believed that all this attention on Mugabe disguised a

Western conspiracy plot against Zimbabwe. 'This thing about the land,' he said, 'it is not about that. It's not about the farms. Forget about tobacco. It's about what's underground. These guys in the West have information about Zimbabwe's mineral wealth. They want our resources. That's what you need to realise.' Why else would the West impose devastating sanctions on us? 'Look up Chester Crocker,' my father told me. Crocker was the US Assistant Secretary of State for African Affairs. According to the Zimbabwean press, Crocker was rumoured to have said to the Senate in 2001, 'To separate the Zimbabwean people from ZANU(PF) we are going to have to make their economy scream, and I hope you senators have the stomach for what you have to do.'

Try as I might, I did not find any evidence of Chester Crocker actually saying that the goal of US sanctions was to make the Zimbabwean economy scream. This quote was manufactured and circulated as part of ZANU(PF)'s propaganda campaign. But the phrase was repeated so often on local news and from my father's lips, it took on the coruscating light of truth. It was, for my father, the searing indictment of the outlandish, enduring, indelible stain of Western imperialism.

Undoubtedly, the Zimbabwean economy was screaming. Hard currency reserves had dwindled. Productivity in the manufacturing and mining industries had nosedived. Unemployment was rampant. Signs of municipal neglect abounded in cities and towns: streets lights blacked out, potholes went unfilled, sewage pipes burst and overflowed, children and dogs rummaged in eddies of debris on the roadside. About half the population needed food aid. Even at a wealthy school like Saints, textbooks were rationed and some students were asked to buy their own hydrochloric acid for chemistry experiments. 'It was', said the international papers, 'the swiftest, most precipitous economic decline on record of any country not involved in a war.'

Was there any truth to ZANU(PF)'s cries about sanctions destroying Zimbabwe? The US government had made no secret of its ambition to punish Zimbabwe's leadership for the land reform programme. Hillary Clinton and Joe Biden were among the co-sponsors of the Zimbabwe Democracy and Recovery Act, known as ZIDERA, in 2001, which basically cut the Zimbabwean government off from international credit lines and suspended debt cancellations. The US government argued that ZIDERA would help Zimbabwe achieve peaceful democratic change and equitable growth. The Zimbabwean government and many other African countries saw this use of sanctions as illegitimate and coercive. Sanctions violated Zimbabwe's sovereignty. The first African American woman to be elected to the House of Representatives in the US Congress, Cynthia McKinney of Georgia, condemned her colleagues, saying that the white farmers who held land in Zimbabwe inherited it through the colonial exploits of Cecil John Rhodes. Like my father, McKinney attacked the United States for its hypocrisy. 'There are many *de jure* and *de facto* one-party states in the world which are recipients of support of the United States government. They are not the subject of Congressional legislative sanctions,' she said. 'To any honest observer, Zimbabwe's sin is that it has taken the position to right a wrong, whose resolution has been too long overdue – to return its land to its people. The Zimbabwean government has said that a situation where two per cent of the population owns eighty-five per cent of the best land is untenable. Those who presently own more than one farm will no longer be able to do so. When we get right down to it, this legislation is nothing more than a formal declaration of United States complicity in a program to maintain white-skin privilege.'

* * *

The world around me, already split into black and white, was ever more colour-blind to any gradations in between. I found it impossible to hold in my head the sheer complexity of what was playing out before me in its full and epic amplitude: the history of land dispossession in the settler colony of Rhodesia; the righteous cause and terrible violence folded into the liberation struggle; the necessity of land reform and the jingoism that occasioned it. I mimicked my father's position, carrying with me a bundle of holier-than-thou arguments that I levelled at the white kids at school: we were the goodies and they were the baddies; we were in the right and they were in the wrong; we were the real victims of history and they were the perpetrators of theft; we would take back the land and they could either accept it or leave.

When I argued with the white kids about the land issue, I defended the government's reclamation of white-owned farms by quoting a speech from the protagonist of Chinua Achebe's novel *Things Fall Apart*, which we had read in my English literature class. 'Let us not reason like cowards,' said Okonkwo. 'If a man comes into my hut and defecates on the floor, what do I do? Do I shut my eyes? No! I take a stick and break his head. This is what a man does.'

Mugabe won the 2002 presidential elections, adding six more years to the twenty-two he had already served as leader of the country. ZANU(PF) again took a parliamentary majority based on votes in rural areas of the country. The election was roundly condemned by international observers for widespread rigging and voter intimidation.

Our headmaster wrote in a newsletter at the end of term that politics in Zimbabwe, from the ballot box to the administration of land tenure, was now thoroughly corrupt. Referencing the presidential and parliamentary elections, he said that 'only an ignorant and naive caveman could, in the confines of his own home, believe that the elections were free and fair.' Only a black person could buy into the delusion that Zimbabwe was still a democracy.

As if to chasten him and prove his point at one and the same time, the government sent its secret police to arrest our headmaster. It was a threatening gesture and he was released after extended questioning and intimidation. My parents thought he had it coming: How can you write such an incendiary, partisan letter to the whole school community with political allegiances across the spectrum?

At a school assembly, the headmaster asked us to pray for him, given his trouble with the government. The white kids gasped in sympathy, the black kids – me included – laughed at his situation. I felt that we had won the upper hand in the struggle for decolonisation.

The ruling party was well aware of the politics at schools like Saints and continued their attack. They argued that Saints and its ilk represented a refusal to fully acquiesce to African leadership. To be fair, they were not entirely wrong – even if, ironically, Mugabe and several of his ministers chose to send their sons to Saints.

The Ministry of Education attempted to implement a state-controlled curriculum that would decolonise education in the country by, among other things, teaching the ZANU(PF) version of history and banning all international exams.

I panicked. I supported decolonisation that transferred ownership of farms, but schools were another matter. I worried that I would be forced to sit local exams that lacked the credibility to earn me university admission to the Massachusetts Institute of Technology. The thought of going to university in Africa had not even occurred to me. To once again echo Dambudzo Marechera, I was still a keen accomplice in my own 'mental colonisation'.

* * *

Then came the exodus.

At the Beitbridge border post, the southernmost point in the country, droves of black Zimbabweans attempted to cross the

Limpopo River into the flat, scrubby, dry valley on the other side of the border in South Africa. This was not an easy journey to make. The winding, potholed road along the Limpopo was used by the South African military, and they did not welcome desperate migrants from their benighted neighbouring country. An endless serpent of razor wire coils tracked the road like a defensive line, a relic of Apartheid's intransigent end of days.

Some Zimbabweans took their chances by crossing into South Africa not at the official border post but elsewhere along the 140-mile-long divide between the two countries. Much of the Limpopo riverbed is parched and empty. One could climb over or cut through the fence separating the two lands and journey southwards through the perilous bush. Game farmers surveying the area in their pickup trucks frequently found Zimbabwean corpses slumped against mopane trees, silent and alone in the desolate expanse of veld.

Other Zimbabweans secured the aid of fixers who trafficked them into South Africa and provided them with makeshift passports, stamps and workers' permits. Those who took the six-hour-long bus ride from the border town of Musina to the metropolis of Johannesburg had to bob and weave their way through a relentless obstacle course in the big city. Threats came thick and fast: crooked cops, an ever-shifting rulebook governing the rights of migrants and asylum-seekers, and hostile locals who targeted foreigners for mob violence. Sequestered in Johannesburg's most run-down neighbourhoods, Zimbabwean migrants built precarious lives on the underside of the economy by selling sundries or their labour at cheap rates. They found shelter in tin shacks, or Apartheid-era servant quarters, or warehouses with overstuffed rooms of naked concrete, or multi-storey buildings without functional elevators and reliable plumbing.

South Africa was not the only popular option. Zimbabweans flocked to Britain. Many of these migrants – who had been bankers and business owners, accountants and engineers, teachers and administrators, secretaries, hairdressers and sales agents in Zimbabwe – could only find work in the UK's care sector, work that was paid under the table and below minimum wage. Back home, they were called BBCs. Not the British Broadcasting Corporation but British Bottom Cleaners: a sobriquet for Zimbabweans employed in residential and nursing homes, wiping the bums of the frail, elderly and incontinent.

On and on it went in a long chain of desperation. Tens of thousands of black Zimbabweans fleeing the country, trying to survive on alien soil, hoping they might one day return home. There was an almost stubborn refusal of Zimbabweans abroad to describe their separation from the homeland as exile, a word that was too definitive, too irreparable. It sounds like being cut off, like a phantom limb. No one wants to live with that kind of pain. Instead, we began to speak of a diaspora of Zimbabweans living beyond the country's borders. Diaspora is much more palatable than exile. Diaspora allows for nostalgia and sentimentality for what once was; it carries an expectation of return.

It is easy to understand the fleeing from political violence and soul-crushing poverty. What else can you do when there are no jobs and no food and the land is barren and speaking out is an offence punishable by prison? But these were not the reasons I left Zimbabwe. My own exodus story unfolded more quietly.

* * *

Towards the end of 2002, I prepared to take my O-levels. While the educational reforms I dreaded had not come into full effect, they had been partly implemented. A rift had worked its way into the educational system. In my O-level history class, for instance, those of us whose families could afford the fees took the international version of the exam. Those who couldn't or didn't want to were moved into a different classroom. They were taught a crash course in local history, delivered over several weeks rather than two years, to be assessed by the local exam board. Some of my classmates, usually the white ones, hedged against the future. They registered to sit their international exams in Zambia or in Botswana, just in case our Ministry of Education decided to yet again ban students from taking foreign exams on Zimbabwean soil. For all that my parents supported Zimbabwean nationalism, they knew that my studies had been disrupted by the politics of a divided country still trying to work out its identity. They understood that I would have better prospects of getting into a Western university if I left Zimbabwe to complete my A-level ('advanced-level') exams – a school-leaving qualification in the UK and many Commonwealth countries taken at about eighteen years old in preparation for university.

I don't know how much they thought through the implications of sending me abroad to study when I was still just sixteen years old. I don't know if they considered the risk that I might leave and come back unrecognisable to them. Or that I might not come back at all. Maybe these were distant considerations, maybe it was a calculated risk but what mattered most to them was securing my future. My parents could live with Zimbabwe's disjointed rhythms; they understood its grooves. But for my life, they wanted certainty and choice. They believed that education was the safest investment in my future, the one thing they could provide that no one could ever take away from me; it was the only thing they 'didn't disagree violently about', according to my mother.

Having been conditioned to look towards a world far beyond Zimbabwe, I was convinced that my real life would begin overseas. And the sooner the better. When a classmate told me that Saints was actually modelled on a Jesuit boarding school in England called Stonyhurst College, and that it looked favourably on Saints boys, I believed that this was where my future lay. I told my parents that this was where I wanted to go. My father wasn't enthused but he didn't object, at least not to me.

I received the acceptance letter from Stonyhurst in November 2002 to start at the school in January 2003. Through pure tenacity, my mother raised the money to pay the school fees (which, at that time, were considerably lower than they are now and were within reach of middle-class families), at least for the first term – later the school offered me a generous stipend. My mother enlisted anyone with means or influence into the project of educating me, including one of her former colleagues, an Englishman called Barry Knight. Barry agreed to act as my guardian when I was at Stonyhurst. He later told me that he was honoured and baffled at being asked to do so, since he really didn't know my mother outside work. I had only met Barry once when I was fourteen and he came over to our house for lunch. He was in Zimbabwe for meetings about a monograph on citizenship and democracy that he was co-authoring with my mother, and he agreed to bring me a Manchester United shirt at my mother's behest. 'I live near Newcastle,' he said, 'I had to hide the shirt when I bought it because Geordies would kill me if they saw me carrying a rival team's colours.' Barry was paunchy with a curly bush on his head. His mind was conspicuously analytical, his sentences were always intricate, he quoted from psychologists and philosophers, statisticians and historians whenever he made a point.

I told Mr J, our housekeeper, that I was leaving as we sat in wicker chairs on the back veranda by the kitchen. He drank black tea and ate white bread. I had a glass of water. I shared with him my ambitions of going abroad and punishing the books en route to my dream university, the Massachusetts Institute of Technology, where I would become a chemical engineer. He marvelled at my schooling trajectory with pride. 'It's good like that,' he said with a look of placid certainty, knowing that this kind of education could never be his.

Since Stonyhurst was a mixed school, I would study with girls for the first time in my teenage years and I fantasised about my first kiss. I might even get a girlfriend or see some boobs. My last month in Zimbabwe was filled with anxious, excited anticipation for the huge change afoot. Everything that had tormented me – the panic attacks, the self-stabbing, the slow-moving estrangement from my father, the separate lives my parents lived in the same house – ebbed into some dim recesses of my psyche. This could all be forgotten. Real life would start now.

Book II: Fire and Ashes

CHAPTER 11

Incredible as it may seem, just after the First World War, an island on the margins of Europe – geographically smaller than Kansas, demographically smaller than metropolitan Tokyo – controlled a quarter of the earth's land mass and claimed a quarter of the earth's inhabitants as its subjects. Throughout the annals of civilisational expansion, no empire has come close to matching the scale and reach of the British Empire. British colonialism in Africa began in the fifteenth century as an unsystematic process of private tenures and holding companies seeking trade with legendarily rich black societies. But by the turn of the twentieth century, Africa's resources had been plundered; natives had been trafficked across the Atlantic for human auction or else coerced into indentured servitude; and settler communities had established themselves on stolen land. All this had taken place with the seal of the British Crown.

For the architects of this colossus, each conquest was as much a moral victory as a material gain. British imperialism promised progress, predicated on a vision of history as marching forward towards universal uplift. Unlike their European counterparts with a conspicuous record of heinous violence in the course of empire-building – think of the pogroms staged by the Belgians in the Congo or the French in Algeria or the Portuguese in Angola – the British conceived of their imperialism as both benign and edifying. Sure, there were blots here and there, but it was worth it for how the British Empire birthed the modern world. As apologists for empire like Niall Ferguson insist, we have the British Empire to thank for the advent of free markets and the rule of law across the globe. The British established relatively incorrupt governments throughout their empire, so the argument goes, and they put Africa's under-utilised resources to productive use at an industrial scale, bringing those lagging behind history out of the dark ages through technology and Western values.

My father always scoffed at the self-regarding cant of defenders of empire. For him, there was nothing redeemable in colonialism, imperialism, neo-colonialism – whatever you want to call it – because they all amount to the same thing: a primal urge, even a lust, for plunder and racial subjugation. Whether he was talking about the modern American empire or the European colonialists before it, my father saw control, control, control. The stupor of power. The entitlement of greed. Like a plague of locusts munching without cease, colonialists devoured the land and the lives of the colonised. Then they belched out the values of liberal democracy with chauvinistic self-satisfaction.

My father's views are hardly eccentric when one looks at the often tragic history of Africa's fateful engagement with the Western world over centuries. Of course, there was the massive, centuries-long trade in slaves. Current estimates suggest about twelve million Africans were trafficked to the Americas, with another six million Africans killed on African soil in the hunt for slaves. On the plantations of the New World, slaves were put to work growing sugar, tobacco, cotton and other cash crops that laid the foundations of the modern global economy. As Daniel Defoe, the eighteenth-century English trader and author of *Robinson Crusoe*, wrote: 'No African trade, no negroes; no negroes, no sugars, gingers, indicoes etc; no sugars etc . . . no continent; no continent, no trade.'

For those natives who didn't leave the continent but were coerced into servitude, the curtailment of their freedom and the conditions of their work were tantamount to slavery. This history cuts close to the bone when I try to piece together the world that shaped my father. It hasn't been an easy task. Eva

Hoffman writes that 'those who are born after calamity sense its most inward meanings first and have to work their way outwards toward the facts and the worldly shape of events.' In my quest as an adult to understand the tortured vein that ran through my family – made worse by the political convulsion in my home country – I have had to turn this history inside out and examine it from different perspectives. I have had to persevere through my parents' uncomfortable silences and mercurial shifts in mood as I urged them to tell me the stories of their lives. I have had to bear my parents' reticence with empathy, to inhabit the stuttering nature of their emotional confusion over how much to share with me, and to think critically about all they said to me – and, just as importantly, all they left unsaid.

* * *

In 1867, a boy named Erasmus Jacobs found a diamond the size of an acorn on the banks of the Orange River in what is today South Africa. More diamonds were soon discovered deeper in the wilderness where the town of Kimberley would eventually form. What followed was a scramble, known as the diamond rush, in which thousands of men from southern Africa, Europe, America and Australia descended on the diamond fields in the quest for unimaginable wealth. Among them was Cecil John Rhodes.

Rhodes set upon the conquest of southern Africa with an obsessive, all-consuming focus. He believed that the British, 'the finest race in the world', could rehabilitate 'the most despicable human beings' if 'they were brought under Anglo-Saxon influence'. Rhodes seized land from Africans and put them to work on it, 'giving them wages that made them little better than slaves', as an early biographer put it. Rhodes wrote often to his mother, regaling her in scrupulous detail with all his endeavours in southern Africa. In one letter he wrote: 'There is great satisfaction in having land of your own, horses of your own, and shooting when you like, and a lot of black niggers to do what you like with, apart from the fact of making money.'

Like British imperialism writ large, Rhodes was Janus-faced. He mastered the art of acquiring power through commerce and legislation in one guise, and through more muscular means in another. Signing treaties and making war was his modus operandi.

Rhodes built alliances and associates among Kimberley's tiny elite. He shored up his operations in the diamond field with capital gathered from speculators who played the London Stock Exchange. By 1888, he was a mining magnate and founder of the De Beers corporation that consolidated the emerging diamond industry. Two years later, he won enough political support in the Cape Colony – a British colony in present-day South Africa – to be elected its seventh prime minister.

Despite his extraordinary success in the diamond field, Rhodes had no intention of returning to the mother country for a more sedate life where he might enjoy the spoils of his African adventure. His eyes were trained on another frontier. North of the Limpopo River, wedged between German South West Africa and Portuguese Mozambique, lay southern Africa's most militarised indigenous state.

The history of human settlement in the region that would one day become Zimbabwe extends deep into the past, as far back as some 2,000 years. By the late nineteenth century, it was the AmaNdebele community, an amalgam of different ethnic groups incorporated over decades according to wars and shifting political alliances, that Rhodes wanted to conquer. Rhodes referred to their kingdom as Matabeleland and thought of the indigenous people as existing in a highly centralised polity with a fierce reputation as warriors. Rhodes spoke in biblical cadences of his destined conquest of the southern African kingdom. 'And when I look down,' Rhodes said, 'this earth shall be English.'

In 1888, Rhodes sent his emissary and business partner, Charles Rudd, to meet with the Ndebele king, Lobengula Khumalo. Rudd signed a concession with Lobengula that ostensibly gave Rhodes exclusive rights to mine Matabeleland. Lobengula famously penned his agreement with a wobbly 'X'. But Lobengula had already issued several such concessions to other prospectors. Moreover, it was not clear what any of these rights actually meant. None of this was a neat business transaction. In reality, there would have been much wheeling and dealing between Africans and Europeans. Some Africans saw opportunities to take advantage of the arrival of the white man while others would have been suspicious of this strange-skinned foreigner. What's clear is that Rhodes had not locked in a major mining business deal in Matabeleland; the idea that he had was a projection of his ambitions.

Why did the region matter so much to him? Rhodes had 'visionary dreams'. In the European competition of empire-building, Rhodes saw Matabeleland as the gateway to the rest of Africa. If he could conquer the storytelling rocks of Matabeleland, then he could extend his dominion over all of Africa from the shimmering gold of the neighbouring kingdom he called Mashonaland to the symphonic Victoria Falls, then onwards from southern Africa to the trees of central Africa's inspirited forests, the humbling peaks of Kilimanjaro, the ancient pyramids of the Nile, the entirety of the continent's uncharted hinterlands. For Rhodes, the colonisation of Africa from Cape to Cairo was a necessary step to conquering the rest of the world and reuniting Britain and the United States. He aspired to nothing short of a world governed by white, English-speaking citizens of the Crown. And if he could have, he would have gone further: 'I would annex planets if I could,' he once said. 'I think of that. It makes me sad to see them so clear yet so far.'

Rhodes deployed a column of 180 white pioneers accompanied by his private army to travel north of the Limpopo River to search for gold and extend the realms of the British Empire.

He had recruited young men, almost all white mercenaries from the Cape Colony, into a fighting force. Despite the Rudd concession, Rhodes planned to invade the Ndebele kingdom and murder its king. He promised his recruits six acres of land, twenty gold claims, and shares of loot from native villages if they carried out his vision. The British government pledged to grant Rhodes' company, the British South Africa Company, a royal charter to exercise sovereign authority on conquered land. The Company had the Crown's blessing to promulgate laws, raise taxes, maintain a police force, build roads and railways and establish an administration.

From his pocket, Rhodes paid for his army's food, wages, equipment and munitions including two Maxim guns, which would prove to be key players in the conflict to follow.

The Maxim gun, first patented in 1884, looks like a small cannon. Hailed at its inception as the most innovative engineering accomplishment in the history of firearms, the Maxim was the first gun to harness the energy of its own recoil to fully automate the cycle of fire, unlock, extract, eject, cock, feed, chamber and lock again into battery. A single pull of the trigger could unleash up to 600 shots per minute, equivalent in firepower to one hundred rifles. The Maxim gun debuted in the theatre of battle in the war against the Ndebele, from 1893 to 1896. In one conflagration, Maxim guns mowed down about 600 Ndebele fighters in just four hours, while only one white man was killed among the invaders.

'We must go on hammering and hunting them,' said Albert Henry George, the 4th Earl Grey and director of the Company, until 'we thoroughly convince them that this is to be a country of the white and not the black'. That's precisely what they did.

A portion of the Company, a column of sixty wagons, headed further north towards the Zambezi River. They trekked through a low and broken grassland, winding their way through 'an unknown country, inhabited by savage tribes', before emerging onto a plateau, about 3,700 feet above the distant sea. The climate was bracing and exhilarating. All around was a magnificent panorama of gently undulating plains and remote hills, extending far beyond the line of sight. They believed that this area they called Mashonaland promised 'limitless agricultural resources' and an 'auriferous region of vast extent'. More than that, as documented by a correspondent for *The Times* in 1890, 'the country has every appearance of being able to support a large white population while making full provision for ample native "reserves".'

The Company annexed the most fertile terrain, dispossessing black people and giving their land to white settlers to build ranches and large commercial farms. The evicted black people were sequestered in native reserves, called 'tribal trust lands'. By 1896, Rhodes had become the stuff of legend. 'The whole South African world seemed to stand in a kind of shuddering awe of him, friend and enemy alike,' wrote Mark Twain on a visit to the region that same year. 'It was as if he were deputy-God on the one side, deputy-Satan on the other, proprietor of the people, able to make them or ruin them by his breath, worshipped by many, hated by many.'

* * *

Family lore has it that about 300 years ago, my paternal ancestors migrated from the Great Lakes of central Africa to southern Africa. They settled in a place that would eventually be known as the Makoni district, named after a powerful Chief Makoni who, according to my father, was one of our forebears. In mid-1896, the rebellion in Mashonaland against Company rule had begun. An imperial Mashonaland Field Force fighting on behalf of the Company targeted Chief Makoni. They rained hellfire on Makoni's settlements with Maxim machine guns. They set villages ablaze, looted cattle and destroyed grain stores. In the space of six weeks, over 700 people were killed.

Makoni surrendered, hoping for amnesty. He was court-martialled in a rapid trial, and the beleaguered chief protested: 'It is very well to call me a rebel but the country belonged to me and my forefathers before you came here.' He was publicly executed by firing squad on 4 September 1896.

Though the chief was the primary target, the persecution of his people – *my* people – continued mercilessly. Women and children, hiding from the imperial infantry in rock crevices, were snuffed out or blown up by dynamite. Some colonial officers admitted that it was 'terrible' and the 'stench from the dead bodies was over-powering'. After the conflict, further casualties mounted up from diseases and famine. Many people were 'mere skeletons'. A local newspaper reported: 'Scarcely a day passes now that the bodies of dead natives are not picked up on the veld near the town, the victims of starvation.' Those who survived did so by eating roots, berries, monkeys, baboons and animal carcasses. A Christian missionary, appalled at the violence and the famine, said, 'I have never seen more miserable specimens of humanity.'

The Company had waged a scorched-earth campaign of 'extreme violence', a scholarly euphemism that stops short of calling the colonial wars in Matabeleland and Mashonaland ethnic cleansing. At a conservative estimate, about 25,000 Africans died during these wars. Can you picture the desolation? Can you picture the flies hovering in the still, hot air over murdered bodies, mutilated and swollen and strange?

* * *

My paternal grandfather was born in August or September during the rebellion of 1896. Without a written record, I can't be sure of the precise date. His mother had been hiding in the caves and was lucky enough not to get blown up. That's why, my father tells me, my grandfather was named Tafiramambo. It means 'we're dying for our king', a statement of defiance (or desperation?) among Chief Makoni's loyalists.

By the end of the failed rebellions of Matabeleland and Mashonaland, mythologised in Shona lore as the First Chimurenga, three to four per cent of the population in the country that would become Zimbabwe had been killed. For perspective, the UK and Ireland lost less than two per cent of their respective populations in the First World War.

In 1898, a new colony born of blood and greed emerged. It was dubbed Rhodesia after one of the world's richest and most ambitious men. Cecil John Rhodes did not live long enough to see what his country would become. He died in 1902, aged only forty-eight. His 'bad heart' had finally failed him. Half a century later, when my father was born in 1951, the last of seven children, he too inherited a name from this epoch: Edgar Tafiramambo Chigudu. But everyone called him Tafi.

CHAPTER 12

The night trains earned their name by running under the cover of darkness. The word FREIGHT was boldly marked on their boxcars. But this was a lie. The ghastly truth was that their cargo was human. In the early twentieth century, the night trains ferried legions of black men from all over southern Africa to the mines and plantations of South Africa. History calls these men 'migrant labourers' because they travelled long distances for low-wage work. But there is something misleading about this label. It is too clean, too polite a way of describing working conditions that closely resembled bondage or modern slavery. It says nothing of the back-breaking labour these men carried out through their waking hours – the heaving of shovels and the rattling of drills deep down in the belly of the earth, as they searched for shiny, evasive stones that would never belong to them. It doesn't convey the rancid stench of unwashed bodies covered in festering wounds in overcrowded workers' barracks. It doesn't hint at how dust and mycobacteria infiltrated workers' lungs until they coughed themselves to death. It doesn't capture the exhausting tedium of picking tomatoes or cotton or fruit on white-owned farms under the scorching glare of the white-hot sun and under the scornful glare of the white foreman. It tells us nothing of the loneliness of the workers' separation from their lovers and children.

My paternal grandfather was a 'migrant labourer' but he was one of the luckier ones. He had started working as a child of nine years old, but that was as a domestic helper on a farm in Rhodesia. They called him a 'houseboy', a term for a black male of any age working as a factotum for a white employer. Racism has a habit of treating children as adults and adults as children. Still, for all its indignities, the life of a houseboy had a grim privilege about it in these brutal times: it spared my grandfather the suffocating dust of the mines and the soul-destroying monotony of the plantations.

In 1919, as a young man, my grandfather left Rhodesia for South Africa. He would, almost certainly, have travelled on a night train. In South Africa, he avoided the mines and farms and found work in hotels in Kimberley, Port Elizabeth, Johannesburg and Cape Town before returning, years later, to Rhodesia. Until 1947, four years before my father was born, my family lived on land that had been theirs for generations. They only moved when the Rhodesian government annexed their land and transferred it to white settlers to start a farm. The family was forcibly relocated to a 'native reserve' close to the eastern borderlands. There, my grandfather built a new house, a brick-and-iron structure, in an arid village surrounded by vast, open woodlands and dry msasa trees. In the language of the time, the family house on the reserves was called their 'rural home'. My grandfather looked for a job in Salisbury, Rhodesia's capital. He leveraged his work experience in South Africa to get hired as a waiter and cook in the city's finest hotels. Perhaps it goes without saying that these hotels only served white people. Since my grandfather worked in the city for a white employer, he was granted single-occupancy 'living quarters' – a dingy bungalow for migrant labourers in a black-only township on the outskirts of Salisbury. He would return to the 'rural home' for long holidays and special occasions.

When my father was a boy, he, his older siblings and his mother would sometimes visit my grandfather at weekends. They crammed themselves into my grandfather's bungalow. Living on top of each other, without space or privacy, was the only way they could steal time together as a family. Even now, this childhood memory conjures an ambivalent mix of indignation and nostalgia in my father. He hated the bungalow's tiny quarters, how it framed a large family in a single man's silhouette. But he also speaks in honeyed tones of their shared intimacy in confinement.

The family eventually lost that bungalow during the early years of the liberation struggle. What stayed with my father was a fearsome disdain for the government that buffeted his family from one home to the next and ultimately tore them apart.

* * *

The Africa of my father's childhood teetered on the fulcrum of historical change. He was five years old when the first sub-Saharan African nation gained independence from colonial rule at midnight on 6 March 1957. Wearing a white skull cap, Kwame Nkrumah announced the independence of the Gold Coast, renamed Ghana in homage to the ancient West African empire. The Union flag was lowered and a new flag of red, green and gold was hoisted in its place. The moment of freedom had arrived. Nkrumah declared that 1957 marked the birth of a new Africa 'ready to fight its own battles and show that after all the black man is capable of managing his own affairs'. It had taken a decade of strikes, boycotts and civil disobedience for Ghana to gain independence, but this was only one battle in the war for African emancipation. 'Our independence', Nkrumah said, 'is meaningless unless it is linked up with the total liberation of the African continent.'

To be sure, in North Africa decolonisation was already underway. The previous year had seen Sudan, Morocco and Tunisia acquire independence, while a war against French colonial rule was raging in Algeria. But the independence of Ghana – only the fourth black nation-state in the world after Haiti, Liberia and Ethiopia – was a signal event in the Black Atlantic. Nkrumah's audience that night included Martin Luther King Jr. and his wife, Coretta Scott King. Nationalists from across the continent like Julius Nyerere of Tanzania joined the celebrations too. One of the premier architects of the civil rights movement in the United States, W. E. B. Du Bois, longed to be in Ghana. But he was barred from international travel because the US State Department had illegally revoked his passport a few years prior, fearing that his stance against nuclear weapons might gain traction and endanger national security in the face of Soviet aggression. Unable to attend the Independence Day celebrations, Du Bois wrote a public letter to Nkrumah and the Ghanaian people congratulating them on hard-won independence and encouraging the new country to don the mantle of the Pan-African movement that he had helped to foster since the turn of the twentieth century. Ghana's independence had arrived mere months after the year-long boycott of the public transit system by African Americans in Montgomery, Alabama. For Du Bois and King, the marching of maids and gardeners through heat and rain, singing 'We Shall Overcome', undaunted by the insults and spit and punches of an onlooking white crowd, sounded the first kicks in the drumbeat of freedom. A drumbeat that now resonated in Africa.

A young Robert Mugabe had moved from Rhodesia to Ghana in 1958. He attended the first All-Africa People's Conference, a gathering of Pan-Africanist leaders and activists from twenty-eight countries and colonies who were all advocating for freedom continent-wide. Mugabe was sceptical of Nkrumah, whom he saw as a militant firebrand. Mugabe's vision of political change skewed conservative, slow-paced and gradual. He was out of touch with the spirit of the times, as Pan-Africanists shared radical dreams for a liberated continent. Nationalism and Marxism were the tools that would dismantle the colonial house, even in fortresses like Rhodesia, and bring about new, liberated societies.

The political leaders who met in Ghana were not the only ones contemplating African nationalism. So too were my grandfather and my Uncle Tinaye, nine years my father's senior. By the early sixties, both men had joined the leading national party at the time, the Zimbabwe African People's Union (ZAPU).

Tinaye went a step further and joined ZAPU's armed wing. He was determined to take down the Rhodesian government *by any means necessary*.

The white-minority governments of southern Africa had other ideas. As the first waves of decolonisation swept through Africa, the European settler populations of South Africa, South West Africa, Rhodesia and the Portuguese colonies of Angola and Mozambique all tightened control of their territories. They were determined to staunch the flow of African nationalism and keep power and wealth in white hands. To them, African leadership augured disaster. An old joke describes white Rhodesia as 'Surrey with the lunatic fringe on top'. In other words, Rhodesia fashioned itself after a posh county in southern England with a golf-club outlook on the world. Its population of over 120,000 white people believed they had created God's Own Country.

Meanwhile, back in England, the British government was breaking up its empire. The world had changed after the Second World War. Britain was not the global superpower it once was. The small island could not afford to finance and administer a large empire abroad while focusing on post-war recovery at home through initiatives like the National Health Service and expanded public welfare. Indeed all of Europe was shrinking inwards, and two new players dominated the international stage: the Americans and the Soviets. During the Cold War, both disavowed the aristocratic European empires of old and framed global politics as an existential contest between capitalism and communism.

Resigned to Britain's fading glory, to the unavoidable truth that the sun was at last setting on the empire, Prime Minister Harold Macmillan admitted that there was no stemming the tide of African independence. He travelled to South Africa in 1960 to warn the white nationalist colonies of the region that Britain could no longer support its empire. 'The wind of change is blowing through this continent,' he said in a famous speech. 'Whether we like it or not, this growth of national consciousness is a political fact.' For African political leaders, the 'Wind of Change' speech was a vindication of their ideals, an overdue recognition of the dignity in black majority rule and self-determination. For the Rhodesian government, it was a bitter betrayal.

The temperature was rising in Rhodesia. African protests against the settler government had escalated from messy and unco-ordinated campaigns into more militant nationalist movements demanding one-man-one-vote. The rising threat of violent nationalism provoked a backlash – or, rather, a whitelash. The hard-right Rhodesian Front party was elected to power. At its helm, as Rhodesian prime minister, was an unlikely hero – a politician of colourless record; a simple man shorn of humour and emotion; a dull speaker with a limited and repetitive vocabulary, as lacking in charisma as he was in fashion sense; an anti-intellectual who preferred cricket to books; and, as it turned out, a tactically astute and bitterly racist demagogue who personified the motto 'Rhodesians never die.' Ian Smith, as man and myth, represented everything my father hated – so much so that I grew up thinking of Smith as evil incarnate and even now, as I write this, I find it difficult to humanise him.

Smith and his supporters styled themselves as besieged Spartans. They ordained themselves the only true Britons left. They cloaked their struggle as white settlers in a decolonising Africa with a false nobility. They were the last good white men standing, as African as any black man, a unique 'breed of men' whose example will 'go some way towards redeeming the squalid and shameful times in which we live'. Their national anthem, stately and august, was intended to evoke a portentous vision of greatness, of godliness, of being on the right side of history. Smith and the Rhodesian Front believed that the country was not 'ready' for black majority rule. They believed that they had earned the right to govern the country as a white settler colony because of their distinguished service to the British. During the Second World War, Smith had volunteered to join a squadron of Britain's Royal Air Force. He was shot down twice while flying Spitfires, first in North Africa and then in Italy. He sustained disfiguring facial injuries, including a broken jaw, that required reconstructive surgery. But he looked at his war record with pride, saying later that 'the things we "Britishers" had been brought up to believe in had triumphed.' What was all this sacrifice worth if the mother country had abandoned its empire and its values? How could the mother country overlook the military dictatorships and civil wars breaking out elsewhere in black Africa while condemning Rhodesian society for not acceding to calls for African independence? What was this if not betrayal of the gravest kind? 'If Churchill were alive today,' Smith said, 'I believe he would probably emigrate to Rhodesia – because I believe that all those admirable qualities and characteristics we believed in, loved and preached to our children, no longer exist in Britain.'

By 1965, Smith's government had decided to break away from the British Empire on its own terms, having reached a stalemate in negotiations with British Prime Minister Harold Wilson about what such a transition might look like. The Rhodies harassed, imprisoned and banned African political activists in a bid to fortify southern Africa as an impregnable bastion of white power. For my father, this was a most difficult time. He was fourteen years old but still in primary school, watching helplessly as his family tried to resist the Rhodesian crackdown. My father's eldest brother was arrested, as was one of his sisters. My Uncle Tinaye had gone to North Korea to learn armed infiltration and intelligence gathering in guerilla warfare. Men like him activated the Rhodesian fear that lurking in the shadow of Europe's declining power in Africa was the insidious advance of communism. Communists, according to the Rhodies, were using African nationalists as a Trojan horse to sack the colonial Troy and capture southern Africa's vast mineral riches. When Tinaye returned to Rhodesia, he was identified as a 'terrorist' by an informer – an

African spy working for the Rhodesian state. My uncle went to prison, at age twenty-three, and remained in captivity for twelve years.

* * *

The story my father told me about his conversion from innocent child to freedom fighter has a fabular quality to it. By this, I don't mean to say that he's being dishonest. What I mean is that his storytelling is driven by a kind of unambiguous morality. He draws clear dividing lines between good and evil: there were heroes who fought for the nation and anyone who stood in the way was a villain. Whether he's conscious of it or not, my father endows his story with symbolism and revelation, with linear causality and progression to self-vindication. It is as much an account of the past as it is a statement about the man he is in the present. It's the story he wants – needs – me to believe if I am ever to understand his enduring nationalist loyalties and the sacrifices he says he has made in my name. To dwell in this story that my father tells is to see the world as he sees it, or as he wants to see it. To dwell in his story is ultimately to see him too. And that story goes something like this.

On 11 November 1965, Rhodesia unilaterally declared independence from Britain – a proclamation that read like a parody of the American Declaration of Independence – replete with lofty 'whereases' and 'therefores' – but in practice, it was a charter for white rule. About three weeks later, my grandfather left his village home to attend a neighbour's funeral. On the way back, my grandfather's party was ambushed. Through the help of an informer, Rhodesian police pinpointed my grandfather as a nationalist with ZAPU. They beat him up, roped him to a motorbike and took him to a holding cell in the nearest town.

My father, who I must stress was only fourteen at the time,

waited at home that evening for my grandfather to return. One evening turned into another. And then another. And then another.

For two weeks, my father and his family heard nothing.

This is life in a country at war. The fear of disaster stalks you, grabs you, sinks its claws into you and refuses to let you go.

Finally, a grey Land Rover rolled into the village. Its doors opened, letting out the familiar hum of a police radio. A bevy of white police officers dragged my grandfather out of the vehicle and dumped him to the ground. Dishevelled, frightened, covered in dust, my grandfather scrambled to his feet. He was told to get a few clothes from the house *chop chop*.

My father saw his dad but couldn't talk to him. Before he knew it, the police had thrown my grandfather back into the car and, as fast as a finger snap, they were gone. The entire episode exists in my father's memory as a bad dream – paradoxically ephemeral and enduring; a distillation of the fear he felt at that tender age.

The police took my grandfather to the country's largest detention site, Gonakudzingwa ('where the banished ones sleep'). On arrival, he was greeted by an aimless congregation of tin huts and boreholes. The site was bounded on the east by the Mozambican border, hundreds of miles from any town, and everywhere surrounded by a dark and howling wilderness where lions and elephants roam free. He was thrown into a small room with walls of corrugated metal. The heat was sweltering during the day, the cold was biting and bullying at night.

In 1966, my father started his secondary education at Murewa High School, in the north-east of the country, founded by Methodist missionaries. My grandfather had left behind enough savings to pay school fees for my father's first year. But in 1967, as my father started his second year, the family savings ran out. There wasn't a penny left.

The missionaries pitied my father and allowed him to continue his schooling if he agreed to do maintenance work on the school grounds during the holidays. My father was bright, though wan and sensitive, as a boy. He was the youngest in the family, the special child, the one indulged by his parents and coddled by his sisters. He struggled to settle into Murewa. Its strict code of conduct was designed to breed men, not boys like my father with manners like flowers.

In the holiday months of April, August and December, my father did not go home. He worked for his tuition by mixing cement or stumping trees or polishing floors or, when he was lucky, filing away paperwork.

One day in August 1968, as my father was ploughing the school fields, a classmate hurried over to him eager and breathless. 'Edgar,' the boy said – the missionaries insisted on the use of Christian names – 'your father has been released.'

My father begged to be excused from the school to go back home and see my grandfather. He took a bus from Murewa to the township nearest to his home. He walked briskly from the bus stop and then sped up to a light jog before breaking into a full sprint as the house came into view. Drowning in an oversized, hand-me-down maroon sweater and dripping with sweat, he threw his arms around his father: 'I saw him, he saw me. We hugged each other. That was it.'

Tinaye was still in prison and the other siblings had scattered around the country. My father was the only child there to welcome my grandfather back from detention. He stayed home for the next three days – one day for each year that my grandfather had been in prison – before he returned to the school and resumed his manual work.

What happened in those few days together? What did my grandfather say about his detention? What did he convey to my father about the unfolding battles in the country? I have no sense of my grandfather's inner life, he is as mythical to me as the downtrodden Israelites of the Old Testament. As for my father, there is something potent if elusive in his recollection of this time. My father's story is flushed with feelings beyond his ability to communicate. I can almost detect in myself his anger, compassion, sorrow, failure, disgust, resentment, betrayal and love, all surging and crashing like waves within him.

The man I grew up with was not one to give himself over to his emotions. I try to imagine him back then, barely seventeen years old, lost and frightened in a hard country. If he felt vulnerable or confused, this is not what he wished to tell me. Instead, he spoke of this moment of existential terror as a Damascene turning point when his internal tumult hardened into political conviction.

Back at school, my father came into his own. He won a scholarship for academic excellence, which covered the costs of his tuition. He distinguished himself as a long-distance runner, became one of the most popular boys at school, and was elected chairman of the Student Christian Movement.

The greatest honour of the chair was to deliver a sermon on one Sunday of the year to the entire Methodist congregation in the Murewa district. My father tells me that he seized this opportunity to preach from the gospel according to Matthew: 'Blessed are ye, when men shall revile you, and persecute you, and shall say all manner of evil against you falsely, for my sake.' As a matter of fact, my father held little religious conviction. He saw Christianity's arrival in Africa as a paradox: for centuries, white rulers claimed moral virtue and superior knowledge of God, and yet they dispossessed, enslaved, imprisoned, infantilised and dehumanised fellow human beings in a way that my father could only describe as evil. To be persecuted by the Rhodesian regime, he now pronounced from the pulpit, was a blessed call to arms because righteousness was on the side of the black man. My father claimed the truth, he knew the enemy, his cause was just.

By 1971, under the spell of high fever, the Rhodesian government had detained, exiled or silenced the most prominent African nationalists. Guerrilla attacks against the Smith government grew more widespread. That year, my father was one of only three students from Murewa to score high enough on his national examinations to continue to the last two years of high school, which he would complete at Tegwani High School at the opposite end of the country in the south-west.

At Tegwani, my father read at a frantic pace late at night. From library books and pamphlets, illuminated by the flame of a paraffin lamp, he absorbed new political ideas about liberation and struggle and decolonisation from Cuba, Chile, the West Indies, the Soviet Union, Indonesia, and other parts of Africa. He had only been at Tegwani for a matter of months when he was summoned to a clandestine meeting down by the river behind the school.

'The main reason why the African people, especially the youth, are now resorting to violence is because they are not allowed a word – not a word – in politics,' said a young man, a guerilla soldier, there to recruit the boys of Tegwani into a demonstration against the Smith government. In a country of six million, white people made up less than five per cent of the population, yet they outnumbered black people twenty to one in all political representation.

My father listened intently at the river meeting, where a plan was formulated to seize the attention of a British delegation in Rhodesia. Britain had declared Smith's unilateral declaration of independence illegal. The British government applied sanctions on Rhodesia as pressure to compel the rebel colony to make more concessions to black majority rule. Lord Goodman and his team had arrived in the country for talks with Smith's representatives about the future governance of the country.

'This is our message,' said the soldier at the river, 'if the British government and the British people still want some friendship with the African people in this country, they must see that they satisfy them by helping to give them freedom.' My father nodded along as the speech continued. 'The only way to reason with Smith is to use violence. And the Africans, we will do it since the British government has refused to use violence. Maybe tomorrow, I'll be behind bars and I don't mind. I am prepared to make such sacrifices and even greater sacrifices for the freedom of the country. Are you?'

Tegwani was among three schools where boys were rallied to demonstrate against racial discrimination. My father and his comrades left the school at 3 a.m. and marched for eight miles to the nearest town of Plumtree. They held defiant placards that read 'Zimbabwe Will Be Free'.

Within moments of entering the city, squads of policemen descended upon them like torrential rain. Barking police dogs, vicious German shepherds, surrounded the protestors in a wide cordon and the police threw tear gas canisters into the crowd. My father and a hundred other screaming boys were rounded up into police cars and taken to court. His sentence was corporal punishment. The Rhodesian government didn't believe in imprisoning minors. They disciplined native children by beating them.

My father spent the night in prison. Stuffed into a cell with eighteen other boys, he couldn't sleep, uncertain and fearful about the next day's flogging.

In the morning, as the dawn's pale sun peered through the cell's window to dispel the twilight, the boys began to stir. The punishment would commence soon. One prisoner climbed on the shoulders of another, and the pair leaned against the wall, edging their way to the window. The lookout on top examined the courtyard scene below to gauge what awaited them. He shouted to everyone else's relief, 'It's not so bad.'

He was wrong.

My father was summoned from the cell and taken to a holding room with another prisoner. There, the police stripped both boys naked. A prison guard wrapped itchy, threadbare cloths over their mid-riffs and buttocks.

At that moment, a banshee cry from the courtyard, high-pitched and bloodcurdling, stabbed the air. My father gasped.

The first round of flogging had been delivered by the police. But as my father was preparing for his beating, a helicopter landed near the prison yard. It delivered what he calls 'the professionals' – his own sinister and clinical codeword for the men who apparently specialised in caning prisoners.

When it was his turn, a prison guard led my father out of the holding room through the courtyard to a large, trapezium-shaped table made of heavy, sun-bleached wood. 'Bend over and spread out,' the prison guard said. My father prostrated his upper half over the table with his limbs splayed out like a starfish. The prison guard tied him down with disturbingly meticulous care.

'You're going to count for me, boy,' said the professional.

'One,' my father croaked, his voice husky with vulnerability.

The cane sliced across his buttocks.

'Aaaaaarghhhhh!!!'

The air vacated his lungs. His chest tightened. A tingling sensation coursed up and down his spine. Sweat ran over his body like a colony of ants. A percussive sound pounded in his ear.

'I said you're going to fucking count for me, boy.'

The word 'two' had barely escaped my father's lips when the cane sliced across his buttocks again. Rivers of sweat and rivers of blood poured in confluence down his legs.

By the fifth stroke of the cane, my father was delirious. His voice had muted. His vision blurred. The colour in his skin drained away.

'Fuck!' he muttered to himself.

After the final caning, a prison guard untied his limp body. Once free, my father jolted back to life. With a burst of energy, he ran. He dashed towards a tap at the other end of the courtyard. He wanted water.

In a flash, the professional who had caned him emerged from the crowd and stared my father down. My father looked into those dull and hateful eyes and froze dead in his tracks. There would be no water for him. He trundled back to the prison cell helpless, humiliated, and so parched he felt he might choke on clumps of dry air.

The prisoners were discharged later that day and told to walk the eight miles back to Tegwani.

***

'I've never experienced such a thing,' my father recalls, still wincing at the memory decades later. And I, listening to this story, felt that something had passed between us. Something complex and difficult to articulate. It was as if I were a child again, sitting with him in the car on the way to school, hanging on his every word, listening with rapt attention to his stories of Muhammad Ali and Pelé, those proud men whose dark skin and athletic prowess stunned the world; of Tracy Chapman and her implacable yearning for black liberation; of generational struggles against the evils of colonialism and the great inheritance that had been handed down to me. His storytelling cast a spell on me. As he underscored the brutality he had endured at the hands of the Rhodies, I felt the weight of history, my life as the gift of his having survived colossal violence.

And yet – and yet – nobody who survives torture is a good witness to their ordeal. The experience is so often ineffable. It is an evisceration of personhood, a breakdown of the self. To be tortured is a fragmented and disorienting experience that is hard to convey in narrative, and to do so – that is, to place a coherent self in the story one tells, as my father did – is to tell a heavily reconstructed story. In this case, a story intended to elicit in me a sense of awe at my father's political coming-of-age and an indebtedness too, a duty to prove myself a worthy heir to his sacrifices, to follow in his footsteps as an unwavering nationalist. Herein lies a strain in our relationship: even moments of vulnerability are freighted with political expectations.

* * *

After the flogging, my father's rear was so lacerated he would have to sit on his thighs for the next two weeks. The walk itself was torture.

A saving grace was that the school's principal, a white British man, had returned to the UK for some ceremonial occasion at Cambridge University. His deputy, a black man called Khumalo, was left in charge. Khumalo supported the nationalist cause. He sent a lorry to pick up the boys, once they were at a sufficiently safe distance from the prison.

The lorry came full of piping-hot food and cold water. 'We ate like baboons,' my father says. 'It was heaven.'

CHAPTER 13

My mother grew up in Kabale, the town she took me to when I was a child, in a picturesque district in south-western Uganda known for its rolling hills and cool climate and sometimes nicknamed 'the Switzerland of Africa'. Her father was a clergyman in the Anglican church and he moved the family around from one home to the next throughout the district according to his work. A career in the clergy was secure but itinerant and impecunious. The family never starved but their means were modest.

I never met my maternal grandfather but I saw his photograph hanging in my Auntie Faith's home whenever I visited. He was seated with his back stiff as a rake, a dour look on his face. He wore a clerical collar and a black blazer with padded shoulders and thick, luscious lapels. He exuded self-seriousness. I couldn't judge his height from the photograph but my mother told me he wasn't tall. I was almost disappointed. The picture in my mind's eye suggested a towering figure. I had merged his physical attributes with his character when I imagined him. But, as a West African proverb puts it, a famous animal does not always fill the hunter's basket.

What I know of my grandfather is that from about the age of twelve, he was raised by Christian missionaries. In the late nineteenth century, while Cecil Rhodes was attempting to conquer southern Africa, the Christian Missionary Society arrived in East Africa. Founded as a social reform organisation in Britain, the CMS had a special vocation: to spread the gospel and to impose their vision of civilisation. Their efforts began under difficult conditions. Many early missionaries succumbed to disease or violent resistance from those bellicose natives. Despite this, the CMS persisted in its quest.

By 1894, Uganda had become a British protectorate, governed under the colonial strategy of 'indirect rule'. The British often created artificial hierarchies by appointing men as 'chiefs' where none had existed and then attributing these inventions to tribal tradition. Sometimes they went as far as dressing up these chiefs in elaborate regalia. Such tactics exemplified the improvisational nature of colonial rule in this part of the continent: a blend of delegated authority and vacuous spectacle.

Missionaries and colonial governors shared overlapping but distinct goals. While the governors sought efficient political control and access to natural resources, the missionaries aspired to the more fundamental project of redeeming black heathens. Some scholars describe this as a colonisation of the soul – a thorough cleansing of the culture from barbarism, of the body from dirt, of the mind from superstition, of the spirit from sin – to align with European ideals of civilisation. When white missionaries arrived in villages, accompanied by translators, they explained that they were not like the new governors sitting in district offices. They had not brought guns but good news. They talked of their god but were often met with confusion. Many people didn't understand the white man's theology and found it absurd, laughable even, that their god had a son but no wife; that he sent that son – supposedly divine – into the world to die at human hands; that he was three but also one. Some people shook their heads at this silliness and walked away. Others saw a threat and attacked the thin-limbed white man who spoke in a strange language that sounded nasal and disgusting. But there were those, like my grandfather, who were drawn into this world of missionary zeal and colonial ambition, who found life's purpose in the foreigner's message of salvation.

My grandfather joined the church and attended mission schools where they flogged children indiscriminately – for being idle or lazy or slow – to instil proper discipline. He wore a singlet and shorts because the people of the living God did not wear bark cloth and animal skins. He shunned the family he was born into as if they had smallpox, and adhered to the words of Matthew 19:29: 'And everyone that hath forsaken houses, or brethren, or sisters, or father, or mother, or wife, or children, or lands, for my name's sake, shall receive a hundredfold, and shall inherit everlasting life.' All this filled my grandfather with an indulgent pride in his identity as one of God's chosen people. He grew up, married a gentle if passive wife, and started a family of his own. His house served the Lord and abided by hygiene as a core tenet of Christian living, an outward expression of inner salvation. 'You can't be a Christian and not have a clean pit latrine. You can't be a Christian and not clean your house very well,' he would say to his family. Likewise, my grandmother would upbraid my mother and her siblings: 'This looks like a dining table of heathens, you haven't cleaned it. You must clean. Be exemplary of what a Christian is.'

Uganda's most elite schools, King's College, Budo for boys and Gayaza High School for girls, were both founded in the early twentieth century by British missionaries. Modelled after boarding schools like Eton College in England, both Budo and Gayaza implanted Englishness into the heart of Africa, right down to holding coronation services where Ugandan pupils lustily sang, 'God save our gracious king ... Send him victorious, happy and glorious. Long to reign over us.' These were the schools that my grandfather wanted his children to attend. For him, 'education meant *everything*', my mother says – a message that has echoed across generations from him through her to me, and that mirrors the same ideas my father internalised when he was growing up.

Unlike her older sisters, my mother did not attend Gayaza. She didn't achieve the grades for admission and instead spent her first four years of high school in Jinja, a city in eastern Uganda. She moved again for her final two years of high school, during which she sat her A-level examinations for admission to university. She went to a boarding school called Tororo Girls, which had been founded in 1965 by the United States government ('A gift from the American people'). Given Uganda's history with Christian missionaries, the evangelical church had deeply embedded roots in the country. Even a school like Tororo, funded by US overseas aid, received visits from charismatic preachers from the US, who would come into Uganda in droves for more modern iterations of missionary work. As my mother remembers it, 'They would come and preach and preach, and we knew God was coming.' She was 'saved' in high school. Being a clergyman's daughter was not enough, my mother had to make the personal choice to accept Jesus into her life as her Lord and Saviour. She took to being born again with alacrity, placing the school's Scripture Union at the centre of her life. And she suppressed whatever tiny doubts or misgivings she had about the rigid ways of the church.

My mother thrived at Tororo. She excelled in the arts and nurtured her passions for creative writing and debate. Popular for her lively, mischievous sense of humour, she made lifelong friends among a close-knit circle of girls, all of whom were born-again Christians.

When my mother was coming to the end of her studies, my frail and sickly grandmother fell ill again. My grandfather took little interest since this was nothing new and he had a church meeting to attend. My mother was back home to care for my grandmother but she was worried and needed extra help. She called her eldest brother – known by his initials, JBK – and asked him to drive all the way from Kampala to Kabale and confront my grandfather. JBK and my grandfather fired verbal shots back and forth until they had run out of ammunition. After the hurly-burly, JBK retreated to a hotel for the night. My grandfather blamed my mother. He found his headstrong daughter exhausting, with her implacable and argumentative spirit. This was not how a good Christian girl was supposed to behave. Why, he might have wondered, was her head so full of nonsense? He convened a court of five village elders to judge his daughter. 'Hope is trying to create tension! To create war between me and my wife,' he said. The pageantry continued for hours, with elders agreeing that my mother was prone to speaking out of turn; she was a troublemaker who believed she could challenge the man of the house. My mother might have seen – if only in hindsight – how foolish my grandfather's court was. But in the moment, she stood there and took it, no doubt telling herself that she would soon go to university and be free of her father's oppressive if earnest sanctimony.

My grandmother also watched on in silence. She had been the cause of the fight but sat on the periphery of all the drama. There was something limp and helpless about my grandmother's role in the family, as my mother depicted her. I have no idea what her relationship with my grandfather was. I don't know if she ever missed his touch when he was on the road proselytising for the church. I don't know if they held each other behind closed doors and took in each other's scent. And when he lashed out at their children, as he did in his kangaroo court for my mother, I can only speculate about what inner turmoil my grandmother might have felt with her loyalties divided between her obstinate husband and impetuous daughter.

***

The fight ended, my grandmother recovered, my mother finished high school. Months passed, and in no time my mother was inserting her key into the door lock of room A5 of Africa Hall. She trembled with so much excitement that she had to steady her right hand with her left just to turn the key clockwise. Two beds, with rigid metal frames and a single-size mattress, fell on either side of a chest-high wood panel that divided the room symmetrically. On both sides: a small wardrobe, a sink, a desk, a chair. The faint but fetid smells of floor polish lingered in the air. My mother walked across the dormitory room and pulled back the curtains. They had once been white but after collecting dust and being scrubbed down repeatedly, the curtains had taken on a straw-taupe hue. My mother looked out from the ground-floor room to see a mound of green earth with a couple of towering trees. Taking in the scene, she thought, *I have arrived at Makerere University* – Uganda's premier university in the bustling capital city.

It was July 1974 and my mother's inward desire for self-liberation mirrored the cultural mood across Africa. For decades, Africans had been rejecting colonial rule and agitating for self-determination. In countries where the battles for freedom were yet to be won, as in Apartheid South Africa, the struggle for political liberation birthed ideas such as Black Consciousness that sought to instil in black people pride and self-confidence. In countries where freedom had ostensibly been won, as in Zaire, there emerged new ideologies of cultural self-assertion such as *authenticité*, propounded by the dictator Mobutu Sese Seko.

These and other ideologies that centred on black self-rule found a ready audience in Uganda's president – a compelling politician from the north of the country, a former army general who had risen to power promising revolutionary change. He claimed he would rid the nation of the corruption and incompetence of his predecessor's regime and the colonial regime before it. Uganda would finally realise its dormant potential. My mother had only the slightest notion of the historical changes afoot in Uganda. As she was finishing high school, the American teachers at Tororo Girls had been sacked and replaced by Ugandans in a tidal wave of government campaigns to transform the country. But my mother was too preoccupied with stepping out of her parents' shadow into the light of burgeoning adulthood. She did not anticipate that the hope and optimism she held for her future would soon be engulfed by the chaotic rule of one of Africa's most notorious tyrants.

CHAPTER 14

In 1973, my father had completed high school and passed his national exams, ranking among the top-performing students in the country. He earned one of the few places available to black students at the University of Rhodesia in Salisbury, the capital city. There, he entered a key battleground for the soul of the nation.

The university was multi-racial but with restrictions placed on its black students – only a limited few could study the sciences or medicine; the majority, including my father, enrolled in the humanities and social sciences. Smith's government felt threatened by the university and its substantial corps of foreign faculty, a community of scholars who spoke out against the parochial madness of the Rhodesian Front. The government disparaged the university as 'the little Kremlin on the hill'. They deported academics who taught black nationalism, Marxism, multi-racialism and other topics of left-wing subversion. Smith's government told its bureaucrats 'that no official publication may state unequivocally that Great Zimbabwe was an African creation'. Those magnificent stone ruins were constructed from unbonded granite quarried from the surrounding hills and are a unique testimony to the sophistication of the African civilisations who lived there for centuries. They contradict, in the most breathtaking terms, the Rhodie propaganda that Africa had no history and its peoples were culturally barren.

White students at the university detested sharing housing and wash facilities with black students. They didn't want to be tainted by African sweat. As campus divisions grew more intense, scores of white students moved out of university digs to Mount Pleasant, a nearby leafy suburb with expansive houses and beds of languid grass. Its name belied the racial animus it incubated.

The Rhodesian Front's Special Branch recruited several students to spy on militant black students who were leading demonstrations against the government. On 7 August that year, the university council singled out a number of my father's classmates for expulsion in a town hall meeting on campus. 'We were standing in the main university court,' my father says. 'They came and announced that the following people had been expelled. Then the riots started.'

Broken glass and loud shrieks. My father was in the thick of it. He saw white shapes running madly towards him. The police, full of blood and venom. All around, black students fell to the ground. Their teeth kicked in by combat boots. Their backs clubbed by batons. My father was rounded up with 150 other rioters. He was sentenced to eight months in prison. Four months suspended, four months with hard labour. He served in Rusape prison, sardined in a cell with twenty other men. After the prison doors were shut at the end of the day, they were not opened until the next morning. If the prisoners were parched, they flushed the toilet and quenched their thirst by drinking the water from the cistern as it flowed into the bowl. Anyone who soiled the toilet bowl was beaten to a pulp.

Each morning, after a fitful sleep, my father woke before dawn. He ate a glob of *sadza* (a thick, doughy maize porridge, a bit like polenta) and drank tepid tea from a metal cup. He was sent out with his prison gang to dig in the fields. After the day's labour, my father was forced to strip naked in front of a sergeant in a holding cell. The memory is still vivid: 'He claps and you make a star jump. He claps again and you open your mouth wide. He claps a third time and you bend over and show him your ass. He makes sure you haven't got any contraband. They did this every time we left the cell. Then the last thing is he kicks you and you go back to your cell.'

The pain and humiliation burrowed into my father's skin and never left him.

* * *

In late November, my father was released early owing to good behaviour. Accompanied out of the prison by Special Branch officers, he was issued an order barring him from coming within about ten miles of Salisbury. So ended his tenure as a student at the University of Rhodesia.

My father spent his first night out of prison in the town of Rusape. He tried to persuade a prostitute to let him sleep in her bed for the night, but she wanted money, and he didn't have any. Instead, he slept outside the railway station with other unsheltered people. They lay on flattened cardboard near the security gates. The next day, he hitch-hiked to the village of his birth to stay with his parents.

Six months passed and he was ready to leave the country. It was now May 1974 and there was nothing left for my father in Rhodesia. Or so he felt. On the day he departed, my grandmother walked him to the gate. My grandfather followed behind, despondent, his body stooped and his eyes glazed with dread. 'My father did not want to look me in the face,' my father says of this moment. 'He knew it was the last time he would ever set eyes on me.'

He took a bus to a depot at Salisbury's edge. Once night had fallen, he made his way to his sister's home in a black township in one of the high-density suburbs for migrant labourers. He stayed there for three days, playing hide-and-seek with the authorities who patrolled the neighbourhoods looking for Africans who dared to break curfew. My father had to decide what to do next. He could not go south to Apartheid South Africa. That was too risky; he would almost certainly be deported back to Rhodesia. He couldn't go east to Mozambique where a war against the Portuguese was still being waged. He couldn't go north to Zambia because it was too difficult to cross the Zambezi River safely without getting arrested by Rhodesian border forces. He resolved to take a train west to Botswana, his only real option.

It was a long journey over two legs, first to Bulawayo and then across to Gaborone, the capital city of Botswana. Trains at that time had no hot water, only cold water that came out of little taps and poured down into a zinc basin that was frequently used by passengers as a urinal. After all, who wanted to negotiate the tumult of the train corridors late at night when looking for a toilet? On arriving in Botswana, the landscape became flatter and flatter, shorn of topographical landmarks; an unchanging emptiness extended as far as the eye could see.

Gaborone was a young city, built in the sixties, and it looked more like a sleepy American college town – a reference that would have meant nothing to my father – than a busy metropolis. Once he arrived, my father claimed asylum at the Botswana Council for Refugees, and he was taken to a refugee camp. With the support of a United Nations refugee scholarship, he applied to universities in the UK and was admitted to the University of Kent in the historic town of Canterbury. But he turned it down. It was July, and he felt too restless to wait around in the camp until September to resume his studies. He had already spent six months in the village with his parents and could not tolerate any more waiting. 'I had never been redundant for such a long time,' my father told me. I now wonder if there was more to it than that. Why was my father so impatient? We might think of the refugee camp as a purgatory, an in-between space where one's sense of time and self can easily dissolve. I imagine that there was no insult greater to my father's dignity than to be told to wait. It was robbing him of his forward momentum. I sense that he had learned to cope with the upheavals in his life by organising his sense of purpose around his revolutionary ideas and his will to change the world, as he knew it, through the project of national liberation. This mattered more than escape or personal freedom, which he might have had if he had gone to the UK. To slow down was risky to the integrity of his self-conception. Slowing down might allow the demons of all he had lost to torment him. He wanted to justify what he and his family had been through in the name of a larger cause. To do that, he had to keep moving. But I can't say any of this for sure.

By happenstance, my father was offered a place to study at Makerere University even though he had not applied there. He didn't even know this university existed and he knew close to nothing about Uganda. To this day, he can't explain how the offer from Makerere came about, but he accepted it for the sole reason that he could start immediately.

With three other young men, all exiles from Rhodesia, and funding from the UN Refugee Agency, my father boarded an aeroplane for the first time. They flew on Air Botswana from Gaborone to Lusaka, in Zambia, where they changed flights to East African Airways. But what my father remembers most from his flight was seeing the pilot, a black man. 'That was a shock!' he says. 'What!? You know, colonialism undermines people. It causes a loss of confidence. We never knew that a black man could pilot a plane.' They travelled from Lusaka to Nairobi, then on to Entebbe. 'I had never thought of something that functioned without whites,' my father says, 'because when we grew up in Rhodesia, everything was done by whites. But here I was in East Africa where blacks were in charge. I didn't see a white man until I got to Makerere University.'

***

My mother walked around Makerere, atop one of the original seven hills that made up Kampala when the city was founded in the early 1900s. A breeze blew through the air, gently moving the leaves of trees and shrubbery. At dusk and dawn, the sun worked its alchemy, lending the campus an incandescent patina of green and bronze as the rosy light bounced off the poinsettia, flame tree and bougainvillea. Sitting at the centre of the campus was the Ivory Tower, a tall and handsome administrative block with white walls and blue-shuttered windows. It was plastered with posters of Uganda's president. My mother looked at the new leader's face. His smile accentuated his sharply angled cheeks, lending him an attractive charm that belied his capacity for terror.

Idi Amin Dada came to power in Uganda via a *coup d'état* in 1971. Hailing from the West Nile region, in the north-western tip of Uganda, Amin was born around 1928. He grew up in and around the bases of the 4th Battalion of the King's African Rifles when the country was still a British protectorate. He officially enlisted in the army in 1946 and quickly became popular among his commanding British officers, who admired his physical prowess and obedience. He rose through the ranks rapidly, attaining the highest office available to Africans in the colonial army.

By the time Uganda gained independence from British rule in 1962, Amin was one of only two commissioned officers in the military. Three years later, he became the head of the Ugandan army and an irreplaceable ally to Uganda's first president, Dr Apollo Milton Obote.

Amin's loyalty was fickle. As Obote's presumed communist sympathies alienated him from Western powers during the Cold War, Amin won tacit support from the Israeli and British embassies to stage a military coup. In January 1971, the charismatic and capricious Amin took to the airwaves of Radio Uganda. Amin was a big man. His voice boomed with rough majesty out of loudspeakers throughout the country. He told his compatriots that he was not a politician but a professional soldier, a man of the people who kept his speeches brief. His message was direct: Uganda was now the first African socialist republic – a 'beacon of freedom and equality where all men are brothers'. Millions believed him.

Amin likened his ascension to the French Revolution. He claimed the same sense of a turning point in history, a clear before-and-after moment that scholars would go on to study as a pivotal event in the chronicles of human civilisation. Once in office, Amin spurned his backers, the British and Israelis who had wanted to be rid of Obote. He spun a compelling David-and-Goliath tale of growing up a poor farmer who picked up a gun to fight the European colonisers and the corrupt African bureaucrats who took over from them.

Despite coming to power in a coup, Amin was unsure of his support in the Ugandan army. He was especially afraid of a possible counter-coup by the ousted Obote. To shore up his position, he conspired to buy loyalty. He ordered a fleet of 200 Mercedes-Benzes for use in the officer corps and installed thirty-six miles of carpet in the military barracks across the country. In August 1972, Amin decreed that 'the Ugandan Africans have been enslaved economically since the time of the colonialists' and that he was now waging 'Economic War' against Uganda's entire Asian community in a bid to 'emancipate the Ugandan Africans of this republic'. Nearly 80,000 Ugandan Asians, many of whom had lived in the country for generations, were told to tidy up their affairs and flee the country within ninety days. Amin distributed over half of the 5,655 factories, estates and houses deserted by the departing Asians to his soldiers. In one fell swoop, Amin crippled the Ugandan economy by expelling the Asian community, which had been a major driving force behind most of the country's formal business.

But you wouldn't know how dismal Amin's rule was if you attended one of his many public rallies. He barnstormed the country, driving a Maserati down the dirt tracks of the countryside. His soldiers trailed him in their slow, camouflaged jeeps. He liked to wear a blue air-force uniform with lacy epaulettes and gold trim when he visited old chiefs and launched one civic campaign after another. He promised to fix bridges and build new schools, even though his government, kneecapped by price inflation, could not afford paper to collect taxes or keep public records. There wasn't enough fuel in the country for officials to visit schools or conduct land surveys. Builders couldn't even get hold of the cement needed to construct new buildings.

Amin delegated the day-to-day administrative labour of running the government to anyone loyal to him. Credentials and expertise didn't matter. He unleashed spies and death squads of soldiers, mercenaries and opportunists of various stripes to hunt down and execute scores of people who he suspected might oppose him. Henry Kyemba, the cabinet secretary at the time, would later write of Amin's killing spree: 'It was impossible to dispose of the bodies in graves. Instead, truckloads of corpses were taken and dumped in the Nile.'

* * *

Like Ugandan society at large, there were spies scattered throughout Makerere's campus: in lecture theatres, libraries, the canteen and the student dormitories. 'You never knew who you were talking to,' my mother says of this time. 'Anyone could be an agent of Amin.' A careless word, an unguarded joke, could be your last. Beyond the pervasive surveillance from his informants, Amin's soldiers sporadically turned up on campus in large black sedans. They would point at young women and curl their fingers in a beckoning gesture. Sexual violence on campus became an anodyne fact of life. 'It was terrible,' my mother says. 'One time, I was kidnapped by a minister. He told his men to get me. They took me to his house and left me with him in a locked room. I told him I was on my period. He didn't want to touch me after that. I think he was afraid of a woman's blood. He thought it was dirty.'

Despite all this, my mother associated Makerere with a vital sense of freedom. As a child, she visited the university often to see her brother, my Uncle JBK, when he was a student and later when he joined the faculty. JBK married another professor, Joy Kwesiga, and they built a home together on campus. So many students flocked to their house, 'talking a language I didn't understand', my mother says. She was in awe of the students' dialect, with all their theories and references to authors and their fancy words. The medical students were the most remarkable in my mother's eyes. 'You remember Dr Grace Kalimugogo? Grace would come to the house, wearing her medical coat, with her friend. And they were talking big. I kept asking myself, will I ever be like them? I grew up admiring them. Admiring, admiring, admiring.'

When campus life was in full swing, my mother built her social circle through the Scripture Union, just as she had in high school and with some of the same friends: 'I didn't attend dances, neither on campus nor outside. I didn't go to parties. Most of my life was at the Scripture Union.' The Union frowned on parties. So my mother and her peers channelled their restless energies and collective anxieties into the passionate worship of God: dancing, singing, shouting in His name. Each weekend at the Scripture Union meetings, my mother tuned in to the timbre of the preacher's voice, deep and manly and always commanding, redolent of her father. As it was in her childhood home, so it was in the Scripture Union: hierarchy was established; the lines of right and wrong were rigidly demarcated; women were told how to comport themselves; and the country's politics were swept under the rug. 'Those are worldly things, you don't get involved in worldly things.'

My mother's degree was in social work and social administration, a mix of apprenticeships and theory. Her most memorable class was on the sociology of development, taught by a sharp-tongued and impious lecturer named Bagamuhunda. An avowed Marxist and an arresting speaker, Bagamuhunda's voice and personality filled the lecture theatre. He quoted radical theorists like Andre Gunder Frank and Walter Rodney from memory, summoning with ease his knowledge of political economy, history and sociology. He told his students that, for all the West's worship of free markets and the United Nations' saccharine rhetoric about a community of nation-states, Africa was not treated as a free and equal player on the world stage. The marauding elites of the former imperial powers still pillaged the continent. Colonialism was as baked into global capitalism as eggs are into a cake.

Bagamuhunda had a reputation as both a radical intellectual leftist and a drunkard. The campus Christians scorned his messages and saw him as immoral. I'm not sure what my mother thought. Still, Bagamuhunda attracted a handful of young men from Rhodesia: black nationalists who had been exiled by Ian Smith's government. They were trying to complete their education at Makerere before returning to the struggle for their country's liberation. Bagamuhunda expected a lot from these young men. They were on the front lines and, with this experience, he thought they would understand politics not only as a battle of ideas but as a battle of *ideals*. In one class, Bagamuhunda gave feedback to his students on an assignment about 'the development of underdevelopment'. The phrase sounds paradoxical. It was coined by Andre Gunder Frank to describe how the prosperity of wealthy, industrialised countries in Europe and North America relied on the impoverishment of poor countries. The former colonies in Africa, Asia and Latin America provided the raw materials, cheap labour and markets for the industrial powers but struggled to build up their own manufacturing sector. The 'development of underdevelopment' helped explain why a country like Nigeria was a net exporter of tomatoes and a net importer of ketchup. Disappointed with one of the Rhodesian students, who failed to grasp the niceties of this concept, Bagamuhunda threw the student's papers into the trash in front of the whole class. 'You're wasting your time here! Go and shoot it out in the Zambezi!' he yelled. Bagamuhunda then made a show of composing himself. He picked up another paper and asked the class, 'Who is Kigundu?'

Bagamuhunda soliloquised for the rest of the morning about the theoretical sophistication of the paper and its robust argument for Africa's political liberation from colonialism and its economic liberation from global capitalism.

My father, glowing inside, knew that it was his paper despite the mangled pronunciation of his name.

***

One day, after Bagamuhunda's class, my mother and her friends walked over to some of the boys sitting on a nearby stairwell, a flirtatious way station for the hubbub of students streaming in and out of lecture halls. In those days, my mother styled her hair in a neat afro. I have only seen a few photos from that time. The images are in black and white but her smile is coy and mischievous. Her dimpled cheeks are exquisite. Her eyes are always wide. They defy the troubles of the times.

'I know this one, this one, this one but not that one,' my mother said, pointing to each of the boys in turn, finally landing her pointed finger at Bagamuhunda's star student. She was in the same class as this intriguing young man and was already enamoured of his intelligence. He was tall, athletic, lean as a plank, and so very handsome. Something about him intimated a depth and a longing that she had not seen in any other man in her life thus far.

'This is a brother from Rhodesia,' said one of the guys in the group.

If he was not being introduced to a beautiful woman, my father might have argued that Rhodesia did not exist, that it was an oppressive fiction of the white man's invention. By right, there was only Zimbabwe. Instead, my father smiled. His pink gums and the slight gap in his front teeth lent his face a gentle boyishness that undercut his severe demeanour.

'Do you drink milk?' my mother said, suggestively.

'Yes, I drink milk,' my father said.

'I'm in A5.'

My father smiled again. There was a milk shortage in the country, courtesy of Idi Amin. He accepted my mother's invitation.

CHAPTER 15

Quite why people are attracted to each other is complicated and unknowable. I am left to guess what my parents saw in each other – I can only extrapolate and imagine from fragments of memories that they have shared with me.

My father visited my mother in Africa Hall often. Sometimes he would accompany her to the Scripture Union. He tucked political pamphlets into his Bible to occupy himself during the rambling sermons. He liked to hang around with my mother and her roommate and he captivated the women with his endless store of anecdotes about his strange upbringing in an exotic land. He has always loved having an audience to enjoy his stories, and my mother willingly obliged. My father bragged about his father: a literate man despite a lack of formal education who loved to cook for his family. My mother was charmed. She noticed how the man before her laughed. The mirth rose from his belly and migrated over his whole body. His shoulders slackened and bounced up and down to a rhythmic cadence. He would lose himself in infectious laughter and he always ended a long chortle by saying, 'What?' in mock self-consciousness before he let out a cathartic sigh.

But how did their romance bloom? Was there a sexual charge between them? Did they hold hands and kiss and dream of a future together?

For most of my life, what I have known about my parents came, as so much does to children, by learning the unspoken family rules: what was safe to ask and what could not be uttered. It's funny and all too common how family dynamics, once set, can endure over a lifetime. When I asked my father to tell me more about his relationship with my mother when they were at Makerere, he clammed up. 'Don't romanticise it,' he chided me as if I were still a boy asking a forbidden question. He only offered sparse recollections. My mother was similarly reticent. 'It's been a long time. It's hard to remember specific details.' Looking into my parents' past, especially their relationship, was like staring directly into a solar eclipse.

Both now and back then, my father preferred to focus on anti-colonial politics and the liberation struggle. This is not irrelevant to the story of my parents' courtship, for they met at an auspicious moment in African history.

* * *

Unlike the other boys on campus, my father was 'exposed'. He told my mother that he had started a degree the year before, in 1973, at the University of Rhodesia, but he didn't last there. 'I was only there for a few months,' he said to her, in that cryptic way of his. Everything he said about himself suggested a complicated backstory; my mother knew he was a man with a vast hinterland behind him. He shared that he had been expelled from the university after protesting against the Smith regime. He spoke ceaselessly about Marxism and Pan-Africanism. He was obsessed with Walter Rodney, the Guyanese historian, thinker and revolutionary, who, in my father's eyes, articulated Africa's predicament with stunning acuity. How could the richest continent on earth in terms of natural resources also be the poorest? My father was fond of posing this question to my mother and her friends and even more fond of relaying Rodney's answer to them. It started with the transatlantic slave trade. This was the engine of European industrialisation, fuelled by Africa as a repository of labour and raw materials. Colonialism continued this system and birthed gigantic monopolies on the backs of African people. Rhodes' company,

De Beers, as well as Unilever, Cadbury, Proctor & Gamble and Barclays, were just a handful of examples. Europe cultivated its celebrated freedoms and human rights while its colonies were exploited and saddled with violence and misery. Racism, of the virulent Rhodesian kind he knew intimately, was a superstructure erected on this base of economic exploitation. After all, my father would say, no people can enslave another for centuries without harbouring a notion of their own superiority.

And, my father would continue, charity was not the answer. The images of African poverty – children with vacant eyes, transparent ribcages, bloated stomachs, skinny limbs – often favoured in fundraising campaigns by Western charities like Oxfam did little more than emotionally blackmail the world's wealthy to continue colonialism by other means.

Nor, for that matter, was Amin the answer. The Ugandan leader might have known how to needle the British. Amin called himself 'Conqueror of the British Empire' and with his friend, Mobutu Sese Seko, the dictator from neighbouring Zaire, the pair renamed historic lakes in Uganda after themselves. Lake Albert was re-christened as Lake Mobutu Sese Seko. Lake Edward became Lake Idi Amin Dada. Amin reassured the crowds gathered at the renaming ceremonies that this was 'another step in the decolonisation of the mind of the people'. Amin presented himself to the world as a champion of racial and economic justice against the evils of white imperialism. He welcomed several prominent African American activists in the civil rights movement to Uganda, including Louis Farrakhan of the Nation of Islam, Roy Ennis of the Congress of Racial Equality, and Stokely Carmichael of the Black Panther Party. They were all, in Amin's words, 'true black Africans who were kidnapped from their motherland more than three hundred years ago'. Some of this amused my father, but he regarded Amin as little more than a dangerous, tin-pot dictator who warped the idea of decolonisation into a self-serving propaganda campaign.

My father's *idée fixe* was Walter Rodney's argument that African liberation required a total break from the international capitalist system. And the way to achieve this total break was for Africans to fight for their land, to claim national sovereignty, to invest in their own industries, to trade with other Third World countries, to turn their backs on the predatory West. My father was possessed with a radical sense of human agency. He believed in revolution, the power of men to make society anew. And I do mean men. Though women were important participants in the liberation struggles of southern Africa, his ideas about who might act out of a sense of historical exigency, and who might be freedom's torchbearers, conformed to conventional gender notions.

My mother was deeply enchanted by my father's intellect and the conviction with which he espoused anti-colonial politics. In the parlance of the time, he was 'conscientising' her and her friends. My mother refers to it now as 'training in politics for idiots'. She was learning that politics was all about power, and it started with questioning who or what had control over her life. Religion had once been the primary means by which my mother made sense of the world. But, increasingly, she found it stultifying. 'I started questioning submission. Submission!' she says. 'I began asking why women should submit. First of all, they are the people who clean, they are the people who feed the priests. They are the people who do most of the things but they are treated so badly. Women were not respected in the church. If anything, they were kind of despised. I thought, no, this is not right. This is not the way it should be.' Her once solid faith began to crack, opening new ways of seeing the world.

* * *

My parents had started a relationship sometime in their first year as undergraduates. Their coupling quickly became a minor scandal on campus. Why was my mother spending so much time with a communist? The Ugandan men could barely understand the attraction. It seemed irrational, even dangerous, that a good Christian woman might be so drawn to an irreverent firebrand. For my mother's friends, it was this very fire that made my father such a spellbinding figure. They talked nonstop about Tafi.

My father, though, was a man divided. He had nestled himself into the warm clutch of his new friends. He spent his first Ugandan Christmas in my mother's home town of Kabale. He had received multiple invitations from my mother and her friends and the young women competed with each other for his company. One by one, they invited him over for a hot meal and offered him a cosy guest room in their parents' homes. He accepted their generosity. He even went to the church services and said grace before dinners. He didn't mind their religious fervour, it kept him out of trouble.

But part of him – the most essential part – had never left southern Africa. He was restless and troubled, reliving his recent past on an endless mental loop.

The same restlessness that spurred my father to leave Rhodesia and then Botswana took hold of him in Uganda. His whole being was alert, tuned in to the frequencies of a distant war. It was a strange longing that he felt: an ardent and romanticised longing to fight, like the old Latin lyric *Dulce et decorum est pro patria mori*, it is sweet and proper to die for one's country. This longing turned each day of my father's exile into a little murder of the soul. His patience with Uganda grew thin. He hated the political illiteracy of those around him. 'They do not know what's happening in the world,' he complained. My mother watched him with increasing anxiety. This thrilling man who had entered her life, at turns full of laughter and full of darkness, was implacable. Not even the lure of erotic love could stifle his desire to leave. Besides, the message from guerrilla commanders to young people who wanted to join the struggle was clear: everything, including marriage, could wait until independence. My father was intent on staking his life in a bush war that my mother did not quite understand.

'To hell with Uganda,' he finally said.

It was now March 1975 and the end of his first year at Makerere. The students left campus for the long vacation and my father boarded a plane back to Lusaka. He wanted to join one of the nationalist movements in exile in the Zambian capital. From there, he hoped to be dispatched to a training camp for guerrilla fighters.

What my father had not appreciated – or perhaps, what he did not want to acknowledge when he told me the story because I might question his judgement – was the deadly rivalry between the nationalists.

By the early sixties, the Zimbabwe African People's Union, or ZAPU, the nationalist party of my grandfather and my Uncle Tinaye, had split. Its spin-off was the Zimbabwe African National Union, or ZANU. Tensions had erupted over how to maintain internal structure and discipline within the ranks; how to balance armed struggle with political negotiation; and who to form an alliance with: the Chinese or the Soviets. Then there was the old-fashioned infighting between big men competing to make their stamp on history or to fuck each other's wives. Both nationalist movements had armed military wings that were essentially competitor armies, habitually shooting at each other on the Rhodesian front lines. Across the board, the liberation movements were riven with factionalism. There's an old quip that a Zimbabwean political scientist used to make: 'If you were to put two Zimbabweans on the moon and visit them the next day, you would find that they had formed three political parties.'

Meanwhile, the Rhodesian Front understood that counter-insurgency required quality intelligence. They devoted vast resources to inveigling nationalists, both high-level politicians and front-line soldiers, to switch sides. African informers for the Rhodesians were known as 'sellouts'. They were reviled as the basest species of traitor and there was a profound stigma against co-operating with the Rhodies. To be marked as a 'sellout' was often to be marked for death. The stigma was not restricted to traitors and informers; it became an epithet for the well educated and well fed in these dire times. In other words, men like my father.

This phase of the struggle was caught up in the geopolitics of southern Africa and the international politics of the Cold War. The Carnation Revolution of April 1974 in Portugal overthrew the authoritarian regime there and helped end Portuguese colonial rule in southern Africa, paving the way for communist elements to come to power in Angola and Mozambique. The Apartheid government in South Africa, hitherto the key regional ally to the Rhodesian Front, entered diplomatic talks with the Zambian government about pressuring the Rhodies to end the war via political settlement. From the South African perspective, it was better to negotiate a peace deal in Rhodesia that would end the fighting and install a moderate government led by the more pliable elements of the nationalist movements. Under South African pressure, the Rhodesian Front agreed to release detained moderate leaders of ZAPU and ZANU for talks in Lusaka. A ceasefire was signed between the warring parties on 11 December 1974.

But there was dissension within ZANU that would lead to the unravelling of the agreement. In late 1974, while key members of the ZANU High Command were away – some in China for training and strategy meetings – a group of mutineers rose up in guerrilla camps across Zambia and Mozambique. They seized military posts and accused the leadership in Lusaka of living in comfort while guerrilla fighters died in the bush with low-grade Chinese rifles and barely enough food to stay upright. They denounced the High Command for abusing female cadres – women who had signed up to fight were instead made to serve as house girls, nannies and sexual playthings for senior men in the movement.

Armed, uniformed in black, the mutineers moved like

insurgents within the insurgency. They abducted fellow cadres, interrogated them as suspected sellouts, and some were killed in defiance of the newly declared ceasefire. When the High Command returned from abroad, they responded with ferocity. A senior commander led a brutal crackdown. The mutiny was crushed. The rebels were rounded up, imprisoned and tortured. As many as 250 were executed.

Just a few days before my father arrived in Lusaka, on 18 March 1975, at around 8 a.m., the chairman of the ZANU war council, Herbert Chitepo, was backing his Volkswagen Beetle out of his driveway. As he did so, his car exploded. Chitepo and one of his bodyguards were killed instantly, their mangled chunks of flesh scattered in the front yard of the house. Another bodyguard survived but with severe injuries. The shockwave from the blast threw part of the car onto the roof of the house, uprooted a tree in the neighbouring yard and injured a child, who died hours later.

Herbert Chitepo's death is a mystery: did the mutineers plant the bomb before they were apprehended? Or was this an inside job, an act of betrayal from an ambitious rival within the war council? The fallout from the rebellion and the spiral of accusations, speculations and confessions around the assassination of Chitepo whipped up an atmosphere of extreme suspicion – as well as shock, grief and fear.

My father landed in Lusaka in the crazed aftermath of the assassination. He was picked up from the airport by a driver and taken to a small township in the north of the city. The neighbourhood teemed with revolutionaries in exile, organised through a network of safe houses and a dizzying array of acronyms. There was a safe house for the ANC of South Africa, Nelson Mandela's party. A safe house for the MPLA, the Angolan nationalists, fresh from their war against Portuguese colonial rule. A safe house for the SWAPO party fighting for independence in Namibia. My father was taken to the large ZAPU safe house. I don't know why he didn't go to the ZANU safe house. Maybe it was family loyalty – my grandfather and Uncle Tinaye had long been with ZAPU. Maybe it was just where the driver was told to take him. Or maybe, in the fractious and paranoid aftermath of Chitepo's assassination, walking into the wrong house with the wrong name could get you killed. It's possible he hadn't made a choice at all. The house had three or four bedrooms at least, reserved for leaders of the movement. My father slept on a stretcher in a living room shared with other subalterns in the liberation hierarchy.

Big, important men passed through the safe house. The future minister of transport was among them, as was ZAPU's representative to Cuba, a man who kept a formidable book collection in the house. And now and then, the biggest of the big men, Joshua Nkomo, ZAPU's leader who had been released from detention in late 1974 for the ceasefire talks, stayed in the safe house. Larger than life in personality and girth, Nkomo commanded each room he occupied. His slate-grey suits and walking stick, his silver tongue and silvering hair endowed him with gravitas. He drew in followers with his paternal charisma and was nicknamed 'Father Zimbabwe'. Nkomo is regarded by many as Zimbabwe's most noble liberation leader.

My father was none too impressed. In the evenings, over the clink of glasses and bottles, he heard the big men converse about the struggle. Their voices grew beer-loud through the night, usually laced with laughter but at times dropping low with secrets. Talk, talk, talk: that's all it was. My father had abandoned everything to join the struggle and now he found himself cooking meat and sadza for a group of blowhards. He cleaned up after them when they went to bed. He was a houseboy. He eavesdropped on their conversations but was never asked for his input. 'Nkomo's legend had been built up by ZAPU and people exaggerated in terms of his abilities,' my father said. Nkomo was a politician and not a warrior. He was a duplicitous pragmatist and not a committed ideologue, or so my father thought. Nkomo was the kind of guy who could have breakfast in Moscow and then lunch in Washington without feeling that something was unhinged.

After three months in the safe house, my father had had enough of all this baroque talk. He thought ZAPU lacked a commitment to fight. But this is a misreading of the struggle. After all, he tried to join the war during a detente that ZAPU was honouring. Moreover, he was grossly under-qualified to advise on political strategy and had no training for combat. Such is the arrogance of youth. My father's time in Zambia did nothing to alleviate his anxiety-ridden experience of life on the periphery of the struggle.

In June 1975, he returned to Uganda to finish his degree.

* * *

My mother waited for him. The long separation had been a grinding torment of anxious anticipation. When my father returned to Uganda, they had a bitter-sweet reunion. A farrago of relief and dread passed between them: *Yes, he is back, but will he disappear again and leave me with this emptiness?* my mother thought. *The struggle continues*, my father thought, *will she understand what I have to do for my people's freedom?*

My father fell back into routine. He studied hard for his economics degree, scarcely vacating the library. In the early mornings or late afternoons, when the sun was pale and timid, that was when he ran. Swift and elegant as a gazelle, my father would stride over long distances in a trance while the rest of the world faded into the background.

CHAPTER 16

A few weeks before my parents graduated from Makerere in 1977, my father travelled to Kenya. Nairobi was bustling. People around the country and the region were moving into the East African capital to start businesses and build homes. New and old, formal and informal, melded together in a rapidly changing urban landscape. Glass-and-steel skyscrapers emerged in the city's business districts but were fronted by second-hand clothes shops. Rickety vegetable stands were popping up everywhere, and ramshackle roadside constructions, stores, mud-brick houses and gas stations extended the city's limits. Minivan taxis, known as *matatus*, swung in and out of the gaps of this urban concatenation as if manoeuvring through an obstacle course. My father criss-crossed through Nairobi to meet Florence, an old high-school friend of my mother.

The pair shopped for clothes. Florence modelled a brown-and-cream-coloured dress for my father. The dress's earth tones complemented her skin complexion with its caramel gloss and dark braided hair. More importantly, it was a perfect fit for her, and Florence's petite dimensions matched my mother's. 'I think she will love it,' Florence said to my father. He bought the dress as a gift for my mother's graduation and also, in effect, as a farewell gift. He was leaving Uganda again but for good this time. He had finished his degree. Now it was time for war, time for him to do what he believed humans had always done when living under tyranny: fight for their freedom.

'He left in March 1977,' my mother says, 'it was horrible.' She gave him a photograph of herself. In it, she stands poised against a blank backdrop. Her dress is patterned in a bold patchwork of floral prints, thoughtfully chosen for this portrait. Her gaze is quietly insistent. She looks miserable, disbelieving pain written across her face. She thought she would never see him again. He thought the same.

Despite his iron resolve to join the liberation struggle, my father's last days in Uganda spun him around in a swirl of emotional vertigo. He had made many friends in Uganda and didn't want to say goodbye. Letting go of this country he'd once kept at arm's length now came with a dismaying sense of finality. The liberation struggle exacted a heavy toll on my father; it asked him to sacrifice everything for the cause. Once he went into the bush, he would be cut off from all communication with the outside world.

Bereft and heartbroken, my mother tried to move on with her life. First, she was hired as a personnel manager on a tea estate just outside Kampala. She later moved back to Jinja, the same city in eastern Uganda where she had been a high-school student for four years, to work for the Uganda Leather and Tanning Industry. Jinja is beautiful. It sits on the north shores of Lake Victoria, at the source of the Nile River. The lake's surface shimmers like beaten silver on cloudless days.

But such tranquillity was a mirage in the last years of Amin's rule.

* * *

Uganda's economy was unravelling. Despite financial aid from Libya and a line of credit from the Soviet Union, the cost of living in the country had risen by over 500 per cent in the late seventies. The United States, disgusted by the human rights abuses of the Amin regime, refused to sell oil to the country. The international price of coffee fell, reducing Uganda's net gain from its most valuable export. All the ingredients were there for economic meltdown: the expulsion of the Asians; the chaotic and unpredictable violence of the army; the loss of the American oil supply; the fall in export revenue; and the circus that was public management. Amin had turned Uganda into a buzzing, anarchic mess. Day to day, most people were getting by through subsistence farming, community markets, petty bribery and bouts of prayer.

In 1977, Amin's soldiers arrested the Anglican archbishop for writing a missive that criticised the president and the pathetic state of the country. Amin was convinced that the church was part of a larger conspiracy with exiled opposition groups to stage a coup. On the same day that the archbishop was arrested, two cabinet ministers disappeared. None of those men were ever seen again. A government spokesman blamed this on a 'motor accident'.

Amin was convinced that rebel guerrillas, those opposition groups that he had exiled to Tanzania, were planning to invade the country. Amin's soldiers pre-emptively annexed a chunk of Tanzania bordering Uganda, a territory that, according to Amin, gave refuge to the rebels plotting against him. His paranoia ran through all of Uganda. It changed the filigrees of unwritten rules that govern how people relate to each other in everyday life. 'Amin's people didn't like us, at all,' my mother says. 'By *us*, I mean people from western Uganda, where I come from. We were seen as opposed to Amin.' In the febrile atmosphere of regional and ethnic suspicion that Amin had so successfully whipped up, ordinary people now regarded each other as potential threats. Where you were from, how you spoke, even your facial features – any sign of social identity – could mark you as a friend or enemy. As my mother puts it, 'Every day you had to be cautious. You watched your step. You went into your house and locked (and locked) the doors; there were many different ways of locking. You minded what you said. Your words mattered. Even a careless word could get you in trouble.'

At night, combatants roamed city streets on the prowl for booze and sex. 'Every day when you went to bed,' my mother says, 'you were afraid that soldiers would come into your house and rape you. So you put whatever object you could behind your door.'

I am struck by this image of my parents in the seventies. They were young, only in their mid-twenties, and had just graduated from university. They were both navigating their way through dangerous and unforgiving mazes of political violence and intimate suspicion, where your protectors could become your persecutors, where charismatic leaders and friendly neighbours could turn on a dime. It was a relentless assault on their sense of safety that rewired them for an ever-present anxiety and emotional guardedness.

In January 1979, the Tanzanian army and a small number of Ugandan refugee fighters invaded Uganda. Mostly travelling and fighting on foot, the troops slowly traversed the country towards Kampala. They faced little resistance from Amin's army, which was in disarray. As one ex-soldier explained, Amin's soldiers had become so accustomed to ransacking their own country and investing in their 'extravaganza lifestyles' that they ceased to be a cohesive, disciplined military force. Rather than face the invading army, many soldiers took their pilfered wealth and vanished.

The Tanzanians had strong international support, including from the British who now, after initially supporting Amin, wanted to see him deposed. Ground attacks were accompanied by aerial bombardment. People evacuated Kampala en masse to escape the violence. One of my mother's sisters was among them. My aunt sought safety in Jinja with my mother. One day, while my aunt was resting, my mother and a friend from work, Immy Rose, went to the market to buy food. On their way back, a bomb fell from the sky. It missed its target: the local army garrison. The bomb landed near the Libyan Arab Uganda Bank, next door to Immy Rose's flat.

For a moment, one of those split seconds that felt like an eternity, my mother and Immy Rose froze with fear. Immy Rose's baby was in the flat with a babysitter.

Pandemonium. A large crowd, weeping and wailing, ran towards them. People pushed against one another, turning over carts and wheelbarrows in their way. Women in colourful sarong-like dresses looked like they were wearing capes as they fled the bombshell. The slapping of shoes and flip-flops on the road sounded like a frantic drumbeat. Turbid dust clouded the atmosphere. My mother and Immy Rose dropped their plastic shopping bags and ran. They left the bananas and groundnuts and beans and vegetables they had just bargained hard for scattered on the ground. The two women must have looked mad, swimming against the tide of the crowd, pushing towards the plumes of smoke and the concrete debris.

They scanned around wildly until they spotted a shaded silhouette: a woman in flight with a tiny bundle tucked into her arms. It was the babysitter and Immy Rose's daughter. Physically unscathed but sweating, panting and crying in terror.

This little group then retreated to my mother's flat to join my aunt. Some other friends and relatives took refuge there too. This was no time to hang around; they had to leave Jinja. They fled on foot and walked for miles out of the city. They kept to woods and brush and tall grass where they could. Other groups were trying to escape, dragging goats and carrying boxes on their heads, kerosene lamps in their hands and rolled-up mats under their arms. Children were clinging to the legs of adults or latching on to backs.

The safest passage was away from the roads where soldiers might be waiting like cats for prey or where more bombs might drop. My mother looked vigilantly for signs of danger: rising smoke meant burning houses, swarms of flies meant corpses. They eventually caught a train heading east and took it to a remote village far from the fighting.

***

Amin's government fell on 11 April 1979. Kampala was ablaze, the air in the capital a booming chorus of rockets and shellfire. Amin and his family set off in a convoy to Tripoli, Libya. They stayed there until Amin fell out with Libyan leader Muammar Gaddafi. The Amin family then moved to Saudi Arabia, where Amin settled with his wives and his forty-three acknowledged children. He retreated from public life and apparently devoted himself to the study of Islam.

Was Amin a terrible anomaly in Uganda's history, a singular force, a one-man cyclone of bloody destruction? The British certainly thought so. Often cited as one of the worst examples of humanity, Amin has variously been reported as a sadist and a racist, a torturer and a fascist, and a bloodthirsty cannibal. He conformed to colonial stereotypes of the African 'big man', a violent, uneducated and primitive tyrant. He personified European anxieties that the end of colonial rule would revert Africa to barbarism. The head of the British Foreign and Commonwealth Office's East Africa Desk at the time wrote that Amin was an 'unregenerate African'. There is irony, of course, in the suggestion that the Ugandan leader's lack of respect for human life apparently had *nothing* to do with the two decades he spent in the British military, where he was trained to kill, where he participated in internal repression against other Ugandans, where he violently crushed the Mau Mau uprising in Kenya in the fifties. Far from being an 'unregenerate African', Amin had been taught by the British, assisted by the British in his rise to power, and was in so many ways just like any of the British soldiers in colonial Africa.

There can be no doubt that Amin charmed and terrified those

who met him and defied those who dismissed him. He had a flair for spectacle with his self-bestowed titles: His Excellency President for Life Field Marshal Al Hadj Doctor Idi Amin Dada VC, DSO, MC Lord of All the Beasts of the Earth and Fishes of the Sea and Conqueror of the British Empire in Africa in General and Uganda in Particular. He was a jester who enjoyed PR stunts like his 'Save Britain Fund', a campaign to send aid from Uganda to assist the mother country through its drawn-out crises of the seventies. But I'm inclined to think that for all that Amin stands out in Ugandan history, he was a symptom of a country unsure of itself, of its direction and identity after colonialism. Amin took the divide-and-conquer logic of British imperialism to its extreme by heightening inter-ethnic tensions, with deadly consequences. A master populist, Amin recruited Ugandans from the West Nile district – historically marginalised during the colonial period – into his army and licensed them to act with violent impunity throughout the country. Later in his life, when Amin was asked if he felt remorse for how he ruled Uganda, he replied: 'No. Only nostalgia.' Nostalgia? For what? 'For when I was a non-commissioned officer fighting against the Mau Mau in Kenya and everyone respected me. I was strong as a bull. The terror of the Mau Mau.' Amin, it appears, never let go of his colonial mentality that power means subordinating Africans.

In 1980, when Obote – a man regarded by the British Foreign Office as Westernised and sensible, his earlier affiliation with communists now forgotten – returned to power, his presidency precipitated a vengeful and paranoid cycle of violence that led to full-scale civil war. My mother had returned to Jinja a few weeks after Amin's ouster. She believed, as had been announced on the radio, that the war was over. But 'then the Obote people came in, and they were even more vicious than Amin', she says.

Anyone associated with Amin was targeted. Throughout the West Nile region of the country, houses went up in smoke, their thatched roofs smouldering in the rain. The sickeningly sweet smell of wet ashes saturated the atmosphere. Bodies lay lifeless on the dirt floors inside huts whose owners were suspected of loyalty to the old regime. Corpses were dumped into rivers, floated along and sometimes washed up on river banks or got caught on snags. Looting, arrests, disappearances and other degrading forms of physical and psychological torture spread through Uganda like an epidemic.

Politics had become zero-sum and public faith in the government was shattered. As one historian described it, the second reign of Obote remains 'shrouded by the smoke of battle and obfuscated by a kind of collective stress disorder'.

The lethality of both political regimes was horrifying: 250,000 Ugandans killed under Amin; 300,000 killed under Obote. So many killed in a population of about fifteen million. So much blood spilled. Who knew blood could be so dark, so thick, so heavy that it covers an entire country like a cloak?

***

A rumour spread through Makerere University that my father, Edgar Tafi Chigudu, had died in the bush war in southern Africa. A memorial service was held for him on campus. My mother was plunged into grief. The origins of the rumour are not clear. Campus culture in a small, enclosed universe like Makerere's quickly became clotted with unsubstantiated gossip.

My mother looked for new direction. Love, religion and politics had all let her down.

It was a novel that would inspire her. The protagonist of *The Women's Room* by Marilyn French is a woman named Mira. Everything that happens to Mira in the book – marriage, pregnancy, childbirth, divorce – is cast through the glassy eye of belated resentment. It's a character study of how a woman starts out submissive and repressed, beholden to other people's expectations of her, and grows into someone liberated but lonely. Despite the book's setting in the United States and its lampooning of white middle-class American men, my mother had never encountered so much of herself on the page. The book conveyed to her that her feelings of intimate betrayal – the feeling that what you should be able to trust can slip away – existed in the world outside herself. The book pushed against the received wisdom that told her anything women did was trivial, domestic or slight, never genuinely important. My mother felt anguished by the unlived lives of women unable to create a path for themselves in an inhospitable time that offered little beyond domestic work and having babies. Decolonisation, for my mother, did not end with sovereignty in the nation-state nor with the elimination of racial hierarchy nor with seizing the means of production. It also had to be about gender equality. French's novel helped my mother to acquire a new acuity of vision that brought injustice into painful clarity. Everywhere she looked, her nascent feminist gaze allowed her to see the raw and brutal, ordinary and intimate, ancient and evergreen ways that women are oppressed. This thing called patriarchy was in the church, in the wars that men fought, in the relationships that she entered. It was as much about the Idi Amins of the world as it was about her father's stubborn refusal to care for her sickly mother.

But the revelation of feminism, though powerful, left my mother at a crossroads. *Where*, she wondered, *do I go from here?*

CHAPTER 17

East African Airways went bust in early 1977. The airline, run jointly by the governments of Uganda, Kenya and Tanzania, folded under a staggering amount of debt (half a billion dollars in today's money) and the political strain of escalating tensions between the three countries. This was a major inconvenience for my father, who was trying to leave Uganda in March of that year. He did not want to go back to Zambia after his previous experience in 1975. This time, he would go to Mozambique, where the Zimbabwe African National Liberation Army, or ZANLA, the armed wing of the ZANU nationalist movement, had guerrilla training camps. There were no direct flights from Entebbe to Maputo, and no way of getting to Mozambique without first travelling through Apartheid South Africa – a dreadful prospect. The South African intelligence organisation suspected any black person trying to get to Mozambique of being a terrorist. But what choice did my father have? He had come to believe, or he believes in retrospect, that his whole life had been building up to this war, and this was all part of what it meant to fight for your country's liberation.

As he anticipated, my father was detained on arrival at Jan Smuts International Airport in Johannesburg, named after a long-serving prime minister of the Union of South Africa. The scene was sickeningly familiar: white businessmen in starched shirts and crisp suits, white women with freshly pressed blouses and long skirts, all moving through this shrine to white accomplishment in southern Africa, paying little heed to the black workers who carried their bags or scrubbed their toilets.

For three days, my father was interned at the airport hotel. 'You cannot go to Maputo if you do not have a return ticket,' they told him, 'but we can send you to Salisbury.' My father refused this offer. The Rhodesians tightly monitored their border crossings, keeping close tabs on who was moving in and out of the country. As a former political prisoner, now travelling on a refugee passport, my father had a huge target on his back. The Rhodesian authorities would immediately identify him as a nationalist fighting the Smith government. He didn't budge from his hotel room.

On the third day of his stay, a white woman from British Airways came to see him, 'a dubious character', my father says. She spoke in the furtive tones of a Rhodie intelligence officer. At least, this is how he remembers it.

'Mr Chigudu, we've got a way out for you.'

'Yes?'

'I suggest we cancel your ticket to Maputo. And instead, we can give you a ticket to Swaziland. How does that sound?'

Swaziland, he knew, was teeming with Rhodesian spies both black and white. But my father agreed to the offer; it was his only option. He took the calculated risk that he could evade detection in Swaziland if he moved quietly in the darkness.

* * *

It was after dusk in Mbabane, the Swazi capital, when my father arrived in the city. He left the airport and went to a small bar with a sparse crowd. He ordered a drink at the counter and noticed an attractive woman in a revealing dress standing close by. She was plying the night trade and eyeing him as a potential customer. He threw her an inviting glance, gently goading her approach. She walked over to him and said, 'So, do you want to do business?' My father flirted a little but soon explained that he wasn't after sex.

Instead, he would offer what little money he had for a bed to sleep in. Somewhere quiet, preferably out of town. A smile blossomed on her face at the prospect of the easy cash. She led my father out of the bar and into the night.

This woman stayed in a surprisingly big house. She had shared it with a lover but kicked him out when he pressured her to marry him. Her ex-lover turned up that very night wanting to talk. He camped in the living room and refused to leave. Meanwhile, my father was upstairs lying awake on the bed with this woman he had just met. 'She slept. She was comfortable. It was me who did not sleep.'

My father lay awake thinking about Uganda and his aching family in Rhodesia, experiencing the emotional churn of wanting to go to war while knowing that his life could be ended before he even set foot in a guerrilla training camp. Maybe the man downstairs was a Rhodie spy, he thought. No one could be trusted. *If I die tonight*, my father said to himself, *nobody in this world would know my fate.*

He rose before the morning's first grey light and snuck out of the house, careful not to wake the woman by his side nor her jilted ex-lover downstairs. He hailed one minivan taxi after another and hitched his way to the nearest border crossing to Mozambique.

Soldiers from the Frente de Libertação Moçambique, the nationalist movement that had just liberated Mozambique from Portuguese colonial rule in 1975, were stationed at the border. They were operating something like a triage system there, directing guerrilla recruits and refugees from Rhodesia and South Africa to makeshift border camps and weeding out potential spies sent by Ian Smith to infiltrate the insurgency.

For the next several weeks, my father was shuttled between various camps in southern Mozambique. He moved through dense forests, wading through thick undergrowth before stopping in a camp run by South African anti-Apartheid fighters. He stayed in that camp for an indiscernibly long period. Days or maybe weeks went by; his orientation was distorted by anxiety and boredom.

One day, all of a sudden, a bus arrived to take my father and others to a ZANU refugee camp. At the camp's entrance, he surrendered his suitcase with his clothes, watch, passport and papers for screening while he joined the throng of refugees.

The camp was an open-air museum of human misery. Thousands of people lay around on the dry, sun-baked earth unshielded from the elements. Mothers looked listlessly at their naked children with bellies taut as globes. The skin over the children's chests and buttocks had turned the tawny colour of weak tea and collapsed into rumpled folds. Spurts of reddish hair was all that was left on their heads. My father took in his surroundings, unsure whether to hold the dead-eyed stare of the moribund people watching him. Everywhere he looked, he saw frightened and contorted faces.

A nauseating stink, the effluvia of human waste and suppurating wounds and putrefaction, prevailed in the atmosphere.

Journalists and relief workers who visited the refugee camp despaired at the lack of even the most basic sanitation facilities. One could hardly find simple medical supplies like iodine, bandages, gauze, vitamin supplements for pregnant women and formula for babies.

The camp was dotted with baobab trees. An old Arab legend has it that the baobab acquired its peculiar shape when the devil plucked it up from the earth, thrust its branches into the ground and left its roots in the air. The baobabs' large trunks had been stripped of their bark. This was one of the few sources of nourishment. People chewed and sucked on the bark for a little water and sugar.

My father went hungry on his first day there.

When meagre rations did arrive, the camp hummed with activity. People milled around in long queues. Many voices talked at once, some were shouting. People were hurrying back and forth, this way and that. My father was given a small portion of sadza and he gave it away almost immediately. He was a new arrival and still strong. People surrounded him begging for his food – they knew he didn't need it as desperately as they did.

At day's end, my father slept in a crowd of refugees bunched together like asparagus on a baking tray. Through the night, if the bodies next to him went still and silent, my father stretched his hand across to see if they were still alive. He had already helped to bury many corpses.

* * *

Early one morning, hours before dawn, my father was pulled out of the crowd. Soldiers had been watching him since he arrived. He was not like everyone else. He carried himself with a quiet self-confidence, the kind of dignity that education bestows. They studied his documents, which only added to their suspicions of him. Why would a man with a university degree volunteer to fight in such horrendous circumstances? He was not gaunt and desperate for survival in the same way as many of the other fighters. It is hard to exaggerate the risks my father had taken to join the struggle. In his single-minded desire to enter the fray, he had chosen the loneliest and most dangerous path to becoming a guerrilla soldier. Now here he was, isolated and vulnerable. I can only imagine the heaviness in his legs, the clenching of his jaw, the trembling of his hands. He had to remain rigid and focused; he knew that any unexplained or unpredictable movement could set off a nervous trigger finger.

'Why did you come here?' asked one of the guerrillas. 'It's only poor people who go to war.'

My father's interrogators had a point. For years now, poor black youth in Rhodesia, sick of unemployment, pathetic living standards and discrimination, had been the primary recruits into the armed struggle against the white supremacist government.

The training camps had become engorged with refugees, and now ZANLA could not shelter, train, equip, feed and clothe all these recruits. Unable to rigorously screen each new arrival at the camp, they picked out people who stood out. The Rhodesians knew this and had been sending spies into the camps to take advantage of the chaos and gather intelligence on plans for guerrilla attacks. The guerrillas were on high alert. The ZANLA soldiers assumed that an educated person, who had spent much time with the whites in Salisbury, was likely a sellout.

My father tried to steady his nerves.

In the background, he heard a small troupe of women singing songs of revolution and bloodshed. The liveliness of the chanting masked the sinister undertones of the message. These songs are sung before somebody is killed.

One soldier glowered at my father throughout the interrogation but didn't utter a word. The soldier spoke with his eyes, tacitly directing my father's attention to the assault rifle he was brandishing – the Avtomát Kaláshnikova model of 1947, or the AK-47: a nine-pound amalgam of forged steel and plywood that will not break, jam or overheat but rather shoot out one hundred lead bullets a minute at a velocity of 1,600 miles per hour whether it's covered in mud or filled with sand. A simple and rugged instrument of death, perfectly suited to war and summary justice. A coil of fear tightened around my father's sternum. The slightest hint of discomfort could betray him, and my father was in the company of men who would think nothing of putting a bullet through his head. He had to remain impassive.

At sunrise, they released my father back into the crowd. His self-control had worked; he had convinced them he was not a spy. In a world beset by intrigue, where my father lived in constant fear for his life, he had mastered a fierce and protective stoicism. Later in life, this emotional habit immured him, his only release coming from a surfeit of drink.

*

Sometime after the interrogation, a bus arrived at the refugee camp to gather recruits for military training. 'Chigudu,' called one of the guerrillas, 'go with them.' My father had been in the refugee camp for a few weeks, maybe a month, and was eager to leave. He had dreamed of military training, and his moment had finally come.

Training started in July 1977, near the city of Chimoio in western Mozambique, close to the Rhodesian border. The Chimoio Operational Base was a sprawling camp of fields and single-storey buildings. It hosted over 6,000 people, not only guerrilla soldiers but children and people with disabilities, along with traditional healers and war spirit mediums. In traditional Shona cosmology, political authority is the gift of the ancestors. They stand at the centre of the moral universe, where they punish wicked actions by restoring order. Sometimes they cause droughts as punishment for incest and witchcraft, other times they lead struggles against foreign invaders. But ancestors have no corporeal form, no materiality and so, to participate in the lives of their descendants, they need earthly representatives. In Shona lore, a widely held belief was that ancestors from the First Chimurenga against Cecil John Rhodes and the British South Africa Company in the late nineteenth century had returned to inhabit spirit mediums or human avatars to guide and inspire the liberation struggle in the 1970s, now known as the Second Chimurenga.

From what I know of my father, this aspect of his cultural heritage was too fey to resonate with him. He revered his ancestors and wanted to honour them but he didn't take the mythology of spirit mediums or prophecy literally. What mattered to him was how the deep past always reasserted itself and would not settle until justice was delivered.

One of the army commanders who dominated the Chimoio training camp went by the *nom de guerre* of Rex Nhongo. He was a taciturn man who wore a black beret, jackboots and a plain green uniform. Nhongo surveyed the training camps and slipped unnoticed into conversations among the cadres. On one occasion, Nhongo sat quietly among a group of soldiers, his face inscrutable as ever. He listened to one of his subordinates unleash a tirade, heavy with bitterness and disillusionment, about the High Command of the nationalist movement. Nhongo restrained himself, allowing this torrent of words to run until dry. Then Nhongo beat him with a stick until the comrade evacuated his bowels.

My father knew better than to speak out of turn. He respected military hierarchy. To be in the trenches meant following strict protocols. There was no room for disobedience.

My father learned close combat, individual tactics, weaponry and long-range shooting. The guerrilla tactics of ZANLA included planting landmines on arterial transport routes, sabotaging power and telephone lines and bombing crucial infrastructure like bridges and fuel stores. They attacked Rhodesian garrisons close to the Mozambican border using mortar bombs, rocket-propelled grenade launchers and machine gun fire. They recruited peasants, who were aggrieved at the loss of their land, into camps in the mountains to take part in all-night pungwes, vigils of singing and dancing that whipped up anti-colonial feeling. These rituals were later used in the 2000s when ZANU(PF) was galvanising its youth militia against white farmers.

After training, my father was made a platoon commander. Once, when he was leading a company of soldiers – marching left, right, left, right – over a long distance, the men happened upon a deserted farm. Three of the soldiers ducked out of the unit to retrieve some lemons. 'Unlike in regular armies,' my father says, 'we were not well fed. It's the hunger that kills you.' It was only when they returned to base, awaiting inspection from commanding officers, that my father noticed the deficit in his company.

'These guys,' the commander said, referring to the three truants from my father's unit, 'where have you sent them?'

My father stood silently. Gripped by fear, he had no answer.

I'm done, he thought to himself. The commanders told him to get a large branch and lie on the ground. He took his beating like a stoic, writhing in pain and clenching his teeth so as not to cry out.

'Discipline your men, Chigudu,' was the parting instruction.

* * *

One morning in November 1977, around 7.45 a.m., the sky over the Chimoio Operational Base erupted like a thunderstorm. The swift roar from the sky receded for a moment before coming back again and again, louder and swifter each time. Rhodesian fighter aircraft dropped their deadly cargo of napalm and cluster bombs on the camp. Paratroopers then raced through the camp, emptying their magazines into ZANLA soldiers trying to escape. Bullets tore through bones. Chests blew open. Human beings were shredded into a splattering red mass.

The assault lasted for three days. Overnight, in their stuttering sleep, the guerrillas could hear the *wah-wah-wah* of aerial bombardment. They would wake up drunk from exhaustion, and more vulnerable to targeted ground attacks. Clouds of dust and napalm fumes enveloped the area. Corpses, disfigured by metal and fire, covered the killing fields, turning the earth black with coagulated blood. Swarms of flies congregated over rotting flesh. It was one of the deadliest massacres of the war. Anywhere between 1,200 and 3,000 guerrillas were killed. My father kept safe from the bombs and gunfire by hiding out a few miles away from the camp.

It would not be the last time the Rhodies used this kind of ambush as a military tactic. As the war went on, they bombed more soldiers and indiscriminately shot civilians too, killing 5,000 to 8,000 people. This was slaughter, pure and simple.

The Chimoio attack reverberated like the aftershocks of an earthquake. The guerrillas became jittery, riddled with fear about the next attack and anxious that the Rhodies had deposited poisons in the areas surrounding guerrilla campsites. It was a rational fear. The Rhodesian army used chemical and biological weapons. Not only napalm, as in the Chimoio massacres, but also parathion (an organophosphate insecticide), thallium (most commonly used in Rhodesia to kill baboons that raided farms), warfarin (a blood thinner used to treat patients who have had a stroke and also to kill rats), anthrax and cholera (bacteria that can infect the skin, lungs and intestines).

These were heavy, gruesome times. War continued at a relentless tempo. A feature of all insurrections is that the closer one looks at them, the messier they become. Neat divisions of the regime on one side and the people on the other belie how widespread violence can become. For rural African peasants in Rhodesia, violence came from all sides. The Rhodesian forces torched villages that they suspected had harboured or fed rebel soldiers. At the same time, peasants who were unwilling or too afraid to support the revolution were intimidated and bullied by the guerrillas: their livestock was attacked, women were raped and old men were doused in petrol and set alight.

Sometime in early 1978, my father was caught in another aerial bombardment, this time at a different campsite. He sought cover in a dense forest. To get under the canopy of trees, he had to cross a river. The explosions from the sky were deafening. Angry flames raged behind him.

He walked along the river bank looking for a place to cross. The ground beneath him was wet and soft, his feet kept sinking into the mud. Eventually, he just waded into the water. He had to hoist himself up on the far bank, frantically grabbing handfuls of grass. It was then that he felt a piercing itch all over his body. Like being pricked by thousands of tiny needles.

'My gun was facing down. I was convinced they had used a chemical weapon. I dropped my guard. Planes were flying over. I thought I was dying. I walked, not even looking for a bush to hide in,' my father recalls, his voice still dripping with dread. He was broken out of his fatalistic reverie when another comrade screamed, '*Ndapinda nepa uriri!*' 'I fell into a grove of buffalo beans!' The buffalo bean is a tropical legume whose pod hairs, called spicules, cause a maddening itch, the kind of sensation that blots out all thought and reason.

My father dived into the nearest bush. He rolled and slid on the ground, his eyes shut tight. His clothes had disintegrated to tatters, and he gave out a groan. The furious itch all over his body had been caused by a plant and not a noxious chemical agent. Bombs continued to fall around him but he was alive.

* * *

A few months later, my father left the guerrilla training camps in Mozambique. He had been selected by his commanders to go to Romania. The Romanian government, along with other Communist states, offered scholarships to support the higher education of refugee students from southern Africa. They believed that a new generation needed technical training to help run the free and independent African states emerging from the gyre of conflict. Romania offered a limited number of university places for ZANLA guerrillas and my father's undergraduate degree made him a strong candidate for one of them.

Before travelling to Eastern Europe, he spent some time in a camp in Maputo. After nearly two years of war, he hardly recognised himself in the mirror. He had always been thin but wiry and lean – a runner's physique. Now he was emaciated. He started eating again, and his appetite and taste buds slowly returned. 'They feed you at camp,' he explained, 'to make sure you're not an embarrassment when you go overseas.'

My father flew to Bucharest with another comrade. They stayed in a hostel for a couple of days while they looked for transport to the town of Cluj-Napoca where they had been told to enrol in the local university's Faculty of Economics. After several stalled attempts, they found the bus that would take them on the long ride between the two cities.

I imagine my father on the bus, sitting by the window and watching the grassy plains of the countryside unfurling. Carts drawn by oxen would slow the bus down on the narrow lanes leading into villages. At each village, when they stopped for rest, the children would point at the vehicle and laugh with glee at the dark-skinned, kinky-haired travellers. Eventually, my father arrived at Cluj-Napoca, in the heart of Transylvania. He noticed the town's eerie stone churches, all wrought with the complexity and detail of Gothic cathedrals.

The task ahead of him was daunting. He had four months to learn as much Romanian as possible before starting his master's degree in economics. He sat in university lectures trying to grasp economic theory and methods in a strange new tongue that bore no resemblance to anything he had studied before.

My father wrote to his family. He had not seen any of them since he first went into exile in May 1974. His brother Tinaye had been released from prison and then sent to Britain.

When the two brothers finally reconnected, Tinaye sent a message: Our father is no more.

My grandfather had been sold out to the Rhodies by an informer. Just like the ambush in 1965 that landed him in prison for three years, he was abducted about two miles from his village home. I have tried and failed to reconstruct this scene: How did my grandfather react when a gun was raised to him? Did he plead for his life or was he resigned to his fate? Did his voice hold steady or crack with fright? Did the killers stand behind or look him in the eye? I don't know if any of this matters when the granite truth is that they shot him in cold blood and jettisoned his remains in a shallow pit.

My father tells me that my grandfather was literate and driven, that he cared for his children and believed in self-improvement through education. But I have no sense of the man beyond my father's broad-brush strokes and a sepia-tinted photograph that sat for many years on the mantelpiece in our living room. I have looked for my grandfather in archives and historical accounts and, through the help of a colleague, I found one passing reference in a book about early nationalism in Zimbabwe. The author interviewed an activist from the Makoni district, who recalled a political meeting in Rusape chaired by 'an old man, now dead, Chigudu, who was just a peasant'. That was the only written trace I could find about my father's father.

Our relationship was unlived, my grandfather's role in my life was absence. A glimmering, heartbreaking absence. Perhaps that was also his role in my father's life.

'I went to bed,' my father said to me as he sank back into the lonely moment he received the news. He didn't want to tell the other student refugees in Cluj-Napoca what had happened – at least, not immediately. He knew that they wouldn't know what to say.

What words were there for a loss so immense?

CHAPTER 18

Margaret Thatcher had little sympathy for the two main nationalist leaders agitating for freedom in Rhodesia. The British prime minister considered Robert Mugabe, the leader of ZANU, and Joshua Nkomo, the leader of ZAPU, to be terrorists.

By 1979, the fighting in Rhodesia had reached a deadly impasse. The war was taking its toll on Rhodesia while the bombing raids into Zambia and Mozambique exasperated the countries hosting Zimbabwe's exiled liberation fighters. Attempts had been made for a diplomatic resolution, including a short-lived period where a conservative clergyman, Bishop Abel Muzorewa, ascended to the prime ministership when the country was briefly called Zimbabwe-Rhodesia, in June 1979. Muzorewa's government was too weak to hold a coalition together. The Rhodies thought Muzorewa could not keep the nationalist insurgents on a tight leash. The nationalists thought Muzorewa was a puppet of the Rhodesian regime. His rule satisfied no one.

Under the charming and pragmatic persuasion of Peter Carington, her foreign secretary, Margaret Thatcher agreed to invite Muzorewa's government, the Rhodesian Front and a joint delegation of ZANU and ZAPU called the Patriotic Front to a meeting in London. More than seventy delegates assembled in Lancaster House, a mansion near Buckingham Palace, that September. Talks began to broker a ceasefire, outline a new constitution, negotiate the terms of land redistribution and plan for a democratic election. These lasted through the autumn and into the winter. It took nearly four months of discussion, but a peace agreement was finally signed on 21 December 1979.

* * *

My father followed the negotiations from Romania. He took a keen interest in Robert Mugabe, the leader of the nationalist movement he had joined. He had never met Mugabe but felt a kindred connection to the man. Mugabe, like my father, was sensitive and bookish as a boy, his mien much older than his years. Mugabe, like my father, had lost an older brother early in life. My father's loss was temporary because his brother Tinaye went to prison and was eventually released, whereas Mugabe's older brother died after eating poisoned maize. Mugabe, like my father, was taken under the wing of missionaries when he was at school – they saw his potential and instilled in him a belief that education was the route to freedom. As black children, their opportunities in Rhodesia were limited. To show academic promise came with lofty, often burdensome expectations. My father admired Mugabe's educational achievements: a bachelor of arts from the University of Fort Hare in South Africa, where Nelson Mandela studied, and several other degrees by distance learning in administration, education, law and science. Mugabe, like my father, had been a political prisoner in Rhodesia. Mugabe, like my father, spent many years in exile – my father in Uganda, Mugabe in Ghana; both men deracinated and longing for freedom; both men falling in love with women in a foreign land; both men seeking to find themselves through the struggle.

Mugabe was not a broad-shouldered combatant but despite his slight frame and thick, black-rimmed glasses, he could be an intimidating physical presence. He spoke in an elegant, commanding manner and showed the steely authority of a headmaster. In fact, that was his nickname: 'the headmaster'.

When the Lancaster House agreement was signed, Mugabe's body was reportedly taut with anger. The agreement did not pledge enough money for the scale of land reform needed in Zimbabwe. The white minority still held half of Zimbabwe's farmland and the Lancaster House agreement imposed a ten-year moratorium on forced redistribution. Instead, it allowed for a limited land reform programme on a willing-buyer–willing-seller basis supported by the British government. The nationalists' anxieties about the land issue were temporarily assuaged when the British and American governments promised to buy and develop even more white-owned land for eventual redistribution to black Zimbabweans. But no amount of money for this compensation exercise was allocated. The shortcomings of this deal would haunt modern Zimbabwe.

An election was planned for early 1980, pitting the Rhodesian Front against the nationalists. To the chagrin of Joshua Nkomo, Mugabe insisted on running a separate campaign, which meant splitting the nationalist vote and strengthening the Rhodesian Front.

In the run-up to the election, the mood in the country was buoyant, even euphoric. Generations of people were on the cusp of having a country they could call their own. Mugabe went on to win a parliamentary majority and premiership as Zimbabwe's leader. This was a global event, not only for black Zimbabweans but for oppressed people everywhere. The new leader delivered a gallant victory speech worthy of Lincoln or Mandela. He said all the right things. Mugabe urged citizens 'to beat our swords into ploughshares, so we can attend to the problems of developing our economy and our society'. He promised never to return to armed conflict. Racial animus was subsumed by the mood of triumphalism and need for reconciliation. He was not showing his teeth, not yet.

Politicians and diplomats in the North Atlantic world placed faith in Mugabe who, as reported by the BBC, was the kind of 'strong, pro-western leader that Zimbabwe would need to embed its new-found independence and democracy'.

***

On 18 April 1980, my father was poised to address 300 young men who had just arrived in Romania from southern Africa for further military training. The session was interrupted by news of Zimbabwe's official independence. Like Kwame Nkrumah, Ghana's first president decades earlier, my father watched tearfully as the British flag was lowered – the last time it flew over an African colony – and a new one of green, gold, red, black and white was raised in its place.

Celebrations erupted throughout Zimbabwe. Bob Marley held a concert in Harare. There is a story that Mugabe would have preferred that Cliff Richard sing at Rufaro Stadium that day. 'In Jamaica,' Mugabe said, 'they have freedom to smoke marijuana, the men are always drunk. Men want to sing and do not go to colleges, some then dreadlock their hair. Let's not go there.' Marley was too uncouth for the bespectacled, suit-wearing, pompous Mugabe.

My father returned to Zimbabwe in 1981. It was a long trip from Bucharest to Vienna, then from Vienna to Johannesburg, and then to Harare. Everything was at once familiar and different. This was the country he had left behind and it was also something new. My father didn't have his bearings. The last time he'd been in the city, in 1974, it was under a cloak of darkness as he'd snuck out of Salisbury and into exile in Botswana. Before that, he knew the university and not much else.

Now he was a free man. Free and poor as a dung beetle. At the airport, he got a ride from a government driver who took him to the new Ministry of Manpower Planning. Like all returning guerrillas and refugees, he could apply for a job in Zimbabwe's new government. My father recognised the secretary at the ministry. She was an old classmate from high school in Murewa and she had also been in the war. She welcomed him back and gave him two dollars, enough for him to take a bus to his sister's place in the same township where he had hidden in 1974.

When my aunt laid eyes on my father, she ran around in circles, overcome by a muddled rush of relief and joy, sadness and passionate grief. Could it be that this harrowing period – the hell of wars, of separation, of waiting and not knowing, of unanswered longings – was now over?

For my father, his return conjured a sense of deliverance that sat, rather queasily, alongside the pain of loss: the birth of a new nation and the pride of survival could not be separated from the realisation of what had been taken away. 'There's no happiness,' my father says, as he is transported back in time, 'there's crying because your father is no longer there.'

Soon after his return, my father fell ill with malaria. A delirium-inducing fever wracked his body. His bones were on fire. He struggled to make himself understood. He got confused about who was in the room, how long it had been, where he was and why.

The family eventually assembled and, when my father had recovered, they went to the common grave where my grandfather's body had been unceremoniously abandoned. Zimbabweans believe that, without proper burial rites, the spirits of the dead are left to wander in the void and torment the living. In the first years of Zimbabwean independence, the remains of fallen comrades were retrieved from battlegrounds to be given a proper send-off. My grandfather was exhumed and buried atop a small hill near his village home.

My father soon settled in a north-western suburb of Harare called Mabelreign. It had been an all-white neighbourhood but with the end of racial segregation at independence, Mabelreign became home to an aspiring black middle class. His bungalow sat in the middle of a thermometer-shaped street with a bulbous cul-de-sac. In the front yard there grew a frangipani tree whose pink flowers blossomed in the thrum and splash of the rainy season and scented the air with a faint sweetness.

All was set for my father's new life. There was just one unresolved matter: the woman he had left behind in Uganda.

***

A year before Zimbabwe gained independence, a postcard had changed the course of my mother's life. It arrived sometime in 1979 at Makerere University, addressed care of Professor Joy Kwesiga, my mother's sister-in-law. The postcard had journeyed a long way to get into my mother's hands. She immediately recognised the handwriting on the back of the card. The elegantly curved, tranquil lettering in black fountain ink, befitting a certain kind of colonial African education, was unmistakable. My father was alive and studying in Romania.

When my father departed from Uganda in 1977, he had left my mother in anguish. His mark on her life was indelible. Friends from that time say that my mother had become more politically aware and that my father's influence extended in ways he could not have foreseen. She began questioning, challenging and pushing against the social structures that she had always taken for granted as fixed and unchangeable. And now, my father's postcard brought something back to life in my mother.

They started talking on the phone but it would still take a few years before my mother decided to reunite with my father and build a life with him in Zimbabwe.

The story of my parents' courtship – or rather the story I pieced together when I was young – was simple and romantic.

My parents' relationship as young lovers had been interrupted by war and my father's noble desire to fight for justice. But their love was so abiding, they were pulled back together once the war was over. It was as if the cosmos willed it so. I was satisfied with this story; its moral about the power of true love was soothing and digestible. I retold this story so often that I believed it was true.

Just before my mother left Uganda in mid-1984, five years after re-establishing contact with my father, her sister questioned the wisdom of her decision to travel to an unknown country to be with a man who was surely, by now, a stranger. Her parents weren't happy either. 'Will we ever see you again?' they asked. 'And when we die, will you come back for our funerals?' Indeed, my mother would not make it back to Uganda for my grandfather's funeral when he succumbed to a hospital-acquired infection two years later.

My mother did not heed her sister's note of caution. She ignored her parents' fears. For years now, her life had stalled. She needed to shake things up, and this was as dramatic a move as she could make. 'It was a big decision. A big and foolish decision,' my mother says, looking back.

She took a bus from Kampala to Nairobi. She spent a couple of days in Kenya, staying in the home of two of her high-school friends, who were sisters. The sisters knew my father from Makerere and, I imagine, were also caught up in the romance of helping my mother reunite with her soulmate.

One of the sisters dropped my mother off at the airport and my mother left East Africa for the first time. She wore a simple dress, a light jacket and spectacles. She wore little makeup, perhaps something glossy on her lips. She looked unassuming but beautiful all the same. She was nervous. Excited too. And curious. There was so much to catch up on, it was a journey laden with expectations.

She landed in Harare in early July 1984, in the middle of a cool, dry sub-equatorial winter. She walked gingerly into the arrivals hall. The beige-and-umber palette of the plastic-tiled floors and wood-lined walls gave the room a drab look. Everything moved much slower over here compared to Kampala. My mother spotted my father. He had barely changed. Still handsome and lean, hair cut short and neatly combed, dressed as she might have expected in smart trousers and a long-sleeved shirt. He was waiting with two other people. A rotund man called Gavi and his sweet-looking wife, Ruth.

My father was nervous, even more nervous than my mother. 'I think Tafi's nervousness was also about what people would say about me,' my mother says.

When they drove from the airport, my mother was struck by how different Harare appeared from Kampala. The soil was dusty and dry, nothing like the moist red earth she knew from back home. The trees were tame, unlike the bursting greenness that sprang up around Lake Victoria. She had left a place of rolling hills, high temperatures, manic energy. Harare was frigid and the city's topography was flat as a lake – a sly intimation of the relationship to follow.

My mother, my father, Gavi and Ruth stopped at a bar near my father's house in Mabelreign. When my mother knew my father at Makerere, he was teetotal. But now he drank. She watched him knock back one beer after another and she grew uneasy almost in inverse proportion to my father's rising Dutch courage. When he was feeling upbeat and confident, buoyed by alcohol, he took my mother to his home, where a gathering of people awaited her arrival.

It was an intimidating start, to meet after five years and then be thrust into a large welcome party the day she arrived. Before they entered the house, my father asked my mother to cover her arms. Her limbs were skinnier than he remembered and she suspected he was ashamed of her. He turned to face her and then said, with a pleading coldness, 'Don't embarrass me in front of my friends with talk of your God.'

There was a celebration that night. Chicken, sadza and vegetable stew were served with beers and sodas. Knowing my father, he would have played sungura music, a Zimbabwean genre with origins in Congolese rumba fused with Kenyan benga and South African township jive. The partygoers danced to the intricate blend of high-pitched guitar lines with pronounced bass and drums and catchy choruses. My father would also have played Lionel Richie, 'All Night Long'. And Dobie Gray and Michael Jackson.

The following morning, my father woke my mother up. In a voice low but insistent, he asked her to join the other women who had already started cooking from an open fire outside. It was chilly and my mother didn't have a coat. This was a bad note on which to rekindle a relationship.

In the days and weeks after my mother's arrival in Zimbabwe, my father left home early for work each morning. My mother lay in bed, cold and alone, until nine in the morning. Normally an early riser, she tended to start her day before dawn but now she wandered about the house in a mental fog until late morning before going outside and sitting in the sun that had at last emerged. She ate her breakfast of eggs and sausages slowly to stretch out the time. Then the rest of the day stared at her in all its blankness. My father would return late, often making a pitstop at a bar en route home. My mother didn't know how to pass the hours. Sometimes she did some cleaning. Sometimes she worked in the garden. Domestic labour being cheap and readily available in Zimbabwe, my father hired a man to help around the house, dusting furniture and polishing floors. My mother occasionally tried to converse with him but the two didn't have much to talk about. With no friends and nowhere to go, my mother felt a stark loneliness enveloping her.

Ruth, Gavi's wife, would pop by from time to time. Like my mother, Ruth was also petite. She liked to wear a long, bright yellow dress with a subtle embroidered pattern. Her hair was fluffy and naturally styled, and she wore large, round glasses that perched elegantly on her nose. She would say she was passing through the neighbourhood and offer to take my mother out. My mother knew that Ruth pitied her and was trying to be kind, that she was not just in the neighbourhood but had intuited my mother's isolation. And my mother gladly accepted Ruth's company.

* * *

My parents married on 31 August 1984, about six weeks after my mother had first landed in Zimbabwe. It was a discreet, almost solemn occasion in the city magistrate's office. Ruth was my mother's matron of honour.

My maternal grandfather sent a message from Uganda saying he did not recognise any nuptials outside the church. And so, to appease him, my parents married again in a church. This time Uncle Tinaye, his wife and my cousins were present too, as were a Ugandan family that my mother had befriended in Harare.

I have never seen any photos from my parents' wedding.

Despite owning a house, my parents had little money. They had no car and could not afford a colour television set. They ate sadza and packet soup. My mother hardly ever left the house on her own.

It was not a tenable situation: my mother needed to find a job, both to earn money and to fill her days. She didn't know the city and had no connections. The easiest line of work to pursue was teaching.

My mother found a job in a high-density township – a former suburb for migrant labourers – in the south-west periphery of Harare. She taught African history to high-school students.

On her first day, she tried to make a good impression on the kids. She went to work in an attention-grabbing frock and she had grown her hair out even longer than Ruth's. It was obvious from her accent that she was not from Zimbabwe. My mother took advantage of this and tried to win over the kids' interest by telling them that she had travelled here from a small but spectacular country in East Africa. A country that lies almost entirely within the Nile basin, enclosed by a horizon-spanning rim of mountains. A country that is always green, no matter what time of year it is. Her home country, Uganda, was rightly called the pearl of Africa.

'And how is my friend, Idi Amin?' asked one of the kids in a smarmy, mocking tone.

'If he's your friend, then you should know,' my mother snapped back, irritated and a little humiliated.

The kids were not interested in learning at all. She hated preparing the lessons because everything she did had to be checked and approved by a micro-managing senior teacher. She hated marking because most students didn't turn in their work, and those who did wrote shoddy, half-hearted essays. She hated how disengaged and unruly the kids were. Once a teacher punished a student by telling him to mow the grass in the school grounds with a sickle, a long metal rod shaped like a hockey stick with a dull blade on its far end. The student took the sickle and hurled it back at the teacher. With hindsight, my mother can see that these were poor kids whose lives had been accelerated and disrupted by war. Their futures remained uncertain despite the country's independence. Their poverty made school learning seem frivolous compared to the daily slog of hand-to-mouth survival. But at the time, my mother could not look past her own misery. After three months, she quit working as a teacher and spent another six months sitting alone at home.

And yet, somehow, my mother didn't pack up her bags and return to Uganda. 'I had left Uganda. I had no job to go back to. I had no life there,' my mother says when she reflects on it. 'But in those situations, you keep thinking it will work. The beginning is hard but it will work.' Another reason she didn't go back might be that she had left a conservative culture in a pugnacious, self-asserting fashion, by defying her parents and older siblings. Was the loss of face too much to bear? And what about my father, did he ask her to stay? Did he think their relationship would get better? Was he also afraid of losing face if my mother left?

It took some time but my mother was offered two jobs, one in the Ministry of Community Development and Women's Affairs and the other in the Ministry of Labour. She took the former. The work aligned with her feminist values and gave her a chance to contribute to nation-building in her new country. For the first time in her career, she thrived. Through the ministry, she was exposed to the challenges facing women across Zimbabwe. The country's economy offered men fancy jobs while women were stuck at home. Arcane laws denied women the right to own property. Married women, legally speaking, were the property of their husbands, and unmarried women of any age were minors. Most people thought that women who wore miniskirts must be prostitutes. My mother opined, loudly and often, about the country and what the ministry ought to be doing. Her manager, a man who spoke in a deep baritone, would occasionally walk into her office and close the door behind him as he whispered, 'You know, people think you're my boss. Could you tone it down?'

In the eighties, there were good reasons to be optimistic about Zimbabwe's prospects. Under colonial rule, Christian missionaries had taken it upon themselves to bring literacy to Africa's benighted children. In the new Zimbabwe, the government would teach grammar and arithmetic to girls and boys in free primary schools. Soon, Zimbabwe provided the best education in Africa, a point of national pride and identity. In large parts of the country that had been left diseased and underfed under colonial rule, the government now established new clinics and nutrition campaigns. The back-breaking labour regimes of the Rhodesians gradually gave way to new laws ensuring more decent working hours, lodgings and minimum wages for black workers. And Mugabe forged strong relationships with international allies in the West. Ronald Reagan credited Mugabe's 'wise leadership' as 'a crucial factor in healing the wounds of civil war and developing a new nation with new opportunities'. Mugabe also forged trading ties in the East, leading to a boom in exports and economic growth. Not for nothing were we dubbed the breadbasket of Africa.

Despite all the forward momentum in the government's quest to transform Zimbabwe, this was still a country born of violence. Over five years in the mid-eighties, hundreds of miles west of Harare, an infantry brigade composed of men in camouflage and red berets went on a killing spree. Their targets were Ndebele people, Zimbabwe's minority ethnic group in Matabeleland that had been conquered by Cecil Rhodes in the late nineteenth century before his Company travelled further north to the land of my ancestors. The massacre of the Ndebele in the eighties was not about tribal hatred, it was far more calculated and sinister. The soldiers accused Ndebele people of dividing the country by voting for ZAPU – the rival nationalist party to Mugabe's ZANU(PF) – in the country's first mass democratic election. They said that the Ndebele people posed a threat to the national security of the country by harbouring dissidents from ZAPU's old military wing and by hiding caches of arms throughout the countryside in the western and midlands provinces as part of a plan to subvert the new government.

Punishment was merciless. 'First you will eat your chickens, then your goats, then your cattle, then your donkeys. Then you will eat your children, and finally you will eat the dissidents,' said one soldier to Ndebele villagers who had been cut off from food supplies. Ndebele men were forced at gunpoint to sing songs of praise to the Mugabe government before they were gunned down.

Huts were burned. Boots stomped on prostrate bodies. Pregnant women's bellies were sliced open with scythes. Even children were killed. The bodies of the dead were piled into mass graves. So many people disappeared, their fate only becoming clear years later. Some were taken from the streets, others from the villages; some from their vehicles, others from schools; some at night, others in the middle of the day. About 20,000 civilians if not more were killed in this operation known as *Gukurahundi* – a Shona word that translates as 'the early rain which washes away the chaff before the spring rains'. A beautiful, life-affirming image – the earthy scent of the first rains falling on dry soil; the cool and fresh air afterwards; the promise of a fecund harvest – now contorted into something necrotic and ugly. A few years after this massacre, Mugabe was knighted by Queen Elizabeth II.

* * *

In Harare, where these events dimly registered, my father had tried and failed to persuade my mother to take the job at the Ministry of Labour. He reckoned it was a much more respectable position than the one in the women's ministry. Tafi confounded my mother. Where was his radical edge? Where was the Tafi who had read Marxist and Pan-Africanist political philosophy and who challenged authority?

Now, they were at odds with each other. My mother was a feminist, 'ready to resist everything', she says, 'and he was also not ready to give in'. She felt hurt and rejected. She knew that she was not the wife my father wanted. My mother told me that, despite living in Zimbabwe for four decades, all the Shona she learned was in her first three months there. As the marriage grew cold, so too did her ability to take in my father's language. I wonder whether my mother's fraught relationship to the language had been passed on to me – passively, subconsciously.

In so many ways, my parents were attempting the impossible. 'At the beginning of the marriage,' my mother says, 'there was nothing to build on. We were trying to build a life without counselling, without support, without even discussing our differences. I kept remembering the person I knew. I thought that where we stopped was where things were. But Tafi had gone through the war. He had gone through so much, which I was not part of. He had come back and maybe his expectations were not met. And I had my own trials and tribulations. There was no one for me to turn to, I didn't have anyone in Zimbabwe. In fact, I think I almost had a mental breakdown. Actually, I *had* a mental breakdown. All these things were eroding whatever was between me and Tafi.'

Whether he realised it or not, my father's life was overshadowed by the struggle. He had lived in a state of autonomic hyper-arousal – in an almost permanent fight-or-flight mode – for so long that he had cut a tender part of himself off. He never revealed too much of what was roiling inside him, his tumult of feeling. But buried somewhere deep within him was the sensitive boy who had been forced to toughen up too quickly. He became a survivor who licked his wounds in private and sustained himself through an unshakeable sense of duty to the nationalist cause.

My mother had a miscarriage. Then another. Eventually, she became pregnant with me. Not only did she have to deal with the queasy mornings in bed, the dull throbbing in her back, the countless visits to the toilet, the sleepless nights and the fear of yet another loss, but she also faced motherhood alone in a place where her life seemed tentative and spare. The casual cruelty of her circumstances grew a hard clot of bitterness inside her.

I was born prematurely in 1986. 'You were the size of an egg, I could hold you in one hand,' my mother liked to say to me.

There's a picture I've seen, taken shortly after my mother was discharged from hospital. My mother is lying in bed, wearing a nightdress and her dimpled smile. My father sits on the edge of the bed. He's dressed for the outside in a beige corduroy jacket and a collared shirt. He cradles me and his face beams with love and pride.

I have known that photo all my life, but until I started delving into my parents' past, I had no sense of the story behind it. I could not have guessed the startling choices my parents had made to get to that point, the point that brought me into the world.

Book III: Exile and Arrival

CHAPTER 19

My life in England began on New Year's Day, 2003. I was sixteen years old, innocent to the point of naivety, ignorant of almost everything worth knowing. I carried a small suitcase packed with clothes: socks and underwear, jeans and T-shirts, a sweater, blue towels and several long-sleeved white shirts. I carried a backpack with my most treasured possessions: my notebook of motivational quotes, a new Discman with the skip protection, and four CDs. DMX, Jay-Z, Nas and Eminem. The essentials.

I carried too, in more ways than I could understand, the oppressive weight of a divided nation, the fractious despair of a troubled family, and a set of expectations too vast to meet. While my father had fought in a revolution of the insurgent guerrilla kind, my mother too was trying to effect a revolution but in her family lineage – revolutionary insofar as she wanted to give me the life she had never had, a life that my grandparents could never have imagined. The South African writer Jonny Steinberg asks, 'How does one carry out such a revolution, when there is no linear path from the world of one's parents to the world one wants for one's children?' My mother's answer was to throw herself into the unknown when she moved to Zimbabwe, and now she placed all her hopes in my education abroad, trusting that this kind of exposure would be my open sesame to the good life.

I took it as my duty to honour all the sacrifices my parents had made. And yet, I could not have spelled out what precisely those sacrifices were. I knew the broad outlines of their history. I knew my father had been to prison and fought in a war. I knew my grandfather had been killed by Rhodies. I knew my mother had left her home country at a time when it was locked in some kind of strife. But I didn't know any of the details.

My parents had told me of their suffering, not through words but through a tempest of dark moods. My mother's unpredictable anxieties and fiery temper, my father's retreat into silence and sorrow – all of it had seeped into me. Somewhere, deep in the boiler-room of my psyche, I had transformed this emotional inheritance into a childish fable about my parents' superhuman strength and endurance. I looked in awe at what they'd built and told myself that since my life was drastically better than theirs, I would have to achieve beyond measure. If nothing else, this knowledge – this burden – gave me a sense of mission so deep that it cut through my being, right down to my atoms. If I put enough work in, my successes would prove that all their losses were worth it.

I did not imagine that my relentless efforts would be foiled again and again, nor could I have guessed that my striving would trap me in an endlessly repeating cycle. No amount of mission could prepare me for the cold strangeness of my new life in England, where I would have to confront questions I did not yet know how to ask.

* * *

My mother and I had travelled together. She planned to take me all the way to Stonyhurst College, my new boarding school. But first we had to figure out where it was. We had flown from Harare via Johannesburg to London Heathrow. The sky was grey. It rained steadily and drearily. I was too excited to see that my mother didn't have a plan. Not really. We had just landed in a foreign country that neither of us knew at all. We didn't know how to use the London Tube or the National Rail train network. We had no access to the internet or to a mobile phone. We held all our cash in chunky bundles of US dollars. It was as if we had just moved a pawn two squares on a chessboard but then had no idea how to play the game.

Although my mother was a seasoned traveller, she primarily relied on her work and social contacts to facilitate practical matters like exchanging currency or arranging transport from point A to point B. On this occasion, she summoned Uncle Tinaye's daughter, one of my cousins who lived in London, to meet us at the airport.

'Hello, Auntie Hope! Hi, Simu!' my cousin called out in the arrivals hall. 'Welcome to England. As you can see, the weather is glorious just for you. God save the Queen,' she said with a laugh. We sat in a Costa Coffee. I drank a hot chocolate with marshmallows and whipped cream. My mother told my cousin that we needed to get to a town called Clitheroe. My cousin had only ever been to London and Birmingham and she argued that surely no place with such a ridiculous name existed. I finished my drink and said I was going to look around. I wandered into a store called WHSmith and bought a magazine, an issue of *FHM*, from the 'Men's Lifestyle' section. It was brazenly horny. The cover story featured a French porn star who posed topless in the magazine's pages. There were also articles about cars and movies. I tucked it into my backpack, hoping my mother wouldn't see it.

Eventually we decided to travel up north, as we knew that this was generally in the right direction. First, my mother and I took the train to Northumberland. There we stayed with my mother's old colleague and co-author, Barry. I had met Barry only once before, back in Harare when I was fourteen years old and he came to the house for lunch. He was just as I remembered him, paunchy with a crown of bushy hair on his head, scruffily dressed and astonishingly articulate. I now met his partner, Christine, who spoke to me with a soft and soulful kindness that never failed to make me feel welcome. And I met Barry and Christine's son, James, a sharp and well-behaved nine-year-old. Before I went to boarding school, he asked his parents to take us all to see *The Lord of the Rings: The Two Towers* in the cinema. I was delighted.

After dinner one evening, we sat by the log fire in the front room. I told Barry and Christine how thrilled I was about Stonyhurst and that I would pass all my exams with a string of A grades before going to university in the United States.

'I'm going to do maths, physics, chemistry and French for A-level,' I said. 'My dream is to go to the Massachusetts Institute of Technology and become a chemical engineer.'

'Oh, right, blimey,' Christine said. She didn't doubt my ambition so much as fear it. I didn't talk like any sixteen-year-old she knew. My mother watched me with pride and added, 'Simu has always been able to do whatever he puts his mind to. If this is his dream, he will do it. You just wait and see.'

Barry didn't say anything. I now know that he felt uneasy about my school. He knew what I didn't – that I was about to step into the parochial, self-regarding world of English boarding schools with people locked in a rigid sense of privilege and tradition. He worried about the pressure and entitlement of that kind of environment. And he knew the peculiar genius for cruelty that the spoiled kids of the wealthy possess. 'You were such a sensitive kid,' he later said to me. It would be a stark and difficult transition.

After Barry and Christine's, my mother and I went to visit a Ugandan family who had lived in Zimbabwe years ago. The same family that had attended my parents' church wedding in 1984. They had now settled in a small market town in Lancashire called Ormskirk. The patriarch of the family was a proud man. He held his head tilted at an acute angle such that his gaze was always pointed downwards as if he were casting Solomonic judgement. Uncle Clem, as I called him, was a professor of medicine at the University of Liverpool – and one of the world's leading experts on hepatitis, he told me. His research yielded many breakthroughs in understanding the biochemistry of viral infections and inflammation in the liver. Like many immigrants who prized education, Uncle Clem saw technical mastery as a shield, a protective barrier against xenophobia. His faith in the impartiality of science was unshakeable. After all, cytokines obey no master other than their molecular truth.

'What does the future hold for you, young man?' he asked when we met. I told him that I wanted to become a chemical engineer. 'Good,' he replied, 'that is respectable.' In his home study, he showed me a sign affixed to the wall. It was an A4 sheet of paper with the words **Excellence is the best deterrent to prejudice** typed out in Times New Roman. 'Let me tell you something about this country, Simukai. The whites will always doubt us. They act polite but you can see that they think we are simple people,' he said. 'Let them think that. You focus on your studies. If there's one thing I've learned, excellence will speak for itself.' I wrote Uncle Clem's motto in my book of motivational quotes.

Uncle Clem and his wife took us to visit Stonyhurst ahead of my first day. I won't ever forget seeing Stonyhurst for the first time. I was wonderstruck. We drove down a long, straight driveway that was flanked initially by stunning green fields and then two parallel ponds. We arrived at imposing charcoal-coloured buildings made of sandstone in both coarse and finely dressed masonry. I got out of the car and looked to my left to see the old infirmary, and on my right was a nineteenth-century church, St Peter's. But standing before me were two brooding towers capped with copper domes encrusted with verdigris. The towers were the architectural inspiration for the granite castle at Saints. The building was huge; I was told it was the second largest building habitable under one roof in England. We were surrounded by sheep fields, and the air smelled of dung. The scene evoked the image of a postcard – bucolic, serene but also otherworldly, something that could never belong to me. Not for the first time, I felt like I had crossed a threshold. If my primary school, Twin Rivers, had been a pantomime version of an elite private school in Harare, like Saints, then Saints was a facsimile of an English boarding school. This was the real McCoy.

Unlike most English boarding schools, Stonyhurst was organised horizontally by age groups, oddly called 'playrooms', rather than vertically by houses. Each playroom had an assigned supervisor called a 'playroom master'. Mine was Dr Terry Bell – the puns write themselves. Dr Bell was also the head of the English department. He welcomed my mother and me and explained that the playrooms took their names from the Roman order of learning, beginning with the Lower Grammar playroom (ages thirteen to fourteen), then Grammar (fourteen to fifteen), Syntax (fifteen to sixteen), Poetry (sixteen to seventeen) and finally Rhetoric (seventeen to eighteen). 'Oh, I see, that's interesting,' my mother said. Dr Bell was tall. He had floppy hair, glasses and a doctorate from Oxford. He had written his thesis on Ezra Pound. He went on to explain that I was now a member of the Poetry playroom. 'He's a Poet and he didn't even know it,' he said while cackling. I later discovered that Dr Bell was an eccentric, choleric man. He called his rising temper 'the five phases of Dr Bell' and warned us students of the wrath he would unleash should we provoke him into phase five. Years later Dr Bell was arrested for having an affair with a student.

My mother left the school by taxi. We said our goodbyes in the front quadrangle, my mother's face crimped with misgiving. I watched her climb hesitantly into the car. As it pulled away, the taxi driver said, 'What has this poor lad done to make you abandon him here?' I imagine he was trying to be affable. But my mother cried all the way from the school to the train station. When she got back to Zimbabwe, she buried herself in work.

***

I spent the rest of my first afternoon exploring the school. All the rooms and passageways were constructed from marble and mahogany. The walls were adorned with paintings of Old Stonyhurst men who had served in the British armed forces and been awarded the Victoria Cross. They had sealed their place in history. I walked around, almost on tiptoe, breathing politely with my mouth shut, subconsciously aware that nowhere in a place like this would I find sacred imagery celebrating the power or valour or intelligence of anyone who looked like me. But being an outsider was part of the bargain. I was here to prove myself. On the school's main notice board was a list of all the Stonyhurst students in Rhetoric who had just been accepted to the universities of Oxford and Cambridge. I pictured my name on that list and felt a flutter of excitement – to be accepted, to make it, to be celebrated. Could this be me?

'You look happy,' someone behind me said. I turned around and saw a middle-aged man, a teacher I presumed.

'Yes, sir,' I said, 'I'm new. It's my first day here, sir.'

'Where are you from?'

'Zimbabwe, sir, I—'

'Oh, are you one of the boys from St George's?'

'Yes, sir, I—'

'Good man! That's a splendid school. We're proud to have you boys here. One does what one can to support such a talented group.' He paused. His eyes filled with pity. 'But it is such a shame, isn't it?' he said.

'Sir?'

'What *Mugabeee* has done to Zimbabwe. A terrible shame.'

'Erm, well, it's been tough, sir. But these things are complicated—'

'It's just awful what's happened there. Ghastly really. That *Mugabeee*. You must hate him. At least you're here now. Welcome to Stonyhurst!'

'Thank you, sir.'

As he left, so too did the tension I hadn't realised I was carrying. I then felt something I did not know how to describe. I allowed myself a quick shudder, then continued sauntering around the school.

That night, at dinner in the canteen, as all the students lined up for food, I was mesmerised by the sight of all the girls. I couldn't believe how pretty they all were. There was a cluster of white kids from Saints who were also in Poetry. They had been at the school since the start of the academic year in September. I knew each of them – George, Liam and Stephen – from Zimbabwe but they were not friends of mine. Still, we had a shared history. George's parents had been teachers at Saints. His father was a curmudgeon who used to raise his fists to students, saying, 'This one will take you to the hospital, this one to the mortuary.' His mother taught me science. She was frosty, not cruel but detached. I remember them as embittered old Rhodies who were hated by the black students. For his part, George had been polite to me at Saints. But I could not erase a tremor of suspicion I had about him. I used to play football with Stephen at Saints. I respected the fact that he was one of the few white guys who played a black sport. Off the pitch, I would give him a nod of recognition when we bumped into each other, but we didn't talk. He hung out with other Rhodies. Liam and I had talked on only two occasions at Saints. I thought he was dumb. Like George and Stephen, I associated Liam with the Rhodies. I recoiled slightly when I saw them all sitting together in the dining hall. I wondered if they even remembered my name. I never trusted white Zimbabweans to remember black people's names.

***

Once classes started, the volume of work to catch up on was formidable. In my physics, maths and chemistry classes, the whiteboards were covered in inscrutable code: letters multiplied by Greek symbols, numbers crowded into parentheses, hexagons sprouting limbs, criss-crossing squiggly and curved lines that apparently explained light's oscillating status between wave and particle. In French, I was asked to research and write an oral presentation on a quintessential aspect of French culture, but I was given three months to do it instead of six.

The work kept piling up. I could feel a familiar uneasiness making an unsanctioned pilgrimage from the pit of my stomach to the rest of my body, clouding my vision, choking up my breathing, unsettling my nerves. I didn't want to lose control again. I had to make myself safe.

I set upon an industrious routine that fitted into the highly regimented ordering of time at Stonyhurst. I woke up each morning at 4.30 before any of the other boys. I studied for two hours in my room. Before breakfast, I went to pray in the Boys' Chapel. The chapel was soothingly dim, full of echoes and mysteries. I took in the sweet aroma of old wood and incense as I practised the breathing exercises that my counsellor in Harare had given me to stave off panic attacks. I went to breakfast. I went to class. I studied in the More Library in all my free periods. I went to lunch. I went to games. I joined the cross-country team, and George was the vice-captain. We ran for miles through the green hills, muddy trails and babbling brooks around the school. To keep spirits up, George sang our old war cries from Saints. Running with him was like contracting malaria; I hurt all over and was losing the will to live. He pushed me to run further and harder than I ever had before. But by the end, even as my body ached, the exertion proved exhilarating. In the late-afternoon break, I studied again in the More Library. After dinner, I prayed once more in the Boys' Chapel. During the evening study session, I sat in my room, completing my homework. I ignored the English boys who rapped their knuckles on my door, yelling, 'Chigudu, the chicken!' and running away in giggles. I reminded myself that I was going to the Massachusetts Institute of Technology to become a chemical engineer. I went to bed early. I woke up early. I did the same each day of the week. Excellence is the best deterrent to prejudice.

*　*　*

It wasn't until I arrived in England that I began to appreciate how colonialism had furnished not only Zimbabwe but Britain too with fiercely held national mythologies. In Zimbabwe in the 2000s, colonialism was the basis of all historic injustice and the scapegoat for all contemporary problems. But in the UK, colonialism had been washed of its sordid history into a clean myth about the country's pre-eminence in shaping the world in its glorious image. At Stonyhurst, I was frequently taken aback by the views of Zimbabwe I encountered. The image of my home country through the looking glass of my new world was warped by ignorance, pity and disdain. If Mugabe liked to claim that colonialism was the cause of all Zimbabwe's problems, then my English classmates were equally simplistic in blaming them entirely on Mugabe, whom they touted as a one-man catastrophe.

I was lounging in the common room on a Saturday afternoon when one of my classmates said, 'Frankly, Zimbabwe would be much better off if we just colonised it again. Clearly, that chap *Mugabeee* and his henchmen are not ready to govern a country. I mean, where is the rule of law? Where is the democracy?' I looked at his bulbous person angrily. This was always the story: Zimbabwe was the naughty child who needed Britain, its helicopter parent, to swoop in and make things right. But I had no comeback at the time. It was dawning on me how little I knew about my country. I felt disarmed and impotent. On top of this, arguing with the English was not like arguing with the Rhodies. I was a minority now and my opponents had a ready-made retort: 'If you don't like it here, then why don't you just go back where you came from?' I can't count the number of times someone has said that to me over the years. It used to sting like a slap across the face.

My classmates parroted the screeds against Zimbabwe that abounded in Britain. Every broadsheet reported on how Mugabe was persecuting white people. In the House of Lords, a Conservative MP said, 'My Lords, the government of Zimbabwe made clear their objective of removing white people who own property in Zimbabwe. Is that not a form of ethnic cleansing?' Even *Hello!*, a celebrity and human interest magazine, devoted a five-page special to Zimbabwe, covering the death of a white farmer. Little to nothing was said, in the media or elsewhere, of Zimbabwe's colonial legacy or the suffering of black people under Mugabe's regime. The political roots of the uprising and the colonial history of land dispossession were glossed over. More subtly, the media depicted the white farmers as human beings with rich stories deserving of compassion. But there was no recognition of black Zimbabweans' humanity in quite the same way. No sense that black people in Zimbabwe also had lives and projects and aspirations and culture, that black people were more than mascots in the unfolding tribulations of the white farmer in Africa.

***

I was an outsider at Stonyhurst in other ways too. The students who had been at the school since Lower Grammar called themselves 'the last of the old school' and sneered at new arrivals like me. This reflected the country's growing anxieties about immigration. In 2002, Zimbabweans made more asylum claims to the UK than any other nationality apart from Iraqis. Within four years, the Home Office estimated that 200,000 Zimbabweans lived in Britain. Other sources reported figures as high as 1.2 million. One classmate told me that if he could, he would shovel all the asylum-seekers arriving in England into a boat rigged with a bomb and then send it off to sea for detonation.

Apart from the occasional sip of wine, I had never drunk alcohol before I came to England. At my first major school event, the Poetry Banquet, hosted by my year group to honour parents and patrons of the school, I discovered how the English drink. I mean, really drink. I couldn't understand how people who were so stiff that they moved like robots could suddenly lose all control. During the after-party, I was baffled to see the logic of cool inverted. I didn't understand why sixteen- and seventeen-year-olds 'danced' by jumping up and down, defying all the laws of rhythm. They yelled along to lame, boring white music: Oasis, Robbie Williams, Bryan Adams, Bon Jovi, and Eagle Eye Cherry. I knew these artists from MTV but had never met anyone who listened to them. But here, each song was like a national anthem; everyone knew all the words except me. They sang them with the same passion and understanding. Why wasn't anyone dancing to real party music? That Dru Hill, Montell Jordan, Destiny's Child, that Jagged Edge remix featuring Nelly.

On another occasion, we had a black-tie dinner in the Top Refectory, the school's opulent marble-tiled hall built in the sixteenth century and decorated with moose heads, a Steinway piano and a table on which Oliver Cromwell slept, in full armour, in 1648. I had dressed for the night in a regal red-and-purple tunic with gold embroidery. My mother had bought it in Uganda and gifted it to me to wear as national dress on special occasions. We bowed our heads to say the Lord's Prayer before the first course. I heard suppressed giggles from the adjacent table and looked over to see what was going on. One of my classmates had pulled his penis out of his trousers while we were praying. If I were being charitable, I might have called this a bit of harmless mischief, or 'banter', as my classmates said. At the time, I thought it was childish and gross. Now what bothers me most is not so much the errant penis as the look of invincibility on his smug face. I'm also convinced – but I have no evidence to prove it – that this same student was the phantom shitter, a menace who surreptitiously defecated in other students' bedroom sinks while they were in class. Mercifully, no one ever shat in my sink.

* * *

By the end of my first few weeks at Stonyhurst, I was exhausted. I had never worked so intensively in my life. I realised too that I was crashing against the extremely solid walls of my limitations in the physical sciences. I could tell from conversations with the students who wanted to study physics, maths or engineering at university that they were different from me in some fundamental way. They saw things in numbers that I couldn't. Their curiosity about the workings of the physical world ran deeper than mine. On top of this, I was lagging behind everyone else after missing the first term. In my maths lessons, the teacher introduced us to integral calculus, but I had yet to grasp the foundational basics of differentiation. My confidence in my plan to study chemical engineering at the Massachusetts Institute of Technology began to waver.

I visited the school's career advisor to ask about applying to university in the United States. She told me the school did not facilitate this, but handed me some pamphlets to read about the Fulbright Commission. My heart sank. I didn't think I could complete my A-levels in a compressed time while preparing for the SATs and navigating an academic system I did not understand. My dream of going to MIT evaporated. I needed a new plan, a new commitment to organise and hold together my sense of self. I felt unmoored without one.

Liam, who was in my maths class, saw that I was struggling. He came to my rescue. We sat in his room, and he talked me through the fundamental theorem of calculus. His explanations were more limpid than anything our teachers or textbooks had conveyed. As it turned out, he was not dumb.

'Look,' he said, 'I don't know anything about MIT. I don't know if you should keep trying to go there. What I can tell you is that *we* are going to *punish* this pure mathematics exam.'

'All right,' I said, 'Let's fucking do it.' I bumped my fist against his.

* * *

'To us in the diaspora,' says the Zimbabwean playwright Tonderai Munyevu, 'death is a phone call.' My mother called me at boarding school to tell me that a dear friend and neighbour, Sarah, who used to go on walks with my mother and me at dusk, had died. When I had told Sarah about my dream to go to MIT and about science programmes I was watching on the Discovery Channel, she nicknamed me 'Mr Cyberspace'. But now, like so many other people in Zimbabwe, her life was claimed by an unspeakable illness. I still remember her dry, barking cough and unnerving weight loss before I left Zimbabwe for the UK. In a country where HIV had infected over a quarter of the adult population, cases like Sarah's were alarmingly common.

I took the news hard. George, Liam and Stephen tried to comfort me. 'People here will never understand what we've been through,' George said, a frisson of anguish crossing his face. He mirrored my grief but was also digging up his own buried feelings of loss and pain. 'I just wish I could be in Zim right now,' I said, fighting an overwhelming urge to cry. 'Time is cruel, nothing stays the same,' Liam said. We all agreed. 'Don't you miss the light?' Stephen asked. We talked about how we hated the wet, dull greyness of the English winter. We needed the incandescence of the Zimbabwean sun. And back home, even when it rained, the deluge from the sky came in warm torrents that could be just as thrilling as the glorious heat.

We sat in Liam's room and gorged on nostalgia, reminiscing about Zimbabwe and ignoring the crisis that compelled us to leave home. Nostalgia needs its illusions. The guys spoke about hosting *braais* (a southern African version of a barbecue) for their friends by the swimming pool, how they missed the smoky taste of roasted meat washed down with a refreshing ice-cold lager. They had lived lives typical of white Zimbabweans. They went on holidays throughout the country, fishing on Lake Kariba or going on game drives through Hwange National Park. They knew many of the same people, traded stories about Valentine's Day kisses, and drew on an endless supply of you-had-to-be-there jokes. I joined in this reverie, even when I knew that their Zimbabwe was not my Zimbabwe.

A memory of a shared experience with Stephen suddenly came back to me.

'Steve, do you remember the time when Muammar Gaddafi came to Zim on an official state visit?' I recalled how the main road outside Saints had been closed to the public and reserved for the exclusive use of Gaddafi's entourage. Steve and I had just finished playing football but we couldn't leave the school through the main black gates. And in those days, without mobile phones, we couldn't even call our parents. 'Do you remember how the teachers took us to a small gate at the back of the school? It was locked, so we had to hop over it to get into the Botanical Gardens. There were like twenty oans in football kit, carrying heavy bags through the mini-rainforest and trying to find the car park.' The image was ridiculous and brought a smile to all our faces. 'I didn't even know who Gaddafi was or why he needed all the main roads in H-town for himself,' I said.

'Ahh, some of the things!' Stephen said. We all roared with laughter. 'Some of the things' was our shorthand for all the uncanny things that happened when you grew up in Zimbabwe.

What bound us was not merely nostalgia for a place but a sense of belonging that we had lost and none of us could quite reclaim. We were now marooned in a centuries-old school that looked like an isolated schloss in the middle of soggy fields in a fog-bound land, left to make do with memories of a period of life that had irrevocably passed. Despite myself, I felt bonded to this group.

Stonyhurst had a pretty relaxed attitude to under-age drinking, so too did the local supermarket in Clitheroe. My guess is that the school thought it was safer for us to drink on site where they could keep an eye on us, rather than having students sneaking off to nightclubs in the nearest city. The guys used to buy stashes of booze for Saturday-evening sessions in the boarding house. When George, Liam and Stephen were drunk and I was stone-cold sober, I found myself swept up in their ritual, singing ballads with unexpected fervour. Our voices rose together for 'Iris' by the Goo Goo Dolls, an alternative rock song that became a pop hit. It was the kind of thing I normally hated, yet it felt raw and accessible when I sang it, arm in arm, with my unlikely band of brothers. The song's lyrics – about longing for connection, the ache of invisibility and the struggle to hold back the tears no one else was meant to see – spoke to something vulnerable and frayed within us. Singing it felt like a release. Even the song's darker images, about feeling so disconnected and numb that you cut yourself until you bleed just to know you're alive, struck a chord – and presaged what was to come in our lives.

CHAPTER 20

During school breaks I returned to Zimbabwe, where life was becoming more difficult each day – for my family and nearly everyone else in the country. Water from the Harare city council flowed intermittently, stuttering from our taps. My parents had installed a borehole in our backyard to compensate, but that only helped until everyone in our neighbourhood did the same, eventually draining the water table. If it wasn't the borehole needing repairs, it was the walls requiring replastering, yet finding skilled handymen and painters was challenging. Cash shortages had become commonplace throughout the country.

The atmosphere in the house felt eerie and quiet. My mother tried to reassure me by saying, 'Tafi and I have started talking a lot more since you left. We only have each other now.' My mother still said that she loved my father. I took her at her word and wilfully ignored whatever doubts I had. She worried about him, that much was clear. She felt sorry for his suffering and wished she could take his pain away. But their relationship never settled into something as comfortable and enduring as real intimacy.

I saw my friends from Saints and received a hero's welcome. We slipped back into our old slang, but they had new words I didn't know. We talked about music. I still loved DMX but was told he wasn't as cool as he once was. Some of my friends now had girlfriends. 'And what about you, bra? Are you punishing white beavers that side?' a friend asked. I mumbled sheepishly and deflected the question. I didn't tell him that I had not even had my first kiss. I shared other stories from England and boarding school. My friends caught me up on what it was like being seniors at Saints. They enjoyed their rising status at the school but complained about the country's crisis affecting everyday life. School fees kept rising; teachers kept leaving. They were all planning to move to South Africa for university. The ground underneath our feet had shifted, and I realised what should have been obvious: our lives were pulling in different directions.

* * *

I returned to Stonyhurst and told one of my teachers about my recent trip home. 'It was nice to see old friends. I felt . . . I don't know. I felt happy to see everyone again. But everyone was also so nervous. The country is in really bad shape,' I said. I told him about destitute families in long breadlines, shuttered stores everywhere, and despair in the thinning faces I saw around town.

'I don't know, sir. It's weird to go home, see how bad things are, then come back to a place like this.'

'I refer you to the gospel according to Luke. In chapter 12, verse 48, he tells us that to whom much is given, much is expected.' His words resonated with my driving sense of mission and my adolescent belief that I could restore a convulsed society if I worked hard and sacrificed enough.

When I was at Saints, students like me, black kids with high academic aptitude – or rather, kids who were good at following instructions and passing exams – were encouraged to pursue medicine as a career. The country's history informed this aspiration as it was passed down from one generation to the next. Few black people trained as doctors under Rhodesian colonial rule. Zimbabwe's most famous hospital used to be called Andrew Fleming Hospital, named after the principal medical officer in the British South Africa Company. It was renamed Parirenyatwa General Hospital at independence in honour of the country's first black doctor. The medical profession was bound up with

Zimbabwe's post-independence project of social uplift, stabilising a black middle class and achieving racial equity. I had initially resisted the idea of going into medicine because I was obsessed with going to MIT. But now that I was shuttling back and forth between a crumbling Zimbabwe and my new world in England, I started to see my future with fresh perspective. A grand truth was revealing itself to me in what I thought was a moment of clarity. Surely, everything was a sign: Sarah's death from AIDS; Uncle Clem's example of excellence as a professor of medicine; my country in need of its best and brightest to help the poor and disadvantaged; the opportunities offered to me through education; my duty to prove myself a successor to my parents' contribution to the nation; living up to the Jesuit motto of being a 'Man for Others'. I knew what I had to do. I would become a doctor. What a relief it was to have a new plan.

And because I was still so intent on high achievement, the ideal place to study medicine was the University of Oxford. This was my new dream. When I drafted my personal statement, I crammed it full of platitudes about my vocation to heal the sick and bring succour to the suffering. One of my teachers cringed when she read it and said, 'It sounds like you're applying to join the seminary.'

Of course, I couldn't detect the more subtle psychology operating beneath my conscious awareness. Choosing medicine under the guise of altruism and making a difference was really a way of managing my doubts and confusion. It was a strategy to wrest away uncertainty. The degree was long and intense. It would focus my attention on doing what I was already good at: studying, taking exams, following a clear line of progression to a defined goal. As long as I was working impossibly hard, there would be no time to sit with anxiety or feeling empty and adrift, unsure of where I belonged. As long as I knew what was expected of me, I could function at a high level. As long as I was given a demanding and all-consuming role, I could hide behind it without asking myself who I was. As long as I set my sights on the noble profession, I was on a path to healing my broken country – not realising that what I truly needed to heal was something much more intimate.

***

I visited Oxford on an open day. It was, reassuringly, just like boarding school. It was a place of cloisters, ancient chapels and stone gargoyles, libraries thick with the scent of old paper and time. Oxford had the same aura of mystique and exclusivity that I associated with an elite education, a more perfect version of Saints and Stonyhurst. I felt a profound pull to this world.

More than fifteen out of eighty students in my Rhetoric playroom at Stonyhurst applied to either Oxford or Cambridge. You can't apply to both universities for an undergraduate degree because they would receive an unmanageable number of applications. Liam and I applied to Oxford to study medicine, and George and Stephen also applied to Oxford to study law and engineering respectively.

I was the first in the cohort to hear back. My letter came in an email in early December 2003 that I read in the school's computer lab. I had been praying for an invitation to interview. The words 'thank you for your application', 'extremely competitive pool' and 'you may be disappointed' winded me like a swift blow to the gut. I reread the email twice, feeling more bereft each time. I did not take academic disappointments well. I had a bad habit of hurling my ring binders at the wall or chucking books to the floor when I didn't get the grades I wanted. I could throw an extravagant tantrum if I missed an A by two per cent. I went to my room and hid. I didn't want anyone to see my misty eyes. I felt consternated by the shame of failing to achieve excellence – at least, as I understood it back then.

A friend slid a note under my door. 'Disappointment never

comes easy for someone with standards as high as yours,' he had written. I clutched the letter to my chest. I eventually left my room. When I saw my friend who wrote me the letter, I hugged him and buried my face on his shoulder, leaving tear stains on his blazer.

Over the next couple of days, the Oxford letters sent by post arrived for my classmates, spreading the virus of rejection around the Rhetoric playroom. I went around the boarding house from one room to the next, asking if anyone had good news. George shook his head when I entered his room and said nothing. When Liam heard my knock on his door, he shouted, 'Leave me alone.' Stephen balled up his letter and threw it in the bin with a mix of acceptance and nonchalance. Our grand school was a little world of cocooned privilege. It incubated the idea that, by right, we, the top students, would be guaranteed an interview at Oxford or Cambridge. Indeed, the school had told us that about ten per cent of each Rhetoric year group would be admitted to the ancient universities. But in ours, only two students were finally accepted to Cambridge and none to Oxford. This was more than a betrayal of expectations; it felt like a metaphysical accident.

The next Saturday night, we had an Oxford rejects party in George's bedroom. Our crew from Saints had become a small centre of social gravity. There were about a dozen boys huddled together with a large stash of booze. I wanted to drink – really drink – for the first time.

After my first pint, I felt light-headed but animated and excitable. After the second, I was woozy and eager to go around the room in a tell-all game of truth. I wanted confessions and consolations and secrets and frustrations.

'Lads, fess up, who has the *Unholy Desires* DVD? I could do with a good wank tonight,' one reject said. 'Shake your grapes. Let me taste some of that fine pussy,' Liam said, quoting a line from that 'movie'. We laughed raucously. Whoever had the DVD was not giving it up. Video porn was a valued commodity in a boarding school, like cigarettes in a prison.

'Where's the strangest place you've ever had a wank?' someone asked the group.

'The library.'

'My car, while driving.'

'The Bayley pub.'

I was three pints down and had lost all inhibition. 'Well, if you must know,' I said, 'it happened when I was flying back to school once. I had a long layover at Schiphol airport in Amsterdam. I was walking around duty-free, looking for the latest *FHM*. But then I saw a cover of *Playboy* with Tori Wilson. I used to watch WWE back in Zim, and she was one of the Divas. She's so fucking hot. I couldn't believe she posed fully nude!' I told them how I dashed to the airport toilets to pleasure myself. Neither the smell nor groans of men shitting in the stalls next to me could break my concentration.

More confessions came, all to do with sex. Which girls had we thought about while masturbating? My answer was nearly all of them. How far had each of us gone with a girl? I kept quiet for that round. And who would we try to hook up with before leaving school at the end of the year? The goal of the hook-up was not only to kiss a girl but to get her to iron your trousers, our euphemism for a handjob.

After four pints, I was wasted.

'Mr Sir. Dr Sir, I mean,' I said to my chemistry teacher who was on duty that night. 'Did you know people call you Dr Layzell, lazy as hell?'

'Oh dear, how much have you had to drink, Simukai?'

'Sir, never have cider before lager. Or was it lager before cider . . . Wait, wait, wait—'

'Go to bed, Simukai.'

'Sir, I had lager before cider. I'm drinking cider now.'

'Someone take Simukai to bed now, please. And make sure he drinks some water. He's gonna have a sore head in the morning.'

'Lager before cider or cider before lager. Why can't I remember...'

When I lay down on my bed, the full force of nausea and head-spin hit me with a wrenching dizziness. A hint of bile rose to my throat, followed by a violent, gushing surge of vomit. I threw up on my pillows and then turned over. I threw up again and passed out.

I woke up a few hours later, around two or three in the morning. My room stank. I went to the toilet at the end of the corridor and saw light creeping from under the door to Liam's room. I gently knocked and then pushed his door open. He was dressed in white shorts and a blue-grey rugby jersey, hunched over his desk, writing manically.

'Simu,' Liam said, 'I've been making notes. I wanted to write this all down before I forget. Hang on, I wrote something for you...' He showed me a chit of paper with a tiny, illegible scrawl. He was trying to note down everything he loved about all his friends. But neither of us could read what he had written.

'Dude,' I said, 'I vommed all over my bed.'

'Oh, mate. Okay, let's go clean it up.'

Before I could say another word, Liam had soaked his towel in the sink and made for my room. He scrubbed down my pillows and said, 'We're going to be doctors, we need to be able to deal with stuff like this.' I stared at him while he toiled away, both of us drunk and out of place in rural England. Something in me swelled with tenderness and gratitude.

CHAPTER 21

The rejection from Oxford shook my confidence in a cutting and profound way. What I had thought of as my uncompromising pursuit of academic excellence was, in truth, a self-flagellating form of perfectionism. I needed to be exceptional to feel safe. I had interpreted Uncle Clem's motto, 'Excellence is the best deterrent to prejudice', accordingly. In a part of my mind, I was still the child from nursery school experiencing rejection from Rhodie kids and private primary schools. I was still the child who needed to hold my family together by making them proud of my academic accomplishments. And now that I had failed to be excellent, my worst childhood fears resurfaced: that I was inadequate, forever out of my depth.

Doubt had entered my mind about my abilities, but it ran deeper than that. Did I really want to study medicine? Was this something I was sincerely driven towards? It was a struggle to admit, even in my most private moments, that the answer might be no. I lived my life under the tyranny of the shoulds. I *should* study medicine because this is what a dutiful son and a good student *should* do. To whom much is given, much is expected.

At heart, however, I was a humanist. I enjoyed my French classes more than physics, chemistry or maths. Reading Albert Camus in my literature lessons felt like an invitation to see the world anew. His idea that life is absurd because humans search for meaning in an indifferent and unintelligible universe was the most provocative philosophy I had encountered, while his belief that we should embrace the absurd and create our own meaning was the most daring. I was desperate to learn more – not just about

Camus but about philosophy and why things are as they are. I was hungry with questions about existence and the world. There was so much I didn't understand: Zimbabwe's crisis, Africa's history, race, identity, displacement, belonging, nationalism, religion, ethics, politics, war. Could it be, I wondered, that there was more to uncover about the peculiar sickness of the spirit that I shared with Liam, George and Stephen? Was it possible that our experiences could be mapped onto a broader canvas of human experience? And how could I possibly find out? I worried that medicine might close off avenues of thought that I was beginning to explore. But back then, I didn't know how to articulate any of that.

The UK's Universities and Colleges Admissions Service allowed high-school students to apply to a maximum of six universities or degree programmes. No more than four of those slots could be used to apply to study medicine. This meant I had two additional slots I could potentially use to apply for something else. I approached my personal tutor for advice.

'Is it too late for me to apply to courses in clinical psychology?' I asked. I saw university in vocational terms, as professional training for a specific career, not as a time for intellectual exploration or self-actualisation. Studying for a degree in French literature or philosophy was a luxury only white people could indulge in, and I carried the immigrant ethos of attaining technical mastery. Clinical psychology was the one professional course I could think of that dealt with the human condition.

'It's theoretically possible,' my tutor said dubiously. 'But listen, someone as bright as you should *not* apply to psychology. It's a poor man's medicine. Maybe Oxford didn't work out but you're bound to get into another medical school.'

He was trying to reassure me. He thought I was taking the wrong lesson away from my failure to get into Oxford. He wanted to remind me that I was talented and bright with a promising future in medicine ahead of me; I just needed to keep the faith and I would bounce back. Still, I felt a bee sting of disappointment when he said this. We were, in hindsight, talking at cross purposes. I was not looking for reassurance that I would get into medical school, I was looking for a way out. I had hoped that my tutor would read my mind.

As my tutor predicted, I received an offer in the late spring to study medicine at Newcastle University. I received this news with a dissonant mix of relief and dread. There was some validation in earning admission to a prestigious programme, but I couldn't silence the siren wailing within me, warning me that I was not ready to commit to a medical degree, let alone a career as a doctor. After accepting the offer, I wrote to Newcastle Medical School asking to defer my entry for a year. I told them that I wanted to take some time to travel, maybe volunteer somewhere. I needed to rest, and I secretly hoped I might use the time to reapply to university to study something else or even revive my ambitions to go to the United States. Time was whizzing by at terminal velocity. My life was moving at a pace I could not control and towards a future I did not want.

When I next went home, for my penultimate vacation before my final high-school exams and the summer break, I told my father about my desire to take a gap year. He shrugged dismissively. An awkward, stale silence fell between us. A few days later, when we spoke again, he was drunk. 'You should not take a gap year, Simu. It's not good to be redundant for such a long time,' he said. He was worried that I would lose momentum in my education and not be able to regain it. I knew my father was terrible at waiting. As a child, whenever we went to the airport as a family – on one of our few collective outings – he couldn't sit still. He would wander away from my mother and me as if his body were allergic to being stationary. What I did not know was how a sense of urgency, of forward momentum, had driven his own journey to university, and had kept him focused during his time in prison cells and refugee camps and in the war. Nothing, in his mind, made you more vulnerable than stopping.

Meanwhile, my mother said she had already saved the money to pay my first-year tuition fees. It would be wise to pay it all upfront because the university would give her a discount. I felt locked in. I would do anything to please my parents, so I stashed my unruly feelings underground. I wrote to Newcastle University to confirm I would take up my place in September 2004 after all. And I told myself that I would do so without complaint. I had to push on, keep studying as if my life depended on it.

* * *

Memory is a protean and slippery human faculty. What's easiest to recall about those last weeks in Rhetoric was how rushed and compressed that period felt. I was working hard to pass my exams, though with less enthusiasm than usual. I went on long runs with George. I played five-a-side football with Stephen. Liam and I broke the rules for once and invited girls into our boarding house to drink with us after lights out. One of them ironed Liam's trousers. I, alas, had to iron my own.

George had a girlfriend called Penny. She was pretty, vivacious and kind. She came from a well-to-do family in a posh part of southern England. Many years after we left Stonyhurst, Penny reminded me of a night that I had long banished to the landfill of memory. When we spoke, images from that night came back to me with frightening intensity but I couldn't put them together. It was like trying to rebuild a vase from crystalline shards of broken glass.

Our groups of friends had been at dinner in the canteen one evening but, unusually, George wasn't there. He didn't join us for our post-prandial promenade along the school driveway, which was one of his favourite rituals. A friend and I went to look for him, thinking he might have gone for a run and come back too late for food. We went into his room. It was empty. Crumpled in his sink was a blood-soaked white towel. Or maybe it was a T-shirt. A box-cutter knife perched on the edge of the basin. George had left a note on his desk that read: 'I am leaving this world where the heart must break or turn as hard as iron.'

I recognised these words. They were from an epigraph to a book by a Catholic priest who had recently visited the school and told us how his time in a Burmese prison had revitalised his faith. God had rescued him at the brink when he was just about to give up on this life.

I don't remember what happened before or after that moment in George's bedroom. I know we panicked and frantically searched for him but I can't quite picture it. I remember my fear, and how it was smothered by confusion, disbelief and the urgent need to find him. My next memory is seeing George in his room, sitting on his window ledge, eyes closed, headphones over his ears blasting Metallica. I tried to shake him awake but he was drowsy. I don't remember if this was on the same night or another occasion. But I have linked these two images and cannot pry them apart.

Penny told the school chaplain what had happened. 'The school knew what was going on. They knew George and other students were hurting themselves and they did nothing. There was such little care and understanding,' she said. George stayed with Penny and her family during a school break. He sat at the kitchen table with Penny's mother who asked him about his family and Zimbabwe. He began to weep, his chest heaved as he laboured to keep silent. But he couldn't. Penny's mother called George's parents who had moved to England too. They were impassive, seemingly indifferent or too damaged themselves to respond to their son's needs. At the time, I watched George's pain from a distance, feeling anguish for my friend. I did not yet realise that I was standing in the same emotional storm.

What was it about Zimbabwe that haunted and followed us?

My white Zimbabwean friends were disoriented by their oxymoronic status: white Africans of Anglo-Saxon stock who felt like exiles in the mother country. Nostalgia for a privileged white childhood in Zimbabwe came with a shame-filled sense of loss. Theirs was a displacement too difficult for them to grasp or explain. I saw George once or twice after Stonyhurst. But he eventually returned to southern Africa and settled in a small beach town with clement weather. I never heard from him again. Liam had adapted by distancing himself from Zimbabwe. His family also left the country. He used to say, 'I am Zimbabwean by birth, Irish by nationality, South African by opinion.' Liam and I stayed friends for many years after Stonyhurst, but our connection quietly faded. Steve and I kept in touch for a while and, in some ways, we became better friends. He was always up for a game of football or watching a film, anything to be part of the gang. But I knew he was unhappy. 'I have little pills that keep me going,' he once said to me over lunch, when we were university students in neighbouring cities. Not long after, I received a call from Penny saying that Stephen had thrown himself in front of a train in the middle of the night. He was the second of my school friends to end his own life. But not the last. Too many in our generation were tormented.

* * *

I finished high school and passed my exams with straight As. I returned to Zimbabwe for the long vacation before beginning university. It was a strange, fallow period. I had nothing to do and no one to talk to. My old friends from Saints were still at school, busy with their own lives. I couldn't drive, and even if I could, I had nowhere to go. Harare was a glum city with its denizens focused on getting by in the ruins of economic collapse. My father was still a fleeting presence in the house. I didn't prepare myself in any way for beginning medical school that September. I filled my hours watching trash TV shows like *The Bachelor* and reading *The Da Vinci Code*. The days passed, loose and unstructured, as if time were a sheet billowing aimlessly in the wind.

In my father's fugitive absences, my mother and I spent a lot of time together alone. We were growing unusually tetchy with each other. Minor irritations escalated into full-blown arguments. 'But, Simu,' she'd say in a high-pitched whine whenever she saw me in the living room, 'don't you have anything better to do than watch TV? It's always TV, TV, TV. No, this is not right!' At points, we found it nearly impossible to get through the day without quarrelling. She was angry that I sat around doing nothing, and I blamed her for my lack of independence. Our relationship was saturated with tension and an inability to hear each other out. I did not tell her about all my emotional confusions from the past eighteen months at boarding school.

One day, my mother and I had gone out to get some groceries. We returned home late in the afternoon. My mother parked in the driveway and motioned to get out of the car but stopped when she noticed that I was looking at her intently.

'What is it, Simu?' she asked, trying to mask her irritation.

'I think we need to talk,' I said. I told her I was worried. Her moods of late suggested that something was wrong. She was too quick to anger and I sensed she was trying to juggle and conceal too much. I could see the toll this was taking on her. 'You might even be depressed,' I said.

I had startled her. She stared into the middle distance without uttering a word. My mother's face was opaque, but I had learned to decipher it when she was carrying more bad news than she was willing to share. After a pregnant pause, my mother said, 'Money is tight.' This I knew, but I sensed there was something more. I wanted to ask, but I didn't say anything. What she didn't tell me was how much money she was spending on my father's farm, a business that was failing. She didn't say how much money she was sending back to Uganda to support one of her sisters through a messy court case and to help rebuild the house of another sister after it had burned to the ground in a freak accident. She was grieving the death of Sarah and so many other people lost to AIDS, including one of her brothers.

'Simu,' my mother said. 'Promise me that when you go to Newcastle, you will not drink. I have seen alcohol destroy lives.' The desperation in her plea hinted at a tidal swell of loss and fear.

'Yes, I promise,' I said without conviction. Neither of us mentioned my father.

CHAPTER 22

At eighteen years old, I was barely an adult when it was time to leave Zimbabwe and return to the UK to start university. I flew into Newcastle's city airport and spent the days before Freshers' Week with Barry, Christine and James in their Northumberland home, in a village just north of the city.

'One of the lads down the terrace wants to take you to the pub tonight,' Christine said. She introduced me to Alan, her neighbour's twenty-year-old son, who was eager for company.

'Hiya, Simu, ye alreet, mate?' he said, by way of greeting. I had trouble understanding his accent.

'I'm good, man. It's nice to meet you,' I said.

'Christine says ye're gannin te dee medicine at the uni. Wey aye, that's champion, that. Ah could neva do owt like that, me. Ah'm too thick, me, like,' he chuckled. 'Reet, shall we gan doon the pub?'

We left the house and wandered through a valley that led to a quaint pub with its own brewery. I noticed heads turning to look at me when we walked in. 'Alreet, lads?' Alan said jovially. Everyone appeared to know each other. As Alan said his hellos, I felt the heat of dozens of eyes on me. I was the only black person there. Were they really watching me, or was I imagining it?

'Simu,' Alan called to me, 'let us introduce ye te Charlotte.' I looked up to see a tall, thin, angular woman with long, flowing blonde hair. *Whoa!* I thought. 'Charlotte's gannin to dee medicine too.'

'Oh, that's great,' I said, facing Charlotte, 'we'll be classmates.'

'I'm so excited about it,' she said. 'Simu is an unusual name, where are you from originally?'

'Zimbabwe. I'm still from there.'

'Your English is amazing!'

'Well, it is my mother tongue,' I said breezily, hiding a twinge of irritation. Charlotte was hot and I wanted to keep talking to her. We swapped numbers and agreed to meet later in the week when we were both at the university. Alan had already downed three or four pints while I had one, and not even finished it. On the way back to the terrace, I said to him, 'Charlotte seems nice.' Alan slowed down a moment. In the darkness of the valley, away from the city lights, I could just about see the stars. It was deathly quiet apart from the rustling leaves and crunch of sticks under our footsteps.

'She's a canny lass, like. Proper shame she's got a bloke, mind,' he said. I laughed. Of course she had a boyfriend.

'I was wondering,' I said, 'did you think it was weird the way she commented on how I talk?'

'How d'ye mean?'

'Well, she said my English was *amazing* in a way that sounded surprised. I don't know. It was like she didn't think a black person from Africa could speak English.'

'I dinna think she meant owt by it. Ways I see it, us lot'd be better off if we stopped stressin' ower what makes us different. Honest, mate, when it come doon to it, we all want the same thing: more sex.'

I dropped the subject, and we continued our walk back.

* * *

The next day, Christine drove me to the university. Over the twenty-minute journey, a queasy sensation stirred in my gut that got worse as we approached Castle Leazes, my halls of residence, a massive concrete block of student digs where I was to live with a thousand other newbies. In the car park, I pulled my suitcase out of the boot and strapped my backpack over my shoulders while Christine studied the legion of students hauling bags and books as well as TVs, stereos, mini-fridges, sporting equipment, all the appurtenances of modern student life. At that point, I was yet to make the unwelcome discovery that my next-door neighbour in halls brought DJ decks with him and liked to play nerve-shattering electronic dance music at three in the morning in the middle of the week.

A guy came over to us, tall and pimple-faced, a second-year student I guessed. He assisted me with my bags as I checked into my new home. His mustard-yellow T-shirt splashed with black lettering, FRESHERS' WEEK 2004, hung loosely over his lanky arms. He bragged about Newcastle's reputation as the UK's number-one party city. 'What degree, mate?' he asked. 'Medicine,' I said. He grimaced. It was a shame to spend the best days of my life as a nine-to-fiver when, like him, I could take a degree in media studies with only six hours of contact teaching a week. 'But don't worry, mate, you're gonna have a great time,' he said with a foolish grin. The alcohol on his breath wafted into my nostrils. I feigned excitement, but I could feel disquiet closing in on me, prowling and circling like a predator.

That evening I walked into the canteen for dinner. I saw row after row of elongated tables, arranged with geometric precision and packed with white students. I almost dropped my tray in shock. At Stonyhurst, for all its remoteness, I had at least met several students who, like me, had come to Britain from Zimbabwe, Nigeria or Hong Kong for education and opportunity. Here, I felt like a misplaced peppercorn in a bowl of salt.

On the Friday of that first week, the students' union hosted a huge welcome party in its four-storey, red-brick building. I attended with Charlotte and a group of her friends. I was the only boy in the group and basked in the female attention. We started drinking at the ground-floor bar. The cocktail special of the night was Skittles, a sickeningly sweet mix of vodka, lemonade and some luminous green liqueur. It went down as easily as a fizzy soft drink. I was drinking cup after cup without realising it. When the lights dimmed, we stood up from our booth. I felt light-headed and almost sat down again. As we walked upstairs to the RnB room on the top floor, I steadied myself on the banister. Just how much had I had to drink? One of Charlotte's friends was climbing the stairs ahead of me. She wore low-rise jeans, and a black G-string was riding up her waist. I felt an intense rush of lust and excitement. I couldn't believe this was my company for the night. In the RnB room, against the background din of Usher and Kevin Lyttle, I leaned into my foreignness as I told stories of growing up in Zimbabwe. To them I was as exotic as a savannah.

'No way, mate, fucking *Mugabeee* hates white people,' said another student. He had been eavesdropping and now came over to interrupt me and impress the women. 'You're probably one of his nephews. You fucked up your country and now you're in this country talking out your arse.' I was gobsmacked. And angry. Why must I take on Mugabe again? Why did I have to be a fucking walking, breathing history lesson for entitled pricks like this?

He was parroting the British press, which continued to portray Mugabe as an icon of evil fixated on murdering white people. I would soon come to understand that Zimbabwe's toxic reputation would accompany me everywhere, always demanding an explanation, an excuse, an argument, an apology.

I would encounter many men like this student throughout my time living in the UK. Years later, a British doctor – someone I'd never met – read an article I wrote in the *Guardian* critiquing colonialism. He didn't like it. Instead of arguing my points, he sent a message to a mutual friend, saying that my father must have enriched himself through corruption while working as a mid-level bureaucrat in Zimbabwe. He even wrote that I carried the 'stench' of a family exploiting Zimbabwe while 'whining about the people who used to exploit the country'. Many British people couldn't fathom the idea of someone like me, from an upwardly mobile African middle-class family.

An argument broke out with this student. Tempers flared. Chests puffed up. Fists waved impotently. I don't remember it. Woozy from booze and the acrid haze of cigarette smoke, I failed to keep track of my thoughts. I was sitting on the stairs leading to the main dance floor in the basement. My arms were folded over my knees and I was crying. Charlotte and one of her friends tried to comfort me but they had to leave to catch the last bus home.

I kept drinking after they left and went looking for a woman – any woman – to hook up with.

I woke up the next morning with a stinking hangover, awash in shame and vomit.

* * *

When Freshers' Week came to an end, I was already hovering on the edge of depletion. I registered at the medical school where I discovered to my dismay that I was the only black man in my cohort of 250 undergraduates and one of sparingly few black faces in the Faculty of Medical Sciences. Before I knew it, our fully packed schedule of lectures was in full swing.

Academic scientists delivered most of the teaching in the first year, introducing us to anatomy, physiology, biochemistry and pharmacology. However, to keep our eyes on the long-term prize, the medical school invited practising doctors from the teaching hospital to give occasional lectures and help us connect theory with clinical practice.

'Cardiology is the single most important speciality you will ever learn,' declared a consultant physician in a guest lecture on the connections between cardiovascular, respiratory and renal medicine. 'Unless, of course, you choose to work in sub-Saharan Africa,' he added offhandedly. The atmosphere in the lecture theatre hummed with eager anticipation as the entire cohort poised themselves to learn about the sexy new technologies used to treat complex cardiac disease. The work that one might choose to do in sub-Saharan Africa was far removed from the collective consciousness. Not for me, though. I was dwelling on our lecturer's throwaway remark.

In Africa, unlike much of the world, heart disease is not the leading cause of death and disability. However, from his dismissive tone, I inferred something far more cynical: a sophisticated understanding of cardiology – from advances in the epigenetics of chronic heart disease to groundbreaking minimally invasive surgery – is neither relevant nor appropriate for a continent where diarrhoea and hunger create a life that is nasty, brutish and short. Even if his remark was not meant to offend, I felt indignant.

When I met with my personal tutor – a gnomish, bald man who lectured in a staccato pentameter – I told him I would not survive in Newcastle for five years.

'Sir, I really don't think I fit in here. I'm the only black man. I have nothing in common with any of the other students. I'm really not sure I should be studying medicine.'

'It's normal to feel daunted in the first year,' he said. A boilerplate reply. 'You need to give yourself time to settle into university life. It's a big change from high school. But once you make some friends, you'll be right as rain.'

I took a moment to digest this. I was not reassured but I didn't know how to press my point. 'Sir, I heard somewhere that there is a student Africa Society—'

'Oh no, no, no! Whatever you do, please do not join an *ethnic* society,' he said, intoning the word 'ethnic' with unconcealed disdain. 'You should try to fit in with the mainstream group of students if you want to make friends.' He offered as an example of insularity the small cohort of Malaysian students in the medical school who largely kept to themselves. 'They don't even drink! Shame really. How can you come to a place like Newcastle and not drink? They miss out on all the fun of being a student. I see it every year. You don't want to be like them.'

* * *

In the months that followed, the days grew shorter. Twice a week, at three in the afternoon, the sun's strength already draining from the sky, I would go into the anatomy lab. It was a sterile realm of stainless steel, the hum of refrigeration, the sharp smell of formaldehyde used to preserve cadavers. I tried to acquaint myself with the innards of the human body. But my focus wavered. I didn't listen to my instructors. I made embarrassing errors like getting confused about which lung had three lobes and which had two. For the first time since my first year of high school at Saints, I was admonished for not reading enough. My textbooks sat with uncreased spines as decorative ornaments in my student room.

The medical school organised visits to the teaching hospitals to give us a flavour of clinical work. Doctors would take us around the wards and show us patients with interesting medical histories. I always slouched at the back of the group of six or seven students, trying to hide my ambivalence. I avoided the doctors' eyes – much like I had avoided the prefects at Saints – and hoped I would not be asked to examine a patient or interpret an X-ray. I was shrinking deeper into myself.

On Saturdays, I often escaped to Barry and Christine's place for a home-cooked meal. They were only a short train journey away. Christine cooked and the kitchen was always filled with the aroma of something delicious: goat's cheese tart, scarlet quinoa with roasted carrots and local honey. It was a temporary escape.

On the return journey, the train was always packed with boisterous passengers: shoppers returning to the city from the out-of-town shopping mall, hens and stags coming into Newcastle 'to get mortal' (blackout drunk) on a night out. Cans of Carling rolled along the floor of the carriage, spilling beer and leaving a tart smell in the air. I took in the city when I walked back to halls. Large crowds in black-and-white-striped football jerseys trekked through the streets on pilgrimage to St James' Park stadium to watch Newcastle United. The chanting was almost infectious: 'Toon! Toon! Black and White Army!' In the Bigg Market, Newcastle's nightclubbing centre, glass bottles smashed against walls, women in tiny skirts and fake tan screamed at each other on the street, men pissed in alleyways and people clobbered each other to a chorus of swearing. Police cars and ambulances rushed past with sirens blasting at a deafening volume. Newcastle seemed to me then such a dark, alien place, especially on those cold, rowdy, rain-drenched and siren-whining nights.

Reaching campus, I would gaze at the multitude of windows that made up the buildings of Castle Leazes. Some were darkened, others flooded with golden light. Each time I walked back to halls, I felt a tremor of loneliness.

* * *

I knew I was nice-looking but I was awkward. I was too sensitive, as my mother had always said, at once too emotionally intense and too cerebral. All this made me a disciple in romantic disappointment. My fleeting crush on Charlotte had passed and we had settled into different friendship groups. I now had a crush on another medical student called Elle. She'd grown up in a village that coincidentally wasn't too far from Stonyhurst. We went on long runs together, as I used to do with George. We sang pop songs and I tried to introduce her to some hip-hop. Elle also lived in Castle Leazes and we often sat together with a large group of students.

At dinner once, another student I hadn't met before joined us. When I introduced myself and told him I was from Zimbabwe and had finished my A-levels at boarding school, he turned to the table and said, 'Is Simu a rah?' As everyone laughed, I kept asking, 'What's a rah?' That only provoked more laughter. I quickly learned that they were calling me a 'rah' because I went to private school, something only posh people did — at least in their experience. The word itself was how they parodied a posh English accent, which sounds like 'rah rah rah rah'. I pushed back and said that I had left a country in crisis and moved to the UK by myself, and it wasn't as if I even had the option of going to a normal state school as they all had. I didn't realise it but, among my new group of friends, nothing else defined me quite as much as the fact that I had spent eighteen months at a private school. Stonyhurst, instead of being a badge of honour, a testament to my parents' commitment to my education, turned into something else I had to defend or explain away — like the fact that I was Zimbabwean.

Elle came to my room in the evenings to hang out. We sat on my bed and watched movies on my laptop. She wore my Stonyhurst leavers' shirt, a maroon-and-white-striped rugby jersey. One night, as we chewed Haribo sweets and watched *Finding Nemo*, she sidled closer to me and rested her head on my shoulder. Her fingers caressed my side. I wanted to reach my arm over her shoulders and pull her close, to feel our mouths pressed together. I wanted to run my fingers through her blonde hair. But I froze. I could feel the sweat pouring from under my armpits and trailing down my ribcage. The moment lingered in the air like thin wisps of smoke, then evaporated into nothing. A few more weeks of hesitancy and miscommunication followed. Then, one night after Christmas, I saw her kissing someone else in the student bar. I felt a stabbing rejection. I was convinced that she thought I was not good enough for her, even though I blew it when she had made her move. I wrote in my diary: 'I am alone and unaccepted.'

* * *

The only communal place to hang out other than the student bar was a place called the Chillout Room. Instead of thumping basslines, soft music played in the background. There was a pool table and herbal tea on offer. People talked without a cigarette or pint in hand. I struck up a conversation there with Mike who helped run the place. He told me that he was part of the Christian Union. Mike spoke in a controlled manner. He was avuncular and possessed a certainty about the world and its divine order. He invited me to join a Bible study group every Wednesday with other students in halls. They were not like the Catholics I had schooled with at Saints and Stonyhurst. They focused on the New Testament and called the catechism heresy. They were more puritan in their moral conduct and deeply committed to the cause of conversion.

Sometime in the late winter, Mike came to see me for a one-on-one chat.

'All right, Simu. How're you going?'

'I'm okay. Well, I don't know. I have this theory that there is a finite amount of happiness in the world.' I laughed, but my lower lip quivered. I hoped Mike had not noticed.

'What do you mean?'

'Sorry, I'm being a little facetious, as my English teacher in Zim used to say. Witty or amusing in an inappropriate manner,' I laughed again. He said nothing and waited for me to continue.

'I guess what I mean is that I'm a bit overwhelmed and not very happy. I feel a bit helpless, you know? Like sometimes, I just, I kinda wish I would be hit by a car. I mean, I don't want to die or anything. Like I'm not suicidal. I don't even want to be hurt badly. I just want to slow things down. Like I want to press the pause button on life but I don't know how to do that.'

Mike listened. He nodded. He encouraged me to keep saying more. By the time I stopped talking, my jaw ached.

'Paul tells us in his letters to the Philippians that if we seek God when we are troubled, then His peace, which transcends all human understanding, will guard our hearts and our minds in Christ Jesus. Simu, do you want the peace of God?'

Before I knew it, Mike placed his hand over me and prayed for my spiritual rebirth. I was born again, again.

The path to redemption is hard and steep. This time, I would take it even more seriously than I did when I was ten years old and got saved in Uganda by Mrs Lubega's intercession. Mike had convinced me that I could do all things through God. But I needed to make Him my priority. I copied the words of a charismatic American missionary into my book of motivational quotes: 'My face is set, my gait is fast, my goal is heaven, my road is narrow, my way rough, my companions are few, my Guide reliable, my mission clear.'

CHAPTER 23

My declaration of love on Valentine's Day 2005 was for the Lord Jesus Christ.

I resumed a familiar pattern of industriousness in my routine but this time I organised it around the evangelical Christian community. On Tuesdays, I went to meetings of the Christian Medical Fellowship to discuss how to practise godly medicine in a secular age. We talked about the need to stand against abortion, euthanasia, stem cell research and needle exchange programmes for injecting users. On Wednesdays, it was Bible study in halls with Mike and other students. On Fridays, I gave up drinking at MedSoc and clubbing in the city in favour of the Christian Union prayer meetings and fellowship at the pub. I finished my week with Sunday-evening services at Jesmond Parish Church, followed by a student dinner with other believers. My language started changing. I used words like 'sin' and 'worldly' to describe the bad; 'godly' and 'biblical' to describe the good; 'grace' and 'accountability' to keep me on the straight and narrow.

Soon after my conversion, on a Saturday morning, I joined a group of students at church. We were going on a weekend-long Bible study retreat at a campsite in rural Northumberland. Splotches of sunlight were breaking through a sky full of drifting cloud as we boarded the minibus. I sat towards the back when we set off. The rumbling of the bus's engine lulled me like a cradle song. I was drifting off to sleep when someone tapped my shoulder.

'What are you listening to?'

'Sorry,' I said. I removed my earphones. 'I didn't catch that?'

'My name's Rob,' he said with a smile, baring a noticeable overbite. 'What are you listening to?'

'I'm Simu,' I said, then pointed at my Discman. 'It's this new rapper called Kanye West. I've never heard anyone like him. Normally I listen to that hard street stuff like DMX. But this guy raps about things like feeling self-conscious and family reunions, but in a cool way. His album is tight!'

'I know Kanye West. He made "Jesus Walks". Great tune.'

Rob and I talked like this for the rest of the journey. Rob was twenty-four years old and he came from Glasgow. He had been living in Newcastle for nearly six years. He worked part-time in the city, and part-time at the church. Most importantly, he liked rap. We dissected how Nas ethered Jay-Z, agreed that Biggie was still the King of New York seven years after his death, debated whether DMX or 50 Cent was the heir apparent to 2Pac, and lamented the low calibre of Christian rap. Rob led the men's discussion groups at the retreat. Broad-shouldered with a thick neck and deep-set eyes, Rob looked like a leader. He told us of his struggle with pornography and how he eventually worked through it with the power of the Holy Spirit and was now happily married to a beautiful woman who was also at the retreat. Maybe, I thought, this could happen for me too?

I told Rob about my crush on Elle and how cut up I was when I saw her with a new fella, a word I would not normally use but had adopted to fit in. 'I understand it hurts now,' Rob said, 'but she's not what God wants for you. He has bigger and better things in store for you. And listen, she needs God more than she needs you and you need God more than you need her.' I took Rob's words to heart. I needed to stop worrying so much about my romantic life, and focus on my relationship with God. I knew too that my sexual desires were unholy. I needed to stop looking at those sinful magazines and repent for all the things I had vividly fantasised about doing but had not done.

* * *

God's timing was immaculate – or so I thought. No sooner had I renounced lust and pledged myself to purity of thought and deed, than I met Fiona at a student dinner at church. We sat at the same table and talked as we ate.

'Everyone always asks me this, so lemme flip the script,' I said. 'Where are you from originally?'

'I grew up near Liverpool,' she said in a light Scouse accent.

'Oh man . . . we were getting on so well. I'm a Man United fan. I guess we can't be friends.'

She laughed and her enormous hazel eyes widened. They glistened with moisture and shone with an almost mineral intensity. Fiona was a second-year medical student who lived in a shared house on a street behind Castle Leazes. I soon saw her everywhere, not only at church and the Christian Union but also at the medical school and in the neighbourhood. I interpreted every chance encounter as a sign. I had done this before, of course, with Charlotte, then with Elle; I had projected my longings for acceptance and belonging onto the person standing in front of me at the right moment. But this time was different. Fiona was everything I thought I wanted – a devout Christian and committed medical student, someone on the same path as me. Fiona did not come into my life by accident, we had met through God's will.

On our first date, we went to watch a film together, *Are We There Yet?*, starring Ice Cube and Nia Long. Part of me hoped the film would be a light-hearted way of opening up a conversation about hip-hop and race – these things about myself that I wanted to convey but didn't know how. But the film was no more entertaining or thought-provoking than a sack of wheat. Fiona drove us back to Castle Leazes and came up to my room, where we chatted. Our conversation was as stilted and bland as the movie. Had I been more honest with myself or perhaps more self-aware, I might have admitted that Fiona and I had almost nothing in common. I didn't even like her that much; she was less a person to me than an idea. I was desperate for my first real relationship and thought she could meet my needs for closeness and belonging. Fiona was also trying to connect with me. She told me that she was sad and suffered from low self-esteem. I didn't quite understand what she meant. I couldn't look past my image of her. If I could, then I might have realised that she was as lost and confused as I was. Before she left my room that night, I asked her to come with me to the student bar. I knew that most of my friends and classmates would be there. I wanted Elle to see that I was dating someone older and beautiful.

Our first kiss took place on a Tuesday after our second date, and it was what I had been hoping for: open-lipped, exploratory, wet, passionate. We lay on her bed and talked. She believed in preserving her sexual purity before marriage and I reassured her that we both did. 'We need to be godly in our relationship,' she added. Then she kissed me again because this was not prohibited in the Bible. A few days later, in the pub after the Christian Union's Friday meeting, one of the student workers, who was close to Fiona, pulled me aside. She handed me a book called *The Relationships Revolution*. She had wrapped it in a brown paper bag to hide what she described as its 'racy' cover – a blurry photo of a couple, bare-shouldered, embracing. The book offered guidance about how to apply biblical principles to modern dating by keeping courtship chaste and oriented towards marriage, preferably at a young age. Marriage, the book said, was the cure for lust and sexual temptation.

The day after, Fiona invited me over to her house for dinner and a film. When I arrived she invited me to her room. I excitedly anticipated more kissing.

'There's summat I wanted to chat to you about,' she said. We were sitting on her bed again. I had angled my body towards hers, ready to pull her towards me, but now I paused and sat up. 'Sure, go ahead,' I said. She sat up too then reached for a sheet of paper full of questions she had written down. I was blindsided. This wasn't a chat, it was an ambush.

'How can we glorify God in our relationship?' she asked. I didn't answer. I was still wondering why I hadn't seen this coming. I should have paid more attention to how close she was to the student workers, how fluently she spoke the language of the church. I had known Fiona for less than a month, and we had only been a couple for four days. The woman standing in front of me, asking to plumb our spiritual depths together and form an immaculate union before God, was a stranger. I could feel the walls closing in on me. I fell silent. I didn't know what to say. She carried on with question after question about the Christian aspect of our relationship, about sexual purity, about courting in a godly way, about using our relationship to bear witness to His greatness.

The following Saturday, Fiona broke up with me. She said I needed time to mature in my faith before entering courtship.

'Where's all this coming from?' I protested, but deep down I knew that our relationship was doomed.

'I think you need to spend time, once a week, with an older Christian mentor. A man who you can be accountable to and who can help you live a godly life.'

'What are you talking about?'

'Maybe you can read the Bible together and figure out how you can best serve God?'

I felt the sting of rejection and failure. I interpreted Fiona's words through the prism of my inadequacy and left her home thinking: What is so wrong with me?

***

The next time I went to church, Rob approached me over dinner. 'Hey, Simu, I wanted to check in with you. Would you be up for meeting regularly? Let's say once a week to talk. Man to man. About the Bible and anything else that's going on? How's that sound?' It was odd that Rob was suggesting this so soon after my conversation with Fiona. Too soon. I wondered if he and the other student workers had been watching our relationship, and if they thought we were both too immature to begin a proper courtship. I wondered too why I had been given a book about how to date according to biblical principles – why this book was handed to me without explanation but with expectation. Who had decided that I needed this?

Over the next weeks, sadness came over me. I wrote in my diary: 'I want to go home. I really want to go home. I am sick of being here. I miss the weather, my room, the TV, the pace of life, Mr J and my parents. I've just had enough of being here. I'm not sure if I want to go to the next lecture. I just can't be bothered doing anything. I feel so lonely and tired and drained.'

Not knowing what else to do, I turned to Rob. Surely, I thought, he had nothing but the best intentions for me. And even if he had interfered in my relationship with Fiona, maybe it was because he knew that we both needed God more than we needed each other? I agreed to meet Rob weekly. We studied the Bible, I confessed to my sins. I once broached the subject of Fiona. I didn't ask if he had intervened in any way, but I told him that I was still reeling from the abrupt way she rejected me. He said, 'You have a deficient attitude towards marriage and relationships,' and I felt like I had been called to the headmaster's room at Saints for cuts.

Rob loomed large in my life. His voice was in my head even when he wasn't there. I began to wonder if every decision I made, every action I took, every thought I had would meet his approval. I felt burdened by guilt if I did anything that Rob might describe as deficient. Doubts, about God or religion, I wasn't sure which, crept into my mind. The evangelical interpretation of the world as embodied by Rob seemed so narrow and specific, and, though I wouldn't say it, controlling. I asked him, in one of our weekly sessions, if there was any chance that we were wrong about everything. For instance, the Bible said we should love everybody but, in the church's teaching, it seemed we should only love those who believed as we believed and condemn everyone else as sinful and blind to the truth. There was an arrogance, even a cruelty, in taking such a sanctimonious position. It reminded me of the racism back home and the xenophobia I had experienced in the UK, this constant looking down on those who are different. I thought too that there was something fatuous in how everyone at church talked about doing things in a godly way. I asked Rob if it really made sense to fret so much about whether students in Newcastle were driving their cars or emptying their garbage in a godly way, when my people in Zimbabwe were dying of hunger and AIDS. Rob's answer was swift: read more books by Christian authors.

And so I did. I bought piles of them from the Christian bookshop – manuals on dating, treatises on why God allows suffering, polemics on the irrefutable case for belief in Christ as the Son of God, and masterclasses on how to spread the word of God most effectively. I read first thing in the morning and between lectures – that is, if I bothered to attend at all. I read at lunchtime and before dinner. One of the books I bought was *What is Truth? Beyond Postmodernism and Fundamentalism*. I didn't understand the subtitle but I thought the book would strengthen my faith in the Truth of the church; I expected a bulwark against my irritating doubts. The book did the opposite. The author warned against those who loudly proclaim certainty, who are intent on ensuring that others believe as they do, who claim that there is only one understanding of the truth and anyone who doesn't see it will be condemned.

When I read this, I slammed the book shut and stowed it away. I doubled down on my commitments to Christ, the way a closeted gay man might perform hypermasculinity. I took to proselytising on campus, trying to turn my non-Christian friends to Jesus. I was almost manic and the feeling was weirdly euphoric. I felt charged with more energy than I could control. My thoughts raced all the time about Jesus and the Bible and spreading the word. I stopped jogging altogether. Every waking moment – all my energy – had to be spent in the service of Christ. The stakes were high. They were existentially high. I had to convert my friends or they might go to hell. I scrubbed my computer of every lurid image. But temptation was everywhere: in each passing glance at a student in a short skirt, in the flickering memory of a kiss. I had to fight my own flesh; no desire could be trusted.

Some of my friends who were not part of the church wondered what was going on with me. But they had never encountered religious zealotry before and didn't know what to say. Instead, they humoured me by coming to Christian events I organised. At one such event, I gave a spoken word performance of a poem I had written, called 'To Whom Much is Given, Much is Expected'. At boarding school, I had understood this phrase as a duty to do good works on earth but now it was entirely about being given God's grace and the spiritual duty to convert the infidels. My friends did not know what to make of the leaflets and tracts I gave them. And I was having my own doubts.

It turns out that trying to live a pristine life is no way to live. I was wed to a childish idea: a desire not to be merely good, but to be faultless, to transcend everything, including the limits of my very being. It was an impulse deeply ingrained in me, and my foray into Christian fundamentalism was its latest expression. One doesn't need much psychological insight to see the dark side of my impulses. I didn't know it then, but underlying my inflexible commitment to purity was a desire for control. Perfectionism was how I had learned to survive, to cope with chaos and uncertainty, and to repress my needs when I felt they couldn't be met. But perfectionism is always doomed to fail. It guarantees a constant gnawing disappointment in yourself that, for me, led to a devastating self-loathing. In the words of Michel de Montaigne, 'the most barbarous of our maladies is to despair our being.'

CHAPTER 24

The medical school had a fail-one-fail-all rule: by the end of the year, we had to pass all our courses to progress to the next stage. If you failed a course, you were called to a pass/fail viva, an oral exam to clarify and test your knowledge of the material taught in the preceding year. If you failed that too, then you had to sit another set of exams over the summer break. And if you failed those, you would be forced to repeat the year.

Having devoted all my time to evangelicalism, I was not doing well academically. I scraped a pass on my written and practical exams but failed one of my take-home assignments. I was invited to a pass/fail viva but I already knew I was going to fail. I was running on empty.

At the viva, I froze in front of the three professors quizzing me. 'What is colostrum?' asked one of them. I said nothing. The man next to him, an Irish anatomist, invited me to a steel table with a series of organs laid out in front of us like a cadaverous buffet. He asked me to identify different structures on each sample, major tissues or blood vessels. I said nothing. He shook his head, vicariously embarrassed for me.

When the medical school published the list of all the students who had satisfied the examiners and could progress to stage two, I was at church. I got a phone call saying that I wasn't on the list. I walked back to halls with a friend and told him all the tragedies that had befallen my family. Each year for the last eight years, starting with Old Man Munro burning up in his house, someone in my life had died. Fires, police violence, AIDS, strokes, suicide, car accidents. Zimbabwe and almost everything I had grown up with was coming apart at the seams. I also knew that in Uganda, my mother had lost many of her siblings to one calamity after another. What did a failed exam matter in the scheme of things? Unlike my parents, I had not been to prison, nor had I lived through a war. Surely, I could get through this?

That night, at the pub with friends, I began sobbing. First, quiet, decent sobbing. And then, long inarticulate weeping.

I wrote in my book of motivational quotes: 'For we are not cast off by the Lord for ever. Though He brings grief, He will show compassion, so great is His unfailing love. For He does not willingly bring affliction or grief to the children of men.' Lamentations 3:31–33.

* * *

I spent the first three weeks of that summer as a volunteer with an education charity, teaching English to children with disabilities in the Hungarian city of Miskolc. Throughout the trip, I felt lost. I drifted in and out of conversation with the other volunteers. My mind wandered, replaying scenes from the last year, unable to weave them into a coherent whole. At night, I didn't sleep. I prayed feverishly for deliverance from the abyss that was opening in me. But with each plea to the Lord, it felt less like praying and more like screaming into an empty firmament. There was nothing out there.

I read one more book of Christian apologia called *Disappointment with God*. I finished it, feeling no comfort and knowing I would never read another book by an evangelical author. I then picked up *What is Truth?* again. This time I read it cover to cover. 'Wherever truth is, it is least likely to be found among fundamentalists, who are best avoided or approached with the greatest caution,' the book said. 'The atheist who is tortured by the problems of the human condition, who is angry with the God he does not believe exists and who devotes his life to the search for understanding may be closer to "living in the Truth" than those who claim to "know the Truth".' I wrote this passage down in my book of motivational quotes.

I returned to Newcastle for the month of August. I lived alone in a five-bedroom student house behind Castle Leazes, on a street parallel to Fiona's. But she had left for the summer. From Monday to Friday I studied in the deserted medical library, trying to learn everything that I had missed during my evangelical fever dream: the Kreb's cycle, the clotting cascade, cyclic AMP, osmolality. Each day of study was as tedious as the next. The same oppressive monotony. In the evenings, I attempted to cook for myself, something I had never done before. My only goal was to make something edible; taste and nutrition were superfluous considerations. After dinner, I visited the Londis, a convenience store down the road where I could rent a DVD. The clerk at the till was an unfriendly, greying woman with precious few teeth and the smell of stale tobacco about her. She grunted when I thanked her. On Saturday mornings, I picked up a purple phone card from the Chinese grocer in town and went to the medical school to use the payphone to call home. Once when I spoke to my father on the phone, I broke down. He responded with the stoic's mantra: 'These are the challenges. You just have to do it.'

I didn't know the details of my father's story at this time. I didn't know that the Rhodies had flogged him mercilessly in Plumtree when he was still in high school. I didn't know about the months he spent sleeping in a crowded cell in Rusape prison after he had been expelled from the University of Rhodesia. All I knew was that he had already been through hell when he was my age. Every time he talked of the struggle and sacrifice, it instilled in me a dogged sense of my own insignificance, a feeling that my problems and fears were trivial compared to the enormity of what he had endured. I had a legacy to honour but here I was: undone by an exam. The shame I felt was crushing.

The faculty building closed at 1 p.m. on Saturdays, and then I had no access to the internet or a landline until the following week. Sometimes I went to church on Sundays but it was now painful to be there. I knew, before I was ready to acknowledge it, that I had lost respect for Rob and Mike, all the student workers and the pastors. They wanted to save my soul but didn't want to save my life.

As usual, I turned to music. I tried listening to DMX but he ended each album with a prayer and a conversation with God. This was not what I wanted to hear. Other rappers I listened to, like Jay-Z and Kanye West, kept bigging up an artist I had never heard of called Talib Kweli. I bought Kweli's album, *The Beautiful Struggle*, because I liked the title. I listened to the CD every day. His style was new to me. It was not braggadocio, it was not gangster mythology, it was not party music for the club. His rhyme schemes were dense and jammed with ideas. I had to concentrate when I listened to him. He rapped about hypocrisy in the church and losing his religion, about poverty and political corruption, and how all he could do was keep on trying. Underneath each virtuosic display of lyrical dexterity, Kweli articulated my black boy blues in pitch-perfect tone.

I struggled to sleep. I began to have a recurrent dream. As I lay in bed, I could sense another presence in the room. I wanted to scream myself awake but I couldn't move. It was terrifying. I now know this phenomenon as sleep paralysis: it occurs when the mind is beginning to wake up but the body is in a relaxed state, and you cannot move for several minutes. I went to see a doctor. I told her about my sleep and how empty I felt when I went to bed and woke up in the morning. My heart raced unexpectedly at random intervals through the day. My hands would get clammy. An unpleasant knot would rise like a balloon from my stomach and push into my chest, squeezing against my lungs until I couldn't breathe. She offered me beta blockers to calm my anxiety but I declined. I couldn't shake the idea that taking a drug to slow down my heart might inadvertently cause it to stop beating altogether. She asked me to take antidepressants but I hesitated – that sounded like an admission that something in me was broken. But the GP insisted. 'You're in a bad way,' she said, 'and you need to sleep.' I eventually agreed to take low-dose antidepressants that also worked as sleeping pills to dull the intrusive thoughts churning and frothing in my mind at night. 'One more thing,' she added, 'the drugs will only get you so far. I think you need to talk to someone. Try the student counselling service.'

The counsellor was a slight woman, much older than the one I had seen in Zimbabwe when I was sixteen. She was soft-spoken and inviting. I told her about my exams and anxiety. And soon more tumbled out of me: my uncertainties about medicine, my longing for home, the people who had died, my mother's depression, my father's drinking – and how everything was made worse by the state of Zimbabwe. 'I think you are dealing with an awful lot of loss,' she said with a kindness that disarmed and unsettled me. It had been so long since anyone had spoken to me so gently. It made me feel intolerably vulnerable. A burning sensation rose through my throat. She let the moment linger but her eyes burrowed into me. I was not ready for this conversation. Did she really want me to say it all? That everything in my world was falling apart? That my parents had deserted me in my most desolate moment? That I was a fuck-up and a failure from a fucked-up and failed country? I looked away to hide the tears welling in my eyes. After three sessions, I didn't go back.

* * *

I persevered and passed my exams, then rejoined my cohort in the second year of medical school. I stopped taking my medication, choosing instead to start partying and drinking much more than I ever had before. One night I drank so much, I woke up in hospital covered in vomit and hooked up to intravenous lines.

A line from the title track of the Kweli album stuck in my head. In the first verse, he raps about someone repeating a cycle of looking for answers – first in the church, then political parties, then community organisations – but coming up short each time, disappointed by lies and broken promises. He then says you're looking for a cure but you don't know what's hurting you. I couldn't fully digest the message of the song, but that line hit me hard. I recognised the feeling he described. The desperate need to remedy a mysterious pain that latches on to your soul. A pain that echoes and hides but refuses to go away.

On a Sunday afternoon in late autumn, I left the city to visit Long Sands beach at Tynemouth village. I walked from the metro station along a wide boulevard, past a primary school and a fish-and-chop shop before finally reaching the shore. The sun hung low in the distance as a cold breeze, salted by the North Sea, pinched my cheeks. Tears streamed down my face. For some time, I sat on the sand and watched the waves scudding outwards and getting lost on the horizon. I imagined the sea's inky depths and icy temperatures.

I had to reorient myself. I couldn't give up or feel sorry for myself. I had to bury my sadness as deep as I could. And, through sheer force of will, I had to finish medical school, no matter what. 'The race goes not to the swift,' I had written in my book of motivational quotes, 'but to those who keep on running.'

CHAPTER 25

In late May 2005, the residents of one of Harare's densely populated townships heard a rumbling ball of sound. It was rolling towards them, slow and placid at first, but growing larger and louder. Then, like a grenade, the sound detonated. Police vehicles surged forward. Bulldozers, some with steel plates and others with short wooden beams like battering rams affixed to front bumpers, tore into the community, destroying houses and kiosks made of corrugated metal, plastic and plywood. With each charge of the bulldozers, people fell back and were trampled. Many were crushed. Their cries were drowned out by the siren skirls and blaring horns of police cars. Survivors of this initial surge massed on the road, fighting helplessly to guard their homes and vending stalls. The air filled with howls of fear, of horror, of anger.

After each 'slum clearance' came confusion: which patch of land had supported whose shack? Which pile of scantlings, crumbled brick or contorted metal was whose to comb through? The entrepreneurial among the displaced scavenged what they could from the wreckage. They hawked building material if it was still viable or else they used the rubble to fill potholes on the road and asked passing drivers for a small tip.

The operation unfolded over three months, leaving the dust and debris of levelled houses everywhere. Township dwellers throughout the country called this wave of slum clearances – this remorseless and spectacular display of state power – 'Zimbabwe's tsunami'. By late 2005, some 700,000 people had lost their homes or livelihoods, often both. A further 2.4 million people starved or were stricken with diarrhoea. I watched it all from Newcastle.

The official purpose of the operation was to clean up the city by eliminating squalor. However, the English and Shona names for the operation signalled a more sinister motivation. Operation Restore Order sounded Orwellian, while Operation Murambatsvina was far more direct; it meant 'to remove the filth'. The operation targeted the urban poor, who largely supported the country's main opposition party, the Movement for Democratic Change. The police commissioner, a loyalist of the ruling party, referred to township residents as 'the crawling mass of maggots bent on destroying the economy'. These individuals were the *tsvina* – the filth, the human waste – that needed to be eradicated to 'restore order'.

Harare's urban landscape shimmered like mica in my memory. I recalled the city through images of sunshine and swimming pools, pine trees and suburban gardens. However, what confronted me on the news was a post-apocalyptic tableau. My country was self-destructing in the most literal sense. 'To whom much is given, much is expected': I held on to this notion, but my medical degree seemed trivial in comparison to the magnitude of the crisis back home. A desperate guilt washed over me. I felt worse when I heard individuals from Zimbabwe, President Mugabe most notably, describe those of us in the diaspora as sellouts who preferred living with imperialists to being in the motherland. He held a particular disdain for Britain.

As British prime minister, Tony Blair labelled Africa 'a scar on the conscience of the world' at a summit in Johannesburg. Blair appealed to the Western world for more foreign aid to help Africa's poor, and more sanctions to punish corrupt African leaders. Mugabe responded to Blair at the same summit, saying: 'We do not mind having and bearing sanctions banning us from Europe. We are not Europeans. We have not asked for any inch of Europe, any square inch of that territory. So, Blair, keep your England and let me keep my Zimbabwe.' At every opportunity, Mugabe blamed Britain and her allies for the poverty and ill health in Zimbabwe: these were the after-effects of colonialism, the consequences of illegal sanctions, the price that a tiny but mighty African country was willing to pay for its freedom. 'Our cause is Africa's cause,' Mugabe said, ever defiant, in interviews. In Mugabe's voice I could hear my father, almost as if they spoke as one. I wanted to take pride in my country standing up for Africa. I condemned colonialism and foreign interference on the continent. But I still could not understand, let alone explain, something as wanton as Operation Murambatsvina. What did that have to do with anti-colonialism?

The questions and insults from English people kept coming. A plumber came to fix the sink in my shared house. I offered him a cup of tea.

'Whe' ya from, like?' he asked, as we waited for the kettle to boil.

'I'm from Zimbabwe—'

'Fookin' Robert *Mugabeee*!'

'Well, yeah, I suppose. My dad's from Zim but my mother is from Uganda. I—'

'Fookin' Idi Amin! No luck for you, son.'

I smiled but didn't say anything.

I needed to read more. If nothing else, I needed to understand the historical context for Zimbabwe's political convulsion and I needed some knowledge to defend my home. I looked for accounts of how colonialism had affected Zimbabwe, but I was startled by what else I found. I had known nothing about the Gukurahundi massacres perpetrated by a unit of the Zimbabwean army over five years in the mid-eighties, which killed as many as 20,000 civilians among the Ndebele people. I had grown up among the Shona majority and in a ZANU(PF) household. In my version of Zimbabwe, as I now discovered, there was an *omertà* when it came to Gukurahundi. This was a double shock, not only at the enormity of the atrocity but at the extent of my ignorance.

I felt a swelling and impotent rage. Zimbabwe was a vast canvas of injustice, bigger than I had previously imagined, and the more I learned, the angrier I became.

* * *

The gap between Zimbabwe and my life in the UK widened with each passing year at medical school, aggravating my feelings of alienation. In my third year, beginning in the late summer of 2006, I started my clinical rotations. The medical school sent us to different hospitals throughout the north-east, organised into geographic clusters called base units. My base unit, named Wear after one of the region's longest rivers, included hospitals in the port city of Sunderland, the cathedral city of Durham and the metropolitan borough of South Tyneside.

On the wards, I encountered another variant of racism. I didn't flinch when a patient called me a 'golliwog' on a ward round. Later, I met with the supervising physician, who peered over the rims of her glasses and said, 'I heard you handled a difficult situation on the ward with exemplary calm, isn't it? I'm from India so I know *exactly* what you're going through. The patients here in Sunderland are from a different generation. They're not used to seeing people like us look after them. When they say racist things, we should ignore them. People like us need to stick together, isn't it?' She awarded me the top grade for my professionalism. I took the grade and didn't tell her I had kept calm because I hadn't understood the patient's accent.

My clinical training prioritised chronic illness, disability and rehabilitation. These were the prevailing patterns of morbidity in the post-industrial, deprived, working-class part of England where I was based. For my internal medicine shifts, I was assigned to a respiratory ward. After each ward round, I had to find a patient, take their history, examine them and report my findings before being quizzed on my differential diagnosis and management plan. One morning, I went to assess a patient called Keith. 'Hello! My name is Simu,' I said to him, 'I'm a third-year medical student. We met during the ward round this morning. I've come by to ask if you have time to chat to me today?' Keith cast his eye over the bay full of old men in pyjamas, each staring vacantly at the ceiling. A cacophony of coughing, gurgling, bubbling and beeping hummed around us. Keith nodded. His blue-tinged lips curled in assent. I felt silly about how I had phrased my question.

Keith had spent decades working in the shipyards that had once powered the north-east's economy. Inhaling unholy volumes of asbestos and tobacco was par for the course. Now, in his old age, his breathing had become laboured. He was barrel-chested and his cheeks were flushed. 'It's me lungs, man. They're knackered,' he said. I listened to his chest through my stethoscope, and I could hear the crackling sounds of alveoli pulling open against fluid and the prolonged wheezing of his breath rushing through narrowed airways. He coughed up foul sputum, stained with tar and blood, and he showed me the pot at his bedside where he kept his expectorated globs.

I met scores of men like this. Men of advancing age who had once worked down the mines or with the ships and were now surviving on a cocktail of medicines and regular sojourns through hospitals. For most, it was not only their lungs that were knackered but their kidneys, hearts, livers, muscles and joints. Alcoholism was a common problem and I saw more than my fair share of cirrhotic patients with yellow skin and bellies distended like a soap bubble at its limits. These men sometimes drowned in their own blood from ruptured oesophageal veins or slipped into ammonia-scented comas.

I had neither the wisdom nor maturity to see it, but patterns of disease always have a social history. What story is this person's body telling us about the world they lived in? How have time and fate left their mark beneath the skin? We are corporeal beings but we carry more than organs within ourselves; we carry traces of the past. The bodies of the men I met in the north-east told stories of heavy industry and hard living, of manual labour's toll. Looking back, I wish I had been more alive to these stories. They might have told me something about the country I was in, the country that I struggled to imagine as my home.

* * *

Try as I might, I found the clinical cases dull and the ward in Sunderland monotonous. Craving something more cosmopolitan, I joined the local chapter of a student global health network with branches at medical schools throughout the UK. Global health quickly filled the space in my life once occupied by religion. I learned the global health creed: 'We believe in human rights. We seek salvation through the Millennium Development Goals.' We incanted slogans like 'Be the change you wish to see in the world' or 'Never doubt that a small group of thoughtful, committed citizens can change the world; indeed, it's the only thing that ever has.' Our rituals were conferences where we affirmed our mission to make a difference. We preached the word on campus through documentary film screenings about the world's many forgotten crises. We targeted new converts: indifferent medical students who were ignorant of the great suffering in Darfur, Congo and Zimbabwe.

One night, I went on a pub crawl with the global health students, trying to raise money for a school in Malawi. I teamed up with another student, a bubbly blonde woman, to approach strangers in Newcastle city centre and ask for donations. 'I'm so glad we're doing this work,' she said when we started, her right palm tapping her chest. 'I spent my gap year in Ghana. I love Africa! Such friendly people and what a beautiful place.' I said I had never been to West Africa, but it sounded nice. White people who liked Africa too much were not that different from those who hated it. Both were condescending.

'Hello!' my friend said to a couple coming out of the theatre. 'Would you like to give money to a charity in Africa?'

The man looked at her, then over her shoulder at me. 'Is he from Africa?' he asked my friend, though his eyes were trained on mine.

'Yes, I am—'

'Then why don't you fuck off back there?'

He held his wife's hand, and they walked away. His words hit me like a sucker punch. I knew this kind of thing would, could and did happen all the time, but I was caught off guard all the same. Drinking had made me vulnerable. 'Fuck him,' my friend said. She didn't wait for me to say anything before skipping along to the next bar. 'Hello! Would you like to donate money to a charity in Africa?' she squawked at someone else. I was trembling with rage and frustration. We joined the rest of the group, hopping from bar to bar. The more wine that flowed, the more upset I became. I drifted away from the group and went scouring around a bar, looking for another black person, it didn't matter whom, to talk to. The only one I found was a brother from Ghana, the toilet attendant selling samples of aftershave by calling out to men who didn't wash their hands:

> No spray, no lay.
> No splash, no gash.
> No Calvin Klein, no sixty-nine.
> No Armani, no punani.

I told him what had happened to me on the street. With an arm slung over my shoulder, the toilet guy drew me in until I could feel his hot, minty breath on my face: 'Ah, my brother, you think I wanna be here? Do you know the kind of abuses I get from these Geordie men? I sit here. I smell the piss and shit every night. I smile and I say, "Welcome, boss. Good evening, sir." Because I'm a hustler. A born hustler. I'm studying business in Sunderland. I will make something of myself. One day, you'll see.' I wanted to go back to the bar, but he held me close for a few moments longer.

* * *

There was the overt prejudice in Newcastle, but also a more subtle kind of racism: irritation from other students if I ever brought up racial politics ('C'mon, don't play the race card'); incredulity at my spoken English ('How come you're from Zimbabwe but you speak so well?'); fascination with my hair ('It's like a sheep'). And, of course, there was the time a student called me 'the whitest black man' he knew – even though the 'only black man' would have been more accurate. All these comments stung. They channelled what the writer Cathy Park Hong calls minor feelings: the negative and dysphoric emotions provoked by low-grade racial slights. What did it mean to call me 'the whitest black man' he knew? I felt anger, as well as shame and paranoia. I turned those corrosive feelings inwards and felt the burning discomfort of my own skin. Was I inauthentic? If I left Newcastle one day to go somewhere with more black people, would they reject me because I had become too white?

I did not know how to describe this scattering of my selfhood. My mother tried to put a nice spin on it, she talked about my childhood travel, my exposure through education, and now my growing interest in global health: 'You are becoming a citizen of the world.' This helped a little but did not quite overcome how frustrated and unsure of myself I felt. The only way to survive in a place like Newcastle was to get good at mimicry, like a chameleon, a watchful creature in disguise.

CHAPTER 26

The medical school encouraged students to spend the summer after their fourth year practising medicine in another part of the world. Most students flocked to places like Australia and New Zealand but all the global health students chose to take their 'elective' in what were euphemistically called 'resource-limited settings'. I thought about going back to Zimbabwe but this was impossible – the British government had issued a travel advisory and the medical school wouldn't insure me to work there.

It was 2008 and Zimbabwe had reached the nadir of its crisis. It had been an election year. The country went to the polls in March and, after a five-week delay, the electoral commission announced a narrow victory for the opposition leader Morgan Tsvangirai at 47.9 per cent of the vote, ahead of Robert Mugabe at 43.2 per cent, with the remainder split between a third-party candidate and spoiled ballots. Since Tsvangirai did not win an absolute majority, a run-off election was called for the end of June. In the interregnum, the army viciously attacked opposition supporters and those who had defected from the ruling party. Bloody beatings, rape, torture with hot irons to the back, kidnappings, disappearances, ransacking of neighbourhoods. The opposition fought back. Politics was denuded of competing ideologies and reduced to a campaign of terror against a bare-knuckle struggle for survival. Inflation had reached the order of several sextillion per cent. We had become a nation of starving billionaires: more than two million Zimbabweans, nearly one in five people, needed food aid from humanitarian organisations. People resorted to eating bark off the trees, like my father had in the refugee camps during the war. Surely this was not the liberation he had fought for.

I flew to Zimbabwe in June to see my parents for a few days before going to South Africa, where I had decided to take my elective. I hired a car with a friend, and we shared the driving on the long journey from Durban to a hospital deep in the rural heartlands of South Africa's Eastern Cape. The hospital setup was rudimentary: three in-patient wards, an outpatient clinic that also functioned as an emergency department, an operating theatre without general anaesthesia, and an HIV unit. I found six doctors on staff; only one was South African. He explained that the hospital was considered a hardship post that local doctors only ever rotated through as part of a government-mandated community service programme. 'I'll be here for eighteen months,' he said, 'that's six months more community service than most South African doctors will ever do.' Of the five other doctors, one was Nigerian and the rest were European expatriates tired of hopping from one disaster to the next as humanitarians for international NGOs like Médecins Sans Frontières. They wanted something more settled and long-term.

A young woman was rushed into the clinic one day. She was in full-blown eclampsia. Her body shook violently while her mouth frothed with pinkish saliva. She had bitten her tongue as she convulsed. At medical school, I was assured that I would never see this disease of pregnancy. Its origins are mysterious, and it preponderates among poor women. Eclampsia leads to protein in the urine, hypertension, seizures and sometimes death, for both mother and child. The treatment is an intravenous infusion of magnesium sulphate and delivery of the child. She was taken to the operating theatre. I don't know if she or the child survived.

Many patients were so sick they had to be carried into the hospital. Cryptococcal meningitis in AIDS patients. Knife and gunshot wounds that had been left untreated for too long and had turned iridescent with gangrene. Acute malnutrition in ghost-like children who were wasting away. I saw a woman, an inmate on medical furlough from prison. She must have been in her thirties or early forties, but it was hard to tell as she had lost the ability to walk. Her legs were dappled with hundreds of tiny holes that maggots crawled in and out of, like overripe fruit starting to rot. The smell was too pungent to bear. I asked to be excused from the room for fear that I might be sick.

All this misery was good experience for the wannabe global health doctor. I learned to suture. I delivered a baby. By turns, I felt exhilarated, mortified and morbidly fascinated.

Marieke, a sandy-haired Dutch doctor with sunburned skin, invited me to see patients with her on one of the adult wards. She wore a jaded and pensive expression as she tested my knowledge of infectious diseases. She asked me to describe the chest X-ray of a young man. He was in his early twenties. I noted the outlines of encysted cavities and the extensive infiltrates that appeared as streaks of white, like cirrus clouds, against a black backdrop. My diagnosis: tuberculosis bacilli had eaten the upper lobes of his lungs. 'Very good,' Marieke said. But there was more to the case, she made clear, as we ambled to his room.

A person with active TB of the lungs harbours hundreds of millions of bacteria, enough to ensure that a small number will be mutants impervious to anti-TB drugs. In a patient who receives only one antibiotic or inadequate doses of several, or who takes medicines erratically or for too short a time, the drug-susceptible bacilli may die off while the drug-resistant strains flourish. The patient becomes a site of rapid bacterial evolution, with drugs supplying the selective pressure. In the gravest cases, like the one Marieke and I had before us, individuals end up infected with bacilli that can't be treated by the two most powerful drugs. Medical science reserves a special name for tuberculosis of that sort: multi-drug-resistant TB, or MDR-TB by abbreviation.

I stood at the door and peered into the patient's room while

Marieke went to see him. Even with protective equipment, she said it was too risky for me to come close to a patient with MDR-TB. Clinically, the case was like nothing I had seen before. I excitedly discussed it with my friend on elective with me, but I sobered up when the doctors disclosed their terror at the next meeting. MDR-TB is a serious illness wherever it appears, but worst, of course, in the places with the fewest resources to deal with it. It is highly infectious among the immunocompromised – one case might be the tip of the iceberg – and it is much harder to treat than regular TB. The doctors feared that there might be a hidden outbreak of MDR-TB spreading in the community where HIV was already rampant. A dual epidemic of HIV and MDR-TB would be catastrophic. I never found out what happened. We were nearing the end of our elective and it would take the doctors weeks or months, if not longer, to investigate an MDR-TB outbreak.

A friend of my mother who worked at the UN sponsored me to attend the International AIDS Conference 2008 in Mexico City that August, at the end of my elective. It was a surreal prospect: me, slated to speak in the Community Dialogue Space, drawing not from expertise, which I lacked, but from my laughably limited experience as a visiting medical student in South Africa. I read what I could to prepare, haphazardly flitting from one article to another in newspapers and academic journals. Like most medical students from my university, I lacked the skills and discipline to marshal evidence systematically to mount a social critique or political argument. By chance, I came across Hein Marais, a journalist, who wrote with measured fury about the South African AIDS epidemic. 'Shelve the abiding fiction that disasters don't discriminate,' Marais wrote. 'Plagues zero in on the dispossessed, on those forced to build their lives in the paths of danger.' I carried his words with me as I boarded my flight to Mexico.

The conference was not what I imagined. It was less a sober meeting than a frenzy of clashing energies. Thirty thousand participants gathered in a blue-glass-and-steel megalith: activists yelling slogans into the air, scientists clutching laptops, sex workers tossing branded condoms into the crowds, politicians striding around with purpose, salsa dancers twirling and defying the seriousness of the conference.

Inside the meeting halls, debates raged that, I soon realised, were not about science but about power. African activists challenged the polished certainty of global health elites over who got to define the problem of AIDS on the continent and, more importantly, who got to define the solution. This was a battle etched in histories older than the virus itself, histories of colonialism, exploitation and race.

Years earlier, in 1996, at the International AIDS Conference in Vancouver, scientists had announced a new treatment for HIV: a trinity of anti-retroviral drugs that promised to suppress the virus and restore immune systems. The results were miraculous enough to be hailed as 'the Lazarus effect', but such miracles came with a price: $10,000 per patient per year. For the Western world, it was salvation. For Africa, where the epidemic was blowing through the continent like fire through dry grass, it was an impossible dream. American pharmaceutical companies joined together to issue a press release about the challenges of distributing drugs in Africa. They couched their concerns in pragmatic language, invoking vivid tropes: mud roads, dirty water and the presumed inability of Africans to tell the time and thus comply with complex treatments. Their logic implied that the real danger lay not in AIDS but in Africans, who might botch their treatment and create resistant strains of the virus that could 'boomerang back to the West'. One could almost admire the efficiency with which these statements distilled centuries of colonial stereotypes into a single document.

It wasn't just pharmaceutical companies that cast doubt about the effectiveness of anti-retroviral drugs in Africa. Around the same time, South African President Thabo Mbeki openly questioned whether HIV was truly the cause of AIDS. For Mbeki, blaming a single virus for the scale of death and misery wrought by AIDS was too convenient – it allowed the West to avoid confronting the structural dimensions of poverty and inequality left in Apartheid's wake. Mbeki was making a profound point about the past. Histories of oppression and subjugation work their way under the skin. His scepticism was, unfortunately, fuelled by a network of fringe scientists and conspiracy theorists. His legitimate critiques were eclipsed by his government's advocacy for treatments like garlic and beetroot instead of anti-retrovirals. To outsiders, this was an incomprehensible tragedy. To Mbeki's supporters, it was a bold rejection of the same Western forces that had for centuries dictated the terms of African life.

By the end of the conference, I was exhausted yet invigorated. Perhaps, I thought, this was where I could find my place: wading into the mess of global health politics as a way of continuing the fight for justice where my parents had left off. It was the kind of thought that felt too grand to say out loud. I pictured myself as the head of a major global health institution like the World Health Organization. I had found a new goal to work relentlessly towards, yet another heavy boulder to push up another steep hill.

* * *

The weeks turned to months, the months to years. Time moved with a pulsating urgency. My resolve to become a global health leader remained iron-clad as I endeavoured to make my CV as impressive as possible. Before I finished medical school, I had helped organise two major national conferences on global health at Newcastle Medical School. I had interned on the Africa desk at my mother's former organisation, the Global Fund for Women in San Francisco. I had taken a year off from my medical studies to gain a research degree in medical and molecular bioscience, which was an excuse to spend four months in Tanzania on a large research project investigating the scale and burden of epilepsy cases in the region around Mount Kilimanjaro. I had become a global health ambassador for the student version of the UK's top medical journal. Global health had become many things to me: a goal to work towards, an identity and a protective cloak against doubt and anxiety.

But even as I was racking up accomplishments, I was still trying to find myself socially, to figure out where I belonged. I moved seamlessly between different groups at the medical school. I went hiking in the Cheviots mountain range on the Scottish border with my friends who enjoyed outdoor pursuits. I had loosened up and allowed myself to experiment with long-held taboos. I went to ecstasy-fuelled raves and chain-smoked with my friends who indulged in Newcastle's nightlife. I had not had any truly intimate relationships, but I had discovered sex. Two nights before my final medical school exams, I escaped to Manchester to see Jay-Z in concert. I knew I was going to pass my exams, but rapping every word of 'Jigga My Nigga' while Hov pointed at me in the front row was my private, limited rebellion against medical school. In moments like this, I wondered what life I might live if the choice were entirely mine, free of pressure and expectation.

I graduated in 2010. My parents came to Newcastle for the celebration. It was the first time since I'd left home eight years earlier that they'd come to see me together. My achievements were the only thing that bound us as a family. My mother ululated when I was awarded my degree; my father quietly observed, undoubtedly proud of me, but emotionally detached and vacant.

When the celebrations were done, I hired a car and picked up my parents from their hotel. The day had finally come to leave Newcastle. I had a job waiting for me as a junior doctor at the John Radcliffe Hospital, Oxford University's main teaching hospital. My father sat next to me in the front passenger seat and my mother was in the back. They were both nervous; it was the first time I had driven the three of us anywhere. I slipped an album into the CD player and the key into the ignition. A rush of relief shot through my body when the horn stabs at the beginning of *Distant Relatives*, a joint album by Nas and Damian Marley, blasted through the car's speakers. The album sketches hip-hop's affinities with dancehall and reggae and traces these genres back to Africa. Marley's roaring patois and Nas' blistering raps bounce off each other as their album portrays African poverty, blood diamonds, slavery, the making of a black diaspora and the hope for better days. All the while, Africa is posited as the land of rebirth and redemption – the album's tone is as inspiring as it is preachy and frustratingly vague in its symbolism. It was the perfect soundtrack for my departure from Newcastle.

***

I worked as a junior doctor for two years, rotating through hospitals in Oxford, Aylesbury, High Wycombe and Slough. Then I embarked on a public health fellowship at Imperial College London. Years earlier, in 2008, during the lowest point of Zimbabwe's crisis, I had come across an article in the *New York Times*: 'Cholera epidemic sweeping across crumbling Zimbabwe'. A horrifying outbreak, caused by a simple bacterial infection associated with the pre-modern era, wreaked havoc in twenty-first-century Zimbabwe – stark proof of how badly my home country had deteriorated. I presented this case to my supervisors as an example of the kinds of topics I wished to research: how political crises can lead to human suffering and preventable deaths. No one at Imperial showed interest. My supervisors preferred that I master epidemiology and biostatistics so I could analyse data on hospital admissions in London rather than explore questions that fell within the realm of political science. I argued that a depoliticised approach to public health would serve no one.

My supervisors asserted that our role was to produce scientific evidence to inform health policy, nothing more. This was not the research I wanted to do; these were not the questions I wanted to ask. I felt a fissure running through me. I needed to understand why I had left Zimbabwe when I did, why the country's crisis had become intractable. Nothing in my education had helped me make sense of my past or the world that had shaped me. Yet again, I felt at sea.

* * *

A friend of mine, Harry, whom I had met when I lived in Oxford and worked at the John Radcliffe, had completed a doctorate in politics at the university and was now working as a postdoctoral researcher. Harry spoke with bombast and tremendous knowledge about Africa: the political machinations behind mega infrastructure projects like dam-building in Sudan; the causes of extreme violence in Rwanda; the popular appeal of militant Islamism in the Horn of Africa; and the astonishing complexity of geopolitics throughout the continent. Meeting Harry was like meeting a human paradigm shift – he was a person of intellect and purpose, who embodied a way of existing meaningfully in the world.

One evening, Harry and I had dinner at an American-style diner near Euston station in London. We both ordered veggie burgers with sweet potato fries and milkshakes. I told Harry that my fellowship at Imperial was not what I'd hoped it would be. I felt stuck.

'I have all this ambition and I don't know what to do with it. I really thought that public health was the answer but the research they want me to do is so boring.'

Harry winced in sympathy. 'This is a waste of your talents, my brother. Have you ever thought about quitting and trying something else? There are so many things you could do,' he said, then had another gulp of his milkshake. I mulled over his words. I had these lofty fantasies about what I could be if I dared to take a risk. But, in reality, I kept myself safe in the world of medicine. Did I have it in me to quit and take a risk on something else? As if reading my mind, Harry said, 'I mean it, Simu.'

For years, I had fixated on the idea of returning to Africa to solve problems and repair what was broken. Conversations with Harry made clear to me just how much I had to learn. He validated my intellectual curiosity in a way that no one else had. It was okay for me to want to be a thinker; there was beauty and truth to be found in the world of ideas.

With Harry's encouragement, I applied for a master's in African studies at Oxford. I poured all my hope, ambition and desire into it. I had had so many false starts; it felt like I was waiting for my life to begin. Could this time be different?

On 30 April 2013, I received a letter from Oxford University stating that, after a gruelling interview process, I had been selected as one of twenty-eight international scholars, drawn from a pool of 1,800 applicants, for a full scholarship that covered my tuition and living expenses. As part of the scholarship, I would be enrolled in a leadership programme to complement my studies. 'You can take pride in being part of such a group,' the letter said. I called my mother that evening. I cried on the phone as I told her that I had made it. I was becoming someone important.

CHAPTER 27

How does one begin to describe a place like Oxford, an institution that is not just a university but a universe unto itself? A place that is at once vast and self-enclosed? A place so freighted with history, expectation and myth?

Everyone in Oxford, at some point, talks about the buildings. They are ancient and majestic, yet intimately interlaced by little stone-cobbled lanes. One can't help but look at them with a kind of reverence. The libraries hold hundreds and thousands of books. The chapels are illuminated by coloured puddles of light from stained-glass windows. The colleges are like portals that open up into manicured quads and landscapes dotted with deer and rivers. It's a place out of the normal flow of time.

Within the Oxford bubble, as everyone calls it, you're sequestered from the outside world. In college accommodation, the cooking and cleaning are handled by uniformed staff from Nigeria or Poland or the north of England. Sports and music and parties and dinners all happen within university walls. It feels so much like being in an adult boarding school. Your classmates are your friends, lovers, rivals and allies. Your professors are your teachers, role models, therapists – and, too often, parental figures.

Like all other students, I had high hopes for Oxford when I started my master's degree in the autumn of 2013. Perhaps unusually, I worried little about being an impostor. My last job in clinical medicine was in a neonatal intensive care unit. I didn't think the pressure of essay deadlines could compare to dying babies. I tried not to take the pomposity of the university too seriously. I shared a private rental flat with Harry. I saw myself as a self-sufficient adult, capable of paying council tax and bleaching my own toilet. At a welcome dinner for graduate students, I ignored everything the principal of my college said in his speech about our community as a home away from home. But then, something he said caught my attention: 'If you are pursuing a postgraduate degree, that means you have unfinished business with the academy.' I understood what he meant because I had unfinished business with the academy. Unlike many of my friends who had finished medical school and had no intention of returning to university, I felt a burning need to get more out of my education. A postgraduate degree was both reinvention and, I hoped, self-actualisation for me. I now tuned into the speech with sharper attention and ingested his blithe self-satisfaction when he added, 'And you have come to the best place in the world to finish it. Just ask the *Times Higher Education* magazine, which has, rightly in my view, placed us at the pinnacle of its world university rankings.'

A funny thing about being 'at the pinnacle' was learning that it was crowded at the top. Getting into Oxford wasn't enough; there was still more jostling to be an elite within Oxford's elite. While undergraduates fretted about the internal rankings among the university's constituent colleges, I stepped into the competitive world of philanthropic postgraduate scholarships. Mine was founded by George Weidenfeld, an Austrian refugee who fled the Nazis in 1938 and then made his life in Britain as a successful publisher and philanthropist. The scholarship's stated mission was to develop young people from emerging and low-income countries 'who are passionate about social change in their home countries'. My cohort included twenty-eight scholars from almost as many different nations, studying everything from law and finance to environmental change and management to plant sciences. The scholarship tried to set itself apart through a leadership programme that included a five-day residential seminar called Moral Philosophy for Leaders. I was quickly learning that the scholarship was not merely financial support; it was aiming at something else. Indoctrination, maybe? That word is much too strong. Perhaps a better word might be inculcation, or maybe enculturation – or better still, assimilation?

The seminar took place at Hartwell House, a Jacobean mansion transformed into a country hotel with sprawling, immaculate grounds. The house once gave sanctuary to the exiled king of France, Louis XVIII, in the early nineteenth century. There, beneath ceilings bearing centuries of aristocratic intrigue, we gathered for close readings of texts from Plato, Rousseau and other canonical thinkers under the tutelage of Oxbridge dons and knighted barristers. Apart from the speech Mandela delivered at the Rivonia trial, which sent him to prison for twenty-seven years, contemporary readings were conspicuously absent, as if anything too modern might dilute the gravity of our discussions. Just as I had once sought to dazzle my high-school teachers with my vocabulary and insight, I was adept at meeting my tutors' expectations by mirroring their language and styles of argument. My peers from Chile or Romania did not know how to perform in this kind of theatre; I could almost see the pearls of sweat on their foreheads when they were asked a question.

'I taught history and philosophy at Cambridge for over thirty years. And, quite frankly, some people are cleverer than others,' one of the tutors told me in the lunch queue, his voice conspiratorial. 'You're very bright, Simukai. But more importantly, you have something that I had when I was your age: independence of mind. It will serve you well if you don't squander it.' He patted my back. After years of striving for recognition, I felt noticed and validated. I basked in the glow of his unsolicited affirmation, untroubled that what he called my independence of mind was really my skill at doing what was asked of me.

Beyond the seminar, the scholarship organised practical workshops for us on public speaking, debate and essay writing, followed by elaborate dinners held in Oxford colleges or among the artefacts of the Ashmolean Museum. Each event was tightly curated and controlled. On cue, the programme director invited us to testify before honoured guests and esteemed patrons about how the scholarship had changed our lives, even when we had only been at Oxford for a few months. In the summer, there was a scholars' Venetian masquerade ball at Blenheim Palace, the birthplace and ancestral home of Sir Winston Churchill. Its grandeur was heart-stopping. And yet part of me knew what I did not want to know: there could be no palace without plunder, no old money without old massacres. I danced in black tie and a gold mask, under a crystal chandelier, listening to a violin quartet and ignoring the hallowed violence behind the cloistered corridors.

The final event of my master's year was a dinner at Brooks's, an exclusive London club founded by Whig nobles in the eighteenth century. A few days earlier, the programme director had invited me for tea and a chat. After the obligatory small talk about the weather and the meadows, she said, 'Simukai, we would like you to give the vote of thanks on behalf of the scholars to Lord Weidenfeld, the donors and the board of trustees.' Of course, this was less a request than an instruction.

I prepared my speech the way a gourmet prepares an *amuse-bouche*. I wanted to achieve a flourish of delicate intimacy, something memorable to whet the appetite without distracting from the main course – after all, the donors would want to have their say. I laced my speech with literary references to V. S. Naipaul but made sure not to quote him verbatim as that would seem over-prepared. I memorised my speech, knowing my audience would appreciate a seemingly extemporaneous toast. On the night, I spoke about home and exile, agency and arrival, about Lord Weidenfeld's life of reinvention after ruin and how he was a lodestar to our generation of scholars who wished to make the world a better, fairer, safer place than the one we were born into. The hearty applause when I sat down felt earned yet hollow somehow. I had bolstered the conceit of the scholarship by telling a polished story of its transformative power.

In only nine months, I had been so easily seduced. Oxford's ways, I was told and began to believe, were superior and ineffable. Each time I shared my story – how I had arrived here, how the scholarship had changed me – I was solidifying a myth, shaping not just how others saw me but how I saw myself. I willingly played the role of grateful scholar, supplicant migrant and emerging leader. With each extravagance bestowed upon me, I became more and more entrenched in this rarefied club of privilege and opportunity. This was an invitation extended only to a few. But I understood the tacit bargain: the door that had been opened to me could just as easily close. To falter in my performance would mean losing my place to others waiting in the wings. I was in the position I had long craved to be in, so why did it feel so . . . icky?

***

As the honeymoon charm of Oxford began to wear off, I felt increasingly aware of the ghosts of Zimbabwe's colonial past lurking all around me. None haunted the place more than Cecil Rhodes, who had been a student at Oriel College in the 1870s, and later gave millions to the university through gifts and bequests. Most striking of these was Rhodes House in central Oxford, a gathering place for recipients of the eponymous scholarship. (To my great unease, the Rhodes scholars I met often referred to each other as 'Rhodies' – a word that still invoked for me a near-breathless hatred.) Rhodes House is a grand building in the style of a Cotswold manor, with one conspicuously incongruous feature: on top of the building's copper-clad dome perches an enormous bronze carving that I recognised immediately – the Zimbabwe bird.

The sculpture is a copy of one of a half-dozen eleventh-century bird carvings stolen in the late nineteenth century from the ancient city of Great Zimbabwe. Rhodes insisted that the technical virtuosity of the original sculptures was so great that they had to have been the work of Phoenicians rather than Africans themselves. Rhodes was the only private individual to ever own one of the birds. He used it as a personal totem. When plotting his conquest of Matabeleland and Mashonaland, he would place the bird on the table and say to his doubtful interlocutors, 'Where this stone bird came from there must be something else.' And, as we know, what followed when he invaded the region was mass killing. In time, I came to see the carving atop Rhodes House as the negative image of what would soon become a much more famous statue: the larger-than-life likeness of Rhodes that peers down onto Oxford's High Street from a niche high up on Oriel College's facade, above a Latin inscription thanking him for his munificence. If the statue of Rhodes portrayed him as a great benefactor, the Zimbabwe bird stood for the wealth extraction and human exploitation on which Rhodes' fortune was built, as well as for the racist ideology that helped justify his colonial programme.

Colonialism continued to shape Oxford in less concrete ways too. I wasn't there long before I learned that the dim view of Africa and Africans held by Rhodes had been shared by many of Oxford's most esteemed historians. Hugh Trevor-Roper, who for a quarter-century occupied the university's most prestigious history chair, infamously pronounced in the sixties that there was no African history, 'only the history of Europeans in Africa. The rest is darkness.' Before Europeans brought history to Africa and places like it, Trevor-Roper went on, there was only 'the unedifying gyrations of barbarous tribes in picturesque but irrelevant corners of the globe'. This was just a touch crasser than what a Fellow at Balliol College said to me at a formal dinner when I told him that I studied African politics: 'What a mess! How could you possibly fix that?'

The handful of Oxford scholars who studied Africa, like Harry, had a nuanced understanding of the continent and shared my disgust at Rhodes. William Beinart, then the Rhodes Professor of Race Relations, quipped that his title was an embarrassment, like being called the 'Goebbels Professor of Communication'. But even though my professors at the African Studies Centre were rigorous scholars, I couldn't help but notice that they were all white. Granted, there aren't many black people in the UK, only about 3.3 per cent of the population. But there are even fewer black academic faculty – about two per cent total, and 0.6 per cent at Oxford in particular. And so a field like African studies has an air of the 1884 Berlin Conference, which heralded the 'Scramble for Africa' – but instead of European powers claiming and trading in different parts of the continent, it's mostly white scholars talking to white audiences about ethnicity in Kenya, democracy in Ghana or refugees in Uganda.

* * *

My studies and my family's history as colonial subjects came together painfully in a seminar on the history of political imprisonment and punishment in Africa. Back then, I had not yet talked to my father at length about his incarceration in a Rhodesian prison during the liberation struggle. All I knew was that the conditions were 'inhuman', as he had once put it when I was growing up. Now, in Oxford, I spent every Friday morning in a basement classroom with Professor Jocelyn Alexander – a white American woman who had been working in Zimbabwe since I was a toddler. Joss, as she liked to be called, guided my classmates and me through weekly discussions about how settler colonial states like Rhodesia locked up their political rivals and tortured, executed and coerced political prisoners into forced labour at an industrial scale. This was how they preserved the colonial order and shored up white political domination in southern Africa. It made me feel sick.

After I finished my master's degree, I proceeded to doctoral studies in the department of international development under Joss' supervision. I wanted to learn as much from her as I possibly could about how to approach problems, do research, argue effectively and think critically. Joss shared my critiques of Rhodes. 'The history of Cecil Rhodes' conquest and government of what became Rhodesia in its earliest days marks the distribution of resources and ideas about race in Zimbabwe up to now,' she once wrote in her characteristically restrained and disciplined style. But she didn't stop there. She also shook my loyalties.

Joss once spoke on a panel hosted by the African Studies Centre with Morgan Tsvangirai, the leader of Zimbabwe's main opposition party, as a special guest. She respected Tsvangirai as a courageous, if flawed, politician. And she was a staunch critic of ZANU(PF), the party my father dedicated his life to. My father called me after the event. 'Tsvangirai is a son of a bitch,' my father shouted on the phone, 'why is he wasting your time in Oxford?'

Every few weeks, Joss and I sat in her office to discuss my work. She, the tall, erudite American professor with a capacious mind amply stocked with historical detail and argument. Me, her naive apprentice. The two of us locked in a Socratic dialogue about Zimbabwean politics. She later said to me, 'I think you should be careful not to accept your father's account of Zimbabwe's history wholesale. He's telling you a very ZANU(PF) version of events.' She was right but this was not an easy thing to hear.

I had absorbed lessons of the past from my father with a childish receptivity. But now, working on my doctorate, I could feel the gap widening between his understanding of Zimbabwe and mine. In my head, I knew he lived with a terrible grief that he processed through total fidelity to the nationalists, and I knew that such a position was a folly. In my heart, I didn't want to judge him, nor did I want to point out the lies and hypocrisy in the party he supported. After all, I am an only child, the designated carrier of my parents' legacy – a burden that I had transported carefully, until that point, with all its history-turned-mythology left intact.

* * *

I had impressed the Weidenfeld committee enough to win further funding for my doctorate. But the scholarship was changing rapidly. After Lord Weidenfeld died, the scholarship started to reshape itself in the image of a new coterie of donors from the business world. The identity of the scholarship became less humanistic and more market-driven and impact-oriented. It scrapped its requirement that all scholars do community service in favour of entrepreneurial challenges. The philosophy seminar remained, but the prior emphasis on close reading was supplanted by the need to learn lessons for today's leadership challenges. Still, I complied. I needed the money. With Joss I was a scholar, but with the scholarship I was a thought leader. This was the paradox of my education at Oxford: it was both liberating and infantilising, both an intellectual awakening and a slow assimilation. I loved it and I loathed it.

And there was no escaping the conflict between what I was studying and where I was studying. The more time I spent in Oxford, the more aware I grew of the university's colonial imprint, of how the awe-inspiring buildings carried within them symbols and sediments of empire. Oxford is strewn with tributes to imperialists and enslavers who have scholarships, portraits, busts, engravings, statues, libraries and even buildings dedicated to their memory. Christopher Codrington, a slave plantation owner, bequeathed £1.2 million in today's money to All Souls College to erect one of Europe's most magnificent libraries (which, until 2020, bore his name). George Curzon, the viceroy of India who presided over the Indian famine of 1899–1900 in which about four million people died, was memorialised at his alma mater, Balliol College. Augustus Pitt Rivers, a nineteenth-century colonial officer, founded Oxford's archaeological museum, which long doubled up as a storage facility for loot stolen during the British Empire. To survive at Oxford, writes the philosopher Nikhil Krishnan, is to take in its skyline of memorialised villains and say, 'Such beauty.' At Oxford, colonialism wasn't a period that had passed, but a historical mass that bent everything around its gravity.

CHAPTER 28

Some 8,000 miles away from Oxford, on 9 March 2015, a student hurled a bucket of human shit at a different statue of Rhodes – one that held pride of place at the University of Cape Town's main campus, just downhill from the convocation hall. I had been to Cape Town a few times, but not since 2005 when I visited some friends from Saints who had started their undergraduate degrees at UCT. I didn't remember the statue, erected to commemorate Rhodes for 'bequeathing' the land on which the university had been founded. What I remembered was how the gorgeous UCT campus tumbled down the side of Table Mountain. The university's Georgian buildings were surrounded by verdant gardens. I remembered soaking up the salty ocean breeze while looking down on the city. In the same year, black South African students had already started agitating for the removal of the Rhodes statue. Nothing had happened in about a decade, but now a reinvigorated campaign had begun. Its slogan was 'Rhodes Must Fall'.

Students walked out of lectures en masse. They occupied administrative buildings. The statue provided a canvas for an outpouring of a generation's growing anger. Students tagged it with graffiti, covered it in black bin bags and sang songs from the anti-Apartheid struggle as they danced around it. I knew that I was witnessing history. History revisited, history challenged, history made. I understood the generational outburst because this was my generation. Like me, the South African students at UCT were 'bornfree' yet feeling the kind of intense historical pain I had carried with me all my life. We were the children of the oppressed coming of age in what was supposed to be a better world and now feeling disillusioned with what we'd found there.

Within a matter of days, the student protests crystallised into a campaign against the supremacy of white culture at UCT, including the Eurocentrism of the curriculum, the dominance of white people on the governing council, the inadequate financial and pastoral support for black students, and the plague of colonial iconography across the campus. They brought all university business to a standstill and, within a month, the statue was taken down. Protests spread throughout South Africa's universities and cities, the largest wave since the country became a democracy in 1994. Enormous crowds with raised fists cried out for black liberation.

As I observed all this, I fluctuated between extremes of emotion. The audacity of these students was compelling and cathartic. It stood in stark contrast to how I was attempting to fulfil the expectations of my own elite institution. I found myself filled with anger and frustration towards Oxford. The shared history of colonialism between UCT and my university was striking. This was a metropole and a colony, with Rhodes as the symbolic lynchpin. It wasn't long before I became a leader in the struggle to transform Oxford.

***

At the beginning, I wasn't interested in taking down statues, however offensive they might be. I thought events in Cape Town could open up some conversation about decolonising the Oxford curriculum but I was not an early advocate of 'radical' action. I met with some friends in a student common room at one of the colleges. There were South African students, including UCT alumni. There were several other African students. There were Rhodes scholars. There were African American students who saw a kinship between decolonial protest and the anti-racism work of

Black Lives Matter in the United States. There were black and brown students from all the main left-wing student groups: the women's office, the student union, the Palestinian solidarity campaign, the Africa Society, the students against climate change, and so on. There were some white students who positioned themselves as allies.

'Something is clearly happening. It's not just about Cape Town. Look at UCL, they have a group called "Why is My Curriculum White?". I think we need something similar in Oxford,' I said to nods of approval. I wanted it to be about more than Rhodes.

I could see one of the South African students scowling. 'I get that there is momentum from UCT,' I added. 'I just think we need our own thing, you know? I don't want us to be too distracted by statues when we're actually trying to change the curriculum or get this place to finally hire some more black professors.'

'That Rhodes statue at Oriel! We need to take it down!' the South African student said.

'Why, though? I can already see the *Daily Mail* headlines: "Much ado about a statue". It's a distraction.'

'Comrade, we did not come to Oxford for fucked-up celebrations of British genocidal history.' His voice shook. He was enraged. I was talking to a student who had grown up in the cramped, claustrophobic shacks of one of South Africa's black townships. In his neighbourhood, most families defecated in plastic boxes that were collected by the municipality once a week. In heavy storms, the rain flooded the township and the wind blew away makeshift homes with their tarp roofs and cardboard-box sidings.

'Rhodes must fall! Ignorance must fall! Fuckery must fall!' he said, more adamant each time.

I told him I understood, but that we couldn't just protest *without* a programme of action. So if we took the statue down, then what?

There was a pause to see which way the conversation would go. Another South African student spoke up. 'Order, comrades!' he said, then shook his head at me. 'I think we should follow the lead of our sisters and brothers at UCT. This is a once-in-a-generation moment. Rhodes must fall in Oxford too. We can't ignore the statue. It's a litmus test. If we campaign to take it down, and people oppose us, then we will know how this university treats black history and black pain.'

I didn't argue. So much in Oxford, I knew, was a monument to the decimation of my ancestors. I conceded that the provocation of targeting the statue was the point, I just didn't want it to be the only thing we did.

We called our work decolonisation. It was an absurd idea. Decolonising Oxford is like 'deboning a skeleton', as Nikhil Krishnan perfectly put it. But absurdity is a weak foe against youthful idealism. Our goal was to slay racist ideologies that still held sway in various disciplines that were too pale, stale and male. We wanted to push the university to bring more black people into academia at every level. And we wanted to end the glorification of men who had dedicated their lives to the colonial project. The scale of these ambitions was core to our politics. We were not interested in half measures or compromises with institutional racism. We borrowed the name of the student movement in South Africa, calling ourselves Rhodes Must Fall in Oxford (RMF). We knew it would be an uphill battle but it also felt like a revolution: urgent, vital and true. One of my friends cautioned me: 'You know what they say about change in Oxford, Simukai? *Change is good. But no change is better.*'

On a Thursday afternoon in late May 2015, I arrived at the Oxford Union Debating Society to meet other RMF students at the members' bar before the debate that evening. I pushed open the heavy wooden door that led into a decorous room. The thick, burgundy curtains had been tied back, inviting the enchanting summer light through large bay windows. The bartenders were stirring and shaking. Behind them, on the wall, was a mosaic display of photographs – a visual catalogue of esteemed guests at the Oxford Union like Mother Teresa, Desmond Tutu, Albert Einstein, the Queen, Emma Watson and Morgan Freeman. Twenty-year-old students dressed in black tie and cocktail dresses milled around, sipping from flutes of prosecco and whispering about free speech. The Union president wore a navy-blue sparkly dress and a tiara, and she strode around looking like a princess. I wore white Converse sneakers, grey jeans, a blue tee with a silhouette of the Notorious B.I.G., and a Nike tracksuit jacket.

'Simukai!' someone called out to me. I rushed over to my crew, seated at a table by one of the bay windows.

'Bro, check this out,' a friend said and handed me a flyer advertising the cocktail special for the evening. It was called the 'Colonial Comeback' and it depicted black hands in manacles.

'Very funny! Y'all got jokes. But isn't this over the top?' I asked.

'It's not us. We didn't make this. That's the actual cocktail.'

I took the flyer and walked over to ask the bartender if this was indeed the signature cocktail. I don't know who was more embarrassed, him or me for him. Our plan that evening was to protest a debate on the legacy of colonialism. We wanted to press the point that colonialism was not a thing of the past and that it lived on in institutional racism, but, to our astonishment, the Union had beaten us to the punch.

Our Rhodes Must Fall in Oxford campaign launched that night. We posted images of the flyer online and it caught national media attention. The next day, every British newspaper ran a story on 'cocktailgate'. Journalists called and emailed asking to speak to us. Our next step was to send out a cryptic email and flood as many mailing lists as possible. The email was written by one of our white allies and edited by members of our group:

Cecil Rhodes has fallen. His statue has been removed and the uncritical memory of his legacy has been discredited at the University of Cape Town, where the Rhodes Must Fall Movement – a movement to decolonize education – targets the still-active tentacles of colonial relations in Africa.

[. . .]

We stand here, in Oxford, in solidarity with all those people on empire's periphery, and bring the world's decolonising fight to its heart.

[. . .]

[F]or Rhodes to truly fall Rhodes must first stand.

Rhodes must be made to stand, revealed for what he really represents: the mutually productive culture of violence, racism, patriarchy and colonialism that to this day remains alive, aided and abetted by the University of Oxford, which continues to stand as an uncritical beneficiary of empire.

[. . .]

Here, in the inner halls of imperialism, Rhodes must fall.

#RhodesMustFallOxford

I shared this email with the 300 students in my department. Two replied. One wrote back to say 'thank you'. The other wrote back to chastise me for the tone of the email. He was condescending when he pointed out that I was a beneficiary of Oxford, as if I didn't know that. He concluded by saying he didn't want to receive any more emails about a 'movement' whose means he found objectionable.

I read the email out loud to another RMF student. 'Can you believe this fuckery?' I said. 'I'm so sick of these white men who get so defensive and dismissive. God forbid that for one day in their privileged lives, they should be made to feel uncomfortable.' I was high on sanctimony and moral certainty. RMF was fast becoming my outlet for years of pent-up frustration. Colonialism was a crime of historic proportions and anyone who didn't see it was an enemy of progress. I worked myself up. My righteous indignation at that moment had merged with other, deeper feelings that had been festering within me for far too long. I let him have it. I started my reply by quoting the Palestinian-American scholar and literary critic Edward Said, about the responsibilities of the intellectual 'to raise embarrassing questions, to confront orthodoxy and dogma (rather than to produce them), to be someone who cannot easily be co-opted by government or corporations and whose raison d'être is to represent all those people and issues who are routinely forgotten or swept under the rug.' This, I argued, was what Rhodes Must Fall was doing. I fired off paragraphs about neutrality and complicity, about the historical and structural dimensions of colonial legacies. Words like 'violence' and 'justice' were all over my email. Finally, I wrote, 'We stand on the shoulders of giants – all those who have fought against racism, colonialism, patriarchy, homophobia and other forms of oppression – we will not be silenced.' Then I hit send.

Needless to say, he did not take my email well. He accused me of promoting 'hate speech'. This upped the ante and I was game to keep going. We exchanged a few rounds before a friend finally asked, 'Will you stop engaging with this guy? There's no point.' I reluctantly agreed. I was angry but I was excited too. I had never been this pugnacious before and it was empowering.

As RMF, we organised student meetings where people talked about their experiences of white supremacy and prejudice. I learned to introduce myself with my pronouns (he/him) and check my privilege as a straight, cisgender, middle-class male, albeit a black immigrant from a troubled country whose history was foundational to Rhodes Must Fall. As I did so, I couldn't tell if this intense focus on individual identity encouraged self-awareness and solidarity or if it slipped into a kind of narcissism of petty differences. Students from South Africa skyped into our meetings and led us in thrilling call-and-response chants. '*Amandla!*' ('Power!') '*Awethu!*' ('To the people!') We enlisted the help of faculty to join our campaign or advise us about how to be most effective. I spoke to Joss and William Beinart, who told me that the Rhodes Trust gave no money to African studies in the university. The trust's only reparative contribution was the handful of scholarships it gave to southern African students, which in any case paled in comparison to the funding for American scholars.

I joined a decolonial study group where, each week, we restlessly argued and debated concepts like neoliberalism, colonialism, capitalism, Zionism, Pan-Africanism, fascism, socialism, imperialism, ableism, casteism . . . -ism, ism, ism, ism until we sounded like buzzing flies. We believed colonialism had shaped everything – from our institutions to our ambitions, from the way history was taught to the way power was distributed. The more we dissected 'coloniality', the more I began to see its fingerprints in places I hadn't expected. 'Everything is political' became a new shibboleth. Even intimacy came under scrutiny, reframed through how white supremacy shaped sexual preference: elevating white women to the summit, relegating black women to the floor.

Matters of the heart remained confusing. I felt a paradoxical, inarticulable longing for and fear of connection. But with decolonisation and politics as my dominant idioms, I was more comfortable with critical theory than with feelings. I didn't know how to express my emotional confusions. I had a talent for dating emotionally unavailable people and little insight into what that said about me. I worried that black women wouldn't like me, or, worse, that they'd see right through me to all my tortured insecurities about identity. That kind of rejection felt unbearable.

With white women, I built a different kind of defence: I treated my budding relationships as spaces for racial education and cast myself as the know-it-all teacher. I asked a white girlfriend once to listen to Kendrick Lamar's 'The Blacker the Berry' with me. 'I think Kendrick might be the GOAT. Listen to that raspy and seething tone in his voice,' I said. 'Listen to the way he speaks under his breath about how he doesn't need black *and* how he wants everything black. This conflict over black identity is the central idea of the song. It's a genius way of conveying Du Bois' concept of double-consciousness.' I told her it was also the story of my life, this divided feeling of looking at myself through the eyes of the white world and knowing that everything I did as a black man was either too much or never enough.

She had not read Du Bois, nor had she read Fanon or Baldwin for that matter. She grew frustrated with how much I talked about race and eventually said, 'I don't think you are trying to call me out, I think you are trying to catch me out.' She was right. Something in me felt broken but I didn't know what. I hoped that ideology would rescue me from my damaged self, that it could provide me with the certainty and clarity I thought I needed. But this was yet another fragile hope.

Despite all the absolutes of student activism, not everyone thought the same way. A contingent of us from RMF tried to start a Black Students Union, modelled on analogous organisations in the United States. Any student who identified as black was invited to a planning meeting. We wanted to come up with a mission statement and charter for this new union, but instead we spent four hours arguing over the meaning of the word 'Black'.

* * *

In November 2015, RMF organised a protest outside Oriel College. Hundreds of students joined and thousands more signed a petition demanding that the statue be taken down and housed in a museum. Protestors condemned the statue as 'an open glorification of the racist and bloody project of British colonialism', and people chanted 'Rhodes Must Fall! Take it Down!'

I tracked the protests from Harare. I was back home conducting field research for my doctorate. My thesis was about the politics of the 2008/9 cholera outbreak that had infected 100,000 people and claimed more than 4,000 lives. A cholera outbreak of that scale – outside a war or environmental catastrophe – was unprecedented in modern history and represented the breaking of all vestiges of Zimbabwe's social contract. In Harare's high-density townships, I spent months gathering testimonies, speaking with doctors, human rights activists, politicians, aid workers, civil servants and community organisers, piecing together an account of how a simple bacterial infection had spiralled into a national catastrophe.

Western governments and media had blamed the outbreak entirely on Mugabe's misrule, citing it as proof of his regime's incompetence and disregard for human life. Some international organisations went further, invoking the Responsibility to Protect (R2P) doctrine and suggesting that military intervention might be necessary to remove him. Mugabe's government hit back with a preposterous counter-narrative, claiming that cholera was not a public health crisis but a biological weapon deployed by the West – part of a racist, terrorist plot to destabilise Zimbabwe and justify neo-colonial intervention. When I tried to talk to my father about this absurd theory, he dismissed it with a casual wave of the hand. The more important issue, he maintained, was that sanctions had crippled our economy and, if anything, it was testament to the strength of Mugabe's leadership that the country was still running. 'No other country on earth could survive the sanctions they put on us,' he said. One of my friends from Saints, who now worked as a doctor in Zimbabwe, saw things differently. 'I am anti-colonial and anti-neo-colonial,' he said ruefully. 'I know that Great Britain is wealthy in part because it plundered countries like ours. Nevertheless, our leadership has failed us.'

I couldn't have put it better.

When I returned to Oxford in January 2016, I quickly entered a closed-loop circle of time-consuming, exhausting and distracting public debates. I participated in a BBC radio show about Rhodes

Must Fall. I was pitted against a crusty, ill-tempered polemicist who was also a seasoned radio interviewee. I sat alone in an empty studio at the BBC offices in Oxford with headphones over my ears and waited to be called on to speak. As soon as I introduced myself, my opponent hit me with a barrage of insults.

'I don't know what is going on in Oxford tutorials these days to produce a legion of historically illiterate young ideologues.'

'If I may,' I said, 'I am from Zimbabwe and I have a different perspective—'

'Well, I need not remind you that your Robert *Mugabeee* is no saint. Maybe you should judge him and not a man who died a century ago and is probably paying for your education. What a waste! Besides, Rhodes was not a racist, he judged peoples by how civilised they were in nineteenth-century terms.'

'That's a disingenuous argument. We're not talking about his views, we're talking about black oppression—'

'Oh, here we go again with this victimhood drivel! Your generation has been brainwashed by this intersectionality and race-baiting gibberish from America. It is having a frightful effect on your intellectual development. In my day, a university education was about learning to think for yourself and taking a stand against real threats. You aren't activists. You are a mindless mob of vandals.'

I left the studio feeling utterly defeated. What had just happened? I had been naive to think this was an honest debate. I had been enlisted into a culture war and what we were doing on radio was not having a rigorous intellectual exchange, it was theatre. To think otherwise was to mine for fool's gold. Other commentators summoned spectres from new and old wars to describe us: fascists, Maoists and ISIS. This was my turning point on the statue: I now wanted that motherfucker taken down.

Public figures from across the political spectrum wrote chin-stroking opinion pieces in the broadsheets with the usual arguments against Rhodes Must Fall: 'it's complicated'; 'Rhodes was not a racist, he was a man of his time'; 'we gave them the railways and democracy'; 'Rhodes Must Fall is a dangerous attempt to erase history.' I collated many such articles and used them as fodder to write my own stump speech that I delivered at colleges, campaign events and other universities: it wasn't that complicated; Rhodes was much worse than a racist, he was a megalomaniacal mass murderer; the railways were built by black labourers; we fought for our democracy. Also, whose history?

'The irony', I was fond of saying, 'is that the white people who accuse us of *whitewashing* history are the ones refusing to confront the history of colonialism. How else can you explain the baffling remarks of Mr Will Hutton, principal of Hertford College, Oxford, who wrote in the *Guardian* that if it wasn't for the legacies of empire that gave South Africa freedom of speech, free association and the rule of law, then the country would descend into unaccountable despotism? Excuse me? One wonders if Mr Hutton has ever heard of a little historical event called Apartheid?' I took aim too at the celebrated Cambridge classicist Mary Beard, who had said: 'The battle isn't won by taking the statue away and pretending those people didn't exist. It's won by empowering those students to look up at Rhodes and friends with a cheery and self-confident sense of unbatterability.' Unlike many of our critics, we recognised that the Rhodes statue was not a sterile historical relic, nor was it some accurate record of the past. It was a piece of self-aggrandising propaganda designed to present an ennobled image of Rhodes for as long as it stood. (There was an analogy here to the way Mugabe had tried to rewrite Zimbabwean history.) If anyone was trying to erase the past – specifically the history of subjugation and suffering on which his fortune was built – it was Rhodes from beyond the grave.

We thought we were making progress when Oriel College pledged to launch a six-month inquiry, gathering evidence and stakeholder opinions to decide the future of the statue. But only six weeks later, in late January 2016, the college reneged on this pledge, stating that it would not remove the statue on the grounds that there was 'overwhelming' support to keep it. It was later revealed in the press that Oriel stood to lose £100 million in donor gifts were it to take down the statue. 'Oxford doesn't care about black life,' wrote one of the South African activists in an online post. I was irritated by the hyperbole and yet I understood it. I was crushed. We had failed. I thought it was all over.

CHAPTER 29

I remained in Oxford. I no longer wrote in a book of motivational quotes, but I kept a photo on my phone that said: 'I got zero time to be a complacent nigga.' I worked like a maniac on my PhD and finished my thesis faster than anyone else in my cohort.

Around the same time, in early 2018, I approached a therapist. I told her that I had just been awarded the title 'doctor' for the second time. I said that I worked hard and had many friends as well as a promising career ahead of me. 'But despite the life I have built,' my email said, 'I am troubled by feelings of loneliness, a sense of dislocation, and anxieties about the future. I have had trouble in romantic relationships, which compounds these feelings. I feel torn about where I belong in the world.'

At our first meeting, my therapist suggested to me that I have a fragmented sense of personal identity. The work of integration, she said, would require me to slow down, to stop striving for one thing after another, to make time to delve into what lives inside me but is hard to acknowledge, to sit with feelings that I rush over, ignore or flee from. I was not ready to hear this. I did not heed her advice to slow down. In fact, I did the opposite. I focused all my energy on trying to convert my doctoral research into a book and get a permanent academic job. In less than six months, near-record time, I went from submitting my PhD thesis to being offered a position as a professor at Oxford.

By the time I began my first year on the job, I was already depleted. Before me was another steep mountain and I didn't have the tools to climb it. I struggled with every aspect of the role. I entered the classroom armed only with the notion that I must surely know something because I have a PhD and I must be able to teach because I've been hired to do so. But I had never been trained to lecture, run a seminar or supervise students. Oxford doesn't bother too much with this kind of professional development; the prevailing attitude is, if you're good enough, you'll figure it out. Asking my colleagues how things worked was futile because you were supposed to learn by osmosis or trial and error or muddling through or by being brilliant. I attended meetings of my departmental management committee and the governing body of my college where I stared dumbfounded at impenetrable spreadsheets and esoteric acronyms. If I asked what these symbols meant, my question was laughed off with a nonchalant 'Oh, no one knows what it all means.' When my students struggled to come up with their own research topics, I felt obliged to do it for them. Not having had any teacher training, I didn't know any other way. And when the invitations came flooding in – to give guest lectures, testify in Parliament or appear on podcasts – I said yes. I had no priority system, nor any clear sense of what kind of scholar I wanted to be. I adapted by working long days and weekends. I neglected my home life. What little food I had in the fridge went mouldy. Grime accumulated on my bathroom basin. On too many evenings, I subsisted on fast food and red wine, then passed out on the couch with *BoJack Horseman* on the TV.

Eventually, inevitably, I crashed. It happened on a Sunday afternoon in late February 2019, about three weeks after I made that appearance before Parliament about Zimbabwe's political crisis. I had gone to the pub with some colleagues. On my way home, I made a pitstop in the department to use the toilet. After washing up, I walked to the door. My hand had curled round the handle but I couldn't pull it open. I let go, leaned against the wall, and slumped to the floor. I don't know how long I sat there for. I picked up my phone and texted a friend:

I'm having a breakdown
I'm having a breakdown
I'm having a breakdown
I'm having a breakdown
I'm having a breakdown
I'm having a breakdown
I'm having a breakdown
I'm having a breakdown
I'm having a breakdown
I'm having a breakdown
I'm having a breakdown

I didn't know what was happening to me and I was scared. I could not yet see the recurring pattern in the relentless forward momentum of my life. I had left Zimbabwe, aged sixteen, in a state of emotional disarray but I suppressed all my needs and redirected my angst and fear into hard work. I did the same thing after I finished boarding school and went to medical school. I did it again after that torrid first year at medical school when I told myself to keep on running no matter what. And on and on through the years of collecting degrees, engaging in global health activism, working as a doctor, trying to be the best at Oxford. I was caught in a loop of tackling one challenge after another without pause or reprieve. I was still looking for the remedy but I couldn't see the ailment.

After my breakdown that Sunday, I was unwilling – or unable – to recognise just how burned out I was. I took a week off work, as if I had a bad cold, but didn't seek any further help. I was more worried about failing to meet the expectations of my department and colleagues, who had entrusted me with a senior academic position at such an early stage of my career.

I tried to suck it up. Perversely, it was the COVID-19 pandemic that forced me to slow down by bringing life as we knew it to a standstill. I felt a modicum of calm and even belonging in the shared grief, outpourings of compassion and mutual support of that terrible period. We were all in it together, trying to get by.

And then George Floyd died.

***

Like most of the world, I had seen the video of the torture and murder of George Floyd, a forty-six-year-old black man from Fayetteville, North Carolina, at the knee of a white police officer. I had felt the shock of watching a violent, twisted, brutal, unspeakable act. I had heard the plea. That simplest, most urgent, most primitive of pleas – 'I can't breathe' – uttered like a prayer.

After my shock came anguish and fury. For days on end, I consumed the news and the frenzied commentary on the killing until my mind was foggy and my body ached. I can't tell you if I thought about my father's father, who was murdered by Rhodesian security forces before I was born. But I felt Floyd's murder in a strangely intimate way.

An atrocity in US policing, one of countless, had uncorked something that had been bottled up the world over during the lockdowns of the COVID-19 pandemic. Seething and unspoken resentments came to the fore. Soon the injustice of Floyd's murder expanded into larger questions about police brutality and its historical repetition, about the social structures that entrench and institutionalise racism. What do we do about the past? How do we step out of the shadows that slavery and colonialism and segregation cast over us?

Days after Floyd's death, the heads of all the Oxford colleges – every single one of them white – wrote an open letter in the *Guardian* claiming that they stood in solidarity with black students and affirmed their commitment to equal dignity and respect. I immediately thought of Gary Younge's piercing observation that white people periodically 'discover' racism 'the same way teenagers discover sex: urgently, earnestly, voraciously and carelessly, with great self-indulgence but precious little self-awareness'.

As one of the few people from the first wave of Rhodes Must Fall who was still at the university, I was asked to speak at an anti-racism protest on 9 June 2020. I stood before a crowd of thousands occupying Oxford's High Street and blocking traffic. Police helicopters flew overhead, and officers on horseback redirected cars coming into the city. I drank the sweet, rich spirit of the crowd. I absorbed the sheer density of its energy. I stood before my audience. I didn't move or say a word until everyone had quietened down into silent anticipation, awaiting my address. It was like a suspension of time. Then the words 'Rhodes Must Fall' came out of my mouth with a guttural force I couldn't contain.

***

It was at the end of that summer that I began to write this book. The public mood in Britain felt charged with both good- and bad-faith debates about the legacies of slavery and colonialism. Oriel College faced enormous pressure to take the statue down and they commissioned another report to decide what to do with it. This time round, the report argued for the statue's removal and suggested several additional measures for advancing academic and public understanding of Rhodes and his legacy. Nevertheless Oriel College reneged again, announcing that it would retain the statue, citing vague legal and financial obstacles to taking it down. I was furious but not surprised. We had been here before. As a concession, the university said it would bolster welfare for students of colour and add some black writers to some syllabuses. It promoted walking tours to highlight the university's complicity in colonialism and the slave trade. It hired a black historian or two. A handful of libraries quietly changed their names, while less attention-grabbing memorials to imperial rogues were removed.

For a while, the polemics around the statue – to fall or not to fall? – bothered me. But the intense anger I had felt could not be sustained. Reckoning would not be a single event but a slow erosion, a tide against a cliff. Or maybe it would not be a tide at all – just people like me, standing at the shore, asking the same questions, waiting to see if the water moved.

What I knew for certain was that the heated rhetoric of the culture wars could never do justice to what decolonisation has meant in my life. I wanted to tell a more complicated story, at once epic and intimate, about colonialism and its aftermath across generations in my family. I wanted to write about the land stolen from my ancestors in what is today Zimbabwe. I wanted to describe colonial oppression in all its sin and ugliness. I wanted to portray the sheer violence of the liberation struggle and the harrowing toll it took on my father. I wanted to explain why my mother became a feminist and how her commitment to women's rights has often rubbed up against her support of African nationalism. And I wanted to reflect on my own coming of age at the end of empire, both in Zimbabwe and as a migrant in Britain.

And, of course, I have pursued these themes in this book. But they are the situation – the context, the contingent facts of history and my life. They are not the story – the wisdom, the insight, the thing I have come to say. What I've been investigating is how personal history is linked to larger history, how political liberation from oppressive rule is not the same as freedom of the self from the burdens of the past. Or, as James Baldwin put it, 'History is not merely something to be read. And it does not refer merely, or even principally, to the past. On the contrary, the great force of history comes from the fact that we carry it within us, are unconsciously controlled by it in many ways, and history is literally present in all that we do.'

But what does acknowledging that we're shaped by history accomplish? What might it take to let that history go? When, in other words, will we be free?

CHAPTER 30

At first, my parents were enthusiastic about the book. 'You could even make parts of it funny!' my father said. But when I sent him my book proposal, he read three pages of fifty before calling to shout at me. 'You cannot use language like "the Mugabe regime", "the Mnangagwa regime". I beg you. You are a professor at Oxford. People will wonder about your allegiance. They will think you have forgotten that you are Zimbabwean and you have been colonised by the British.' I couldn't take his barking. I hung up.

The long silence that followed was the chasm between him and me.

I tried to think of my father historically. Here was a man who had fought in the war. He had been through so much that I was still trying to understand. His experiences of prison and torture, exile and guerrilla warfare – sacrifices born of his unwavering commitment to national liberation – perhaps granted him a set of emotional permissions I ought to respect. In his quivering insistence that I must not use the language of imperialists against the nation of my blood, I felt the ache of an old freedom fighter whose thinned skin is stretched over an open wound. His voice carried a child's frustration at not being understood and an ageing man's fear that his son might sully his life's work.

I eventually flew to Zimbabwe to see him in March 2022. I drove ninety miles east out of the capital, heading deeper into Manicaland, a traditional tobacco-farming area. Alone in the car, I thought about Hisham Matar and his plaintive ode to his father. 'With every passing day the father journeys into his night, deeper into the fog, leaving behind remnants of himself and the monumental yet obvious fact, at once frustrating and merciful,' Matar writes, 'that no matter how hard we try we can never entirely know our fathers.'

I arrived at my father's farm soon after lunch. I had not been there for years and it was less shabby than I remembered. He gave me a tour, starting outside. Water sprinklers had greened the lawn. He had constructed a beautiful dry garden filled with succulents, herbs and shrubs with pink and lilac plumes, all hemmed in by tasteful rock displays. In his own small way, my father had reclaimed the Africa of the white man's dreams, where nature can be subdued inside a compound and where the bush extends just beyond the fence in all its thrilling wildness. The tour ended as always with his library. By now, my father had accumulated thousands of books. But in his collection he kept no novels or anthologies of poetry or literary memoirs or essay collections. His shelves carried historical monographs about Africa, mostly about Rhodesia and the liberation war. It's as if his memory was scouring the past, looking for something to cling to against the slide of time. I wanted to scour the past with him too, but I wanted to move beyond the dry historical facts printed in books – I wanted to uncover the history etched in his soul.

We sat down in his bedroom with two bottles of brandy to lubricate the conversation, and memories of his youth flowed out of him like a gushing river. It was only when we turned to Zimbabwe's post-colonial trajectory and our family that he began to falter.

'Can I tell you something?' he asked. 'When you said you want to talk to me, I really didn't know what you were going to ask. If you noticed, I was leaving some gaps in my story. Do you get what I'm saying?'

'I get what you're saying but I also don't know what we're talking about.'

'Let me tell you. When people become vague, it means there are some sensitivities.'

'You know, in our family—'

'Because I am thinking, I don't know how you will handle it.'

He kept going on like this, elliptical and abstract. I could feel the temperature rising within me. I was losing patience and I pushed.

'Are you and Hope still together?'

I had used my mother's first name. I was distancing myself from their parental roles, and I wanted my father to know this.

'What do you mean?'

Where his words had earlier been rich and full, now they were muffled by regret and denial. Not in so many words, he was saying: it's not a child's place to ask about the parents' marriage. I became angry; why couldn't he give me a straight answer? Something snapped within me. I felt a flash of burning resentment. In that moment, I saw my father as a courageous war hero and an emotionally absent coward. I wanted to know if we were still a family, if we had ever been. I knew that my parents had stayed together for my sake even when they had grown apart. But I wanted him to say it. I wanted him to admit that he had withdrawn from the family, that he had not been there for me when I needed him. Years of repressed anger and feelings of abandonment came out of me. I began to shout.

'Why won't you tell me? Tell me! What happened between you and Hope? Why did you leave me?'

'This was the reaction I was afraid of—'

When he said that, I smashed the empty bottle of brandy on the coffee table. His whole body flinched. The sweet smell of liquor filled the room.

'Answer my fucking questions!'

I pushed and pushed, urging him to go where it hurt, to speak of a suffering he did not know how to describe. I had asked him to face the collateral damage that comes to everything a man possesses – his marriage, his family, his loyalties, his sense of self – when he dares to defy a racist regime and lives long enough to watch a victory of liberation turn sour and carnivorous. He laid it on thick with self-righteousness and self-justification, with a litany of grievances about a life riven with hope and bitter disappointment.

'Everything I've done in Zimbabwe, I've done for you,' he said at last.

'What?' I screamed. 'I didn't want a country, I wanted a father!'

* * *

My mother and I spoke several times for this book. We met in Uganda, where I interviewed her in her apartment and in cafes. We took frequent breaks so she could cry and recompose herself. 'Thinking about all this,' she said, 'it evokes memories that . . . that one buries.' We travelled together to her childhood home town of Kabale. We walked along muddy roads lined by banana trees. We visited her old schools. We went to see the tombstones of her father and mother and all the siblings she had already lost: Joy, Godfrey, Monica, Florence and Ambrose. My mother was more open than my father but still not wholly forthcoming. It was difficult for her to be fully candid. A life marked by such loss, then masked by overwork and professional achievement – something I knew all too well – is difficult to open up to scrutiny.

I grew frustrated with her. She was holding too much back, only partly filling in the gaps of my childhood. I confronted her after speaking to my father. I wanted to know more about the marriage, why my father was so embittered, why she had stayed with him, what was at the root of our familial dysfunction. I knew that none of this was straightforward but I wanted something more than deflections and platitudes. When my mother refused to engage with me, I stopped talking to her.

We became distant and went for a long time without seeing each other.

* * *

In *East of Eden*, John Steinbeck writes: 'When a child first catches adults out – when it first walks into his grave little head that adults do not have divine intelligence, that their judgments are not always wise, their thinking true, their sentences just – his world falls into panic desolation. The gods are fallen and all safety gone. And there is one sure thing about the fall of gods: they do not fall a little; they crash and shatter or sink deeply into green muck. It is a tedious job to build them up again; they never quite shine. And the child's world is never quite whole again.'

How strange that, despite being an adult in my mid-to-late thirties, I felt like a child while researching and writing this book. It compelled me to experience the raw ache of seeing my parents as full human beings – flawed and astonishingly scarred. These were undoubtedly lessons I should have learned earlier. Yet I have done the bulk of my learning in enclosed institutions that have not encouraged this kind of searching. Whether in boarding school, church, medicine, global health or academia, I was repeating a pattern that began in childhood: redirecting any familial or personal pain I was experiencing into the arduous work of perfectionism, self-righteousness and achievement. I sought control through intellectual mastery. This strategy soothed me when I felt afraid, rewarded me with praise when I needed reassurance, and provided me with a sense of direction when I felt lost and confused. The distinctly colonial flavour of my education, combined with my relentless drive to push myself on and on, transformed me into a particular kind of person – someone hard-working, able to process information quickly and articulate arguments fluently, but also someone who conforms to institutional expectations, adopts their values, and confuses high performance and academic validation with acceptance, belonging and love. My drive, combined with the opportunities I've been fortunate to have, both enlarged my horizons and limited my capacity to fully embrace my feelings and develop a more rounded understanding of myself. And yet, no amount of achievement could quell the pain and restlessness within. I was coming to see that willed forgetting is a double-edged sword. Sometimes it allows us to keep moving, but sometimes it can lead us to overlook the roots of our distress until that distress brings time to a shuddering halt.

* * *

A year and a half later, in October 2023, my mother came to visit me in the UK, seeking to reconnect. I pointed out, stingingly, that this was the first time in two decades that she had come to see me without there being a graduation or conference to attend.

We went for a long walk through Oxford. My mother was enthralled by the sheer beauty of the architecture. It induced a kind of awe in her.

'Wow, Simu, can you believe you work here?'

For a passing moment, I thought about showing her the Rhodes statue and the obnoxious plaque beneath it that was installed after the 2020 protests. (It reads: 'Some of his activities led to a great loss of life and attracted criticism in his day and ever since.' That was one way to put it.) But then I changed my mind. I smiled weakly at my mother and didn't say anything. I saw the beauty of Oxford and appreciated it. But the university's mystique had faded.

My position at Oxford had not magically relieved me of my pain and confusion. No institution nor authority figure – certainly not my parents – could do that for me. I had to do the hard work of reckoning with my past if I wanted to live with a greater sense of freedom in the future. 'You have to look deeper, and you have to look back,' my therapist had impressed upon me. 'No matter how agonising, even and especially when it goes against your strongest impulses, you have to look back.'

The walk with my mother ended in my office. It was a Saturday and the building was empty. This was the only place in the city centre where we could find some privacy. My mother apologised for everything – for the truths withheld; for the times I felt abandoned, always unwittingly; for how much fear I'd had to live with as a child. She was at last speaking honestly. 'I was broken. Tafi was broken. We built a broken home in a broken country. And in the midst of that brokenness, we had you.'

* * *

I moved out of Oxford in spring 2025. My routine there felt constricted. I split most of my days between my rental home and my department without much of a life in between. I needed to get out and had saved enough to pay a deposit on a small flat in London. In the twenty-two years since I had first arrived in the UK, I'd moved house nearly twenty times. Finally, I had a home of my own. I wished I could tell Mr J about it, but he had died a few years earlier. He would have said, 'It's good like that.'

On the day I picked up my keys from the estate agency, I walked through my new neighbourhood. It had boutique cafes and a lovely little greengrocer. I tried to guess which pub would become my local once I had my bearings. It was mid-afternoon and young mothers pushed their prams along a tree-lined pavement. Most of the houses were terraced Victorian-style conversions, but there were some modern apartment blocks – like the one I was about to move into – dotted in between them.

I stepped into my building expecting to feel a rush, but what churned in me was an ambivalence I couldn't put my finger on. In the new pad, I took photos to send to friends, announcing that I was a Londoner once again: yeah baby! The flat had south-facing floor-to-ceiling windows and I basked in its light for a few moments. I then started making a list of everything I needed to do. I had to organise a deep clean and notify my bank of my new address. I needed to sort out insurance and council tax and utilities and mortgage repayments. And I needed to buy furniture. Where to begin? Feeling overwhelmed, I sat on the carpeted floor of the bedroom. I leaned against the wall and slipped my headphones on. I had made a playlist to celebrate my move. I wanted to feel this moment as one of triumph: a possession of my choice, agency, and the long labour of gradual arrival. The music filled my ears, but, to my frustration, it didn't hit like I thought it would. I cycled through my jazz-infused hip-hop favourites: The Roots, Little Brother, Blu & Exile, Kendrick Lamar, Little Simz, Dave. The songs were all too dense or too fast or too upbeat. None fit my mood.

I stopped the playlist and put on Tracy Chapman instead. I listened to 'Bridges', a haunting slow-paced acoustic song with a sparse arrangement. Her voice was rich, soulful, earnest. She transported me into an ethereal plane of nostalgia and regret. With each line, it sounded like she was talking to me, imploring me to sit still, be quiet and remember every painful moment I tried to forget, every connection I had lost and couldn't repair.

I remembered what it was like to leave Zimbabwe at sixteen. My generation had scattered. The world I grew up in no longer existed. The country had changed irrevocably. It could never be my home again. I recalled that New Year's Day, landing at London Heathrow in January 2003 – with my four CDs and book of motivational quotes in my hand luggage. I reflected on all the different phases I had been through in the years since, how many times I'd reinvented myself in search of belonging.

EXILE AND ARRIVAL

I stared across the room, through the door that opened onto the balcony. The wind blew through the branches and leaves of a tall tree outside my flat. Thick grey-white clouds clogged up the sky. The music played on. I surrendered to Tracy's voice. I allowed the song to wash over me. It was time to stop running.

Acknowledgements

I must have been a year into this project when I first discovered the critic Vivian Gornick and her treasure trove of essays on the art of personal narrative. Her meditations on truth and craftsmanship delighted me with their wisdom and clarity. I thought I had found my navigational help through the murky waters of life writing. But the more I read, the more trepidatious I became. Gornick offered more than inspiration; she issued chastening warnings to the aspiring memoirist. Where I had not properly understood the ethical and aesthetic demands of memoir, Gornick impressed upon me that this was not a genre to be taken lightly. It was not for the faint-hearted. It was a genre whose rewards lie on the far side of arduous self-examination, a tolerance for risk, exposure and the inevitability of causing hurt to oneself and others. For Gornick, memoir can only attain the status of art when it delivers on the question 'Who am I?' This delivery, she hastened to add, was not something as coarse or improbable as a definitive answer – let alone a mere recital of events – rather a depth of inquiry: the labour of a rigorous and supple consciousness shaping the raw material of life into meaning. As she put it with her characteristic elegance: 'What happened to the writer is not what matters; what matters is the larger sense that the writer is able to *make of* what happened.'

Whether I have risen to Gornick's challenge – whether I have succeeded in writing a memoir whose larger meaning transcends the experience at hand – is not for me to say. I leave that to the reader's judgement.

What I can say is that in the five years I spent writing this book, I have had to muster as much energy, discipline and writerly imagination as I could humanly manage to push through the many doubts, frustrations, anxieties and setbacks that plagued me at every step. In the process, I have accrued an overwhelming number of debts to colleagues, institutions, writers and friends who, knowingly or otherwise, have guided me through the toughest task I have ever undertaken. It would be impossible to pay adequate tribute to everyone whose work or insight or support has had some hand in this book.

My intellectual debts begin with a vast body of scholarly and literary texts that scaffold the histories, political contexts and emotional terrain of this narrative. I will not attempt to list all these books and essays here, but I can offer a few key recommendations for those interested in further reading.

For a background to Africa's deep history, I recommend Howard W. French's *Born in Blackness: Africa, Africans, and the Making of the Modern World, 1471 to the Second World War*. For an understanding of Africa's trajectory through the twentieth century, I recommend three outstanding works of scholarship: Frederick Cooper's *Africa Since 1940: The Past of the Present*, Adom Getachew's *Worldmaking After Empire: The Rise and Fall of Self-Determination* and Mahmood Mamdani's *Citizen and Subject: Contemporary Africa and the Legacy of Late Colonialism*.

I can't overstate the tremendous influence Jocelyn Alexander has had on my understanding of Zimbabwe. I drew heavily on her impressive body of scholarship, and also on that of my colleague and friend Miles Tendi, who has written authoritatively on Zimbabwe's liberation struggle and its legacies. I fully recommend their work to the academically inclined. For those who want more literary renderings of Zimbabwe, I benefited greatly from reading novels and memoirs that grapple with the messiness of the country. Among the most inspiring to me were NoViolet Bulawayo's *Glory*, Tsitsi Dangarembga's *This Mournable Body*, Novuyo Rosa Tshuma's *House of Stone* and Peter Godwin's *Mukiwa*. On Uganda, I recommend Richard Reid's monograph, *A History of Modern Uganda*, and the stunning photo-book by Derek Peterson and Richard Vokes, *The Unseen Archive of Idi Amin*.

ACKNOWLEDGEMENTS

To help me understand how political violence and trauma distort memory, fragment identity and ramify across generations, I read a wide body of creative non-fiction dealing with struggle and war in different contexts. Some of these books included Eva Hoffman's *After Such Knowledge* (Poland), Patrick Radden Keefe's *Say Nothing* (Northern Ireland), Tracy Kidder's *Strength in What Remains* (Burundi), Carolyn Forché's *What You Have Heard is True* (El Salvador), Amos Oz's *A Tale of Love and Darkness* (Israel and Palestine) and Jonny Steinberg's *Winnie & Nelson* (South Africa).

And finally, I learned about memoir writing in the finest of literary traditions: by imitating those who have mastered the form. Hua Hsu's *Stay True*, Dina Nayeri's *The Ungrateful Refugee*, Safiya Sinclair's *How to Say Babylon* and Lea Ypi's *Free* all expanded my sense of what is possible in this genre.

***

I had long aspired to write beyond the academy but was prompted into taking this ambition seriously by an inquiring email from a literary agent who had heard me speak at a public event and intuited that I had a book in me. From our earliest conversations, Carrie Plitt encouraged me to develop my writing from inchoate musings to a proposal and eventually to a full manuscript. I am grateful for how skilfully she championed my work with publishers, taking care of the business side of book writing and allowing me to concentrate on cultivating my voice.

Through Carrie, I have met a wonderful team of literary agents at Felicity Bryan Associates in Oxford, including Angelique Tran Van Sang who represented me when Carrie was on leave. Carrie also introduced me to Zoë Pagnamenta, at Calligraph literary agency in New York, who helped secure a publishing deal for this book in North America. I am grateful to them all for their support.

Any writer should be so lucky to have their book handled with the passion, commitment and wisdom of my editors: Will Hammond at The Bodley Head and Amanda Cook at Crown. Will and Amanda saw what this book could be long before I did, and they worked with such patience and diligence in coaxing the very best out of me. They urged me to reconfigure the architecture of the story and improve its pacing. They challenged me on every page to balance exposition and immersion in a scene. Crucially, they helped me develop the double perspective that this book inhabits, of life as lived and life as reconstituted through memory and maturity. Likewise, I am grateful to Juliet Brooke who joined the editorial team at The Bodley Head and worked with me on the final draft of the book. My editors improved this book immeasurably. It has been a privilege to work with them. But, of course, all shortcomings and mistakes are mine alone.

I thank Duncan Heath for copy-editing this book. I thank Leah Boulton, Joe Pickering, Stuart Williams and the team at Vintage. I thank Katie Berry and the team at Crown.

* * *

I've been the fortunate recipient of institutional backing and funding that have supported my creative work.

The first iteration of this project was a long-read essay in the *Guardian*, published in 2021. I thank David Wolf for commissioning this work and Alex Blasdel for his incisive editing. Working with Alex was like going through a writing bootcamp and I am all the better for it.

In 2022, I was awarded a British Academy and Leverhulme Trust Senior Research Fellowship that granted me a year of research leave. I spent the year as a Fellow at the Center for Advanced Study in the Behavioral Sciences (CASBS) at Stanford University: an idyllic and stimulating setting in which to write. I had the joy of working among a community of scholars dedicated to advancing our understanding of the human condition.

ACKNOWLEDGEMENTS

Before leaving the US, I was nominated by my editor Amanda to participate in a memoir-writing workshop at Aspen Summer Words chaired by Ashley C. Ford. Through example and instruction, Ashley taught me so much about how to write about childhood with honesty, perspective and compassion. I thank her and all my fellow participants for workshopping the first chapter of this book. At the conference, I had the pleasure of meeting Claire Dederer, who wrote me an illuminating email about turning my *Guardian* long-read essay into a full-length book.

I received generous invitations to share my work in progress through research lectures and seminar presentations at different universities. I thank colleagues at UC Berkeley, Brown, Princeton, Stanford, the University of Edinburgh, the University of Sheffield, the University of Warwick, and Kellogg College and All Souls College, Oxford.

I have been studying and working at the University of Oxford for over ten years. I thank Jocelyn Alexander for supporting and challenging me to be a sharper and more confident thinker. I am also grateful to Max Bolt, Amogh Dhar Sharma, Dan Hodgkinson, David Jackman, Didi Ogude, Lena Reim, Diego Sánchez-Ancochea, Albert Sanghoon Park and Tom Scott-Smith who all helped me with this book directly and indirectly. I thank Doug Gollin and Cheryl Doss, former Oxford colleagues, for their intellectual and emotional support over the years. I thank all my doctoral students for their encouragement and patience: Biruk Terrefe, Vyoma Dhar Sharma and Joshua Parker Allen watched this idea develop from the start and they kept asking penetrating and thoughtful questions at different stages of its development. Through her good humour and conscientious administration, Elizabeth Gilbert made my working life easier and helped me through a difficult phase of my career.

Many other colleagues in the academy have supported me professionally. Thank you, for various reasons, to Jean Allman, David Anderson, Shreya Atrey, Paul Betts, Joel Cabrita, Cécile Fabre, Nandini Gooptu, Gabrielle Hecht, Dorothea Kleine, Gabrielle Lynch, Dan

Magaziner, Sloan Mahone, Ambreena Manji, JoAnn McGregor, Mpho Molefe, Akasemi Newsome, Terri Ochiaga, Woody Powell, Astrid Rasch, Eugene Rogan, Simon Rushton, Priya Satia, Toni Schmader, Ricardo Soares de Oliveira, Christine Sypnowich, Vladimir Unkovski-Korica, Megan Vaughan and Lea Ypi.

* * *

My friends are my greatest source of community, belonging and intimacy. I have mentioned several friends above already. In addition I thank Adam, Anne I., Anne M., Arturo (RT!), Bella, Chris (You there!), Dan S., David (the Vidad oan), Diana, Diane and Bruce, Faith, Florence, Harry (Dr V.), James, JanaLee and Ian, Jean, Jeff, Joe, Jono, Kieran, Kirsten, Kuukuwa, Lisa, Lucy, Maisha, Martin (the one and only Martinelli), Michaela ('Collord'), Mihika (Emcee), Nitsan, Pascal, Peace, Sa'eed (what it do blood?), Sanjeev, Sophie, Stacy, Steve, Sylvia, Tess and Tom (Tomonopolous Poe).

I thank Ankita, Ella and Myfanwy for holding me and all my weirdness with such tenderness and care.

I thank Jonny Steinberg for his mentorship, for pushing me harder than anyone else to be the best writer I can be.

I thank my therapist who believed in this project from the beginning and without whom I would never have managed the depth of introspection and self-understanding needed to complete this book.

I thank my found family: James, Barry and, always, Christine.

And I thank my family. All my aunts, uncles and cousins, especially Tafa, Tonde, Rudo and Don.

This book is dedicated to my parents. I wrote this book for them with all my love.